GEORGE III'S CHILDREN

ALSO BY JOHN VAN DER KISTE

Historical biography

Frederick III: German Emperor 1888 (Alan Sutton 1981)
Queen Victoria's family: a select bibliography (Clover 1982)
Dearest Affie: Alfred, Duke of Edinburgh, Queen Victoria's second son, 1844–1900
[with Bee Jordaan] (Alan Sutton 1984)
Queen Victoria's children (Alan Sutton 1986; large print edition
ISIS 1987)
Windsor and Habsburg: the British and Austrian reigning houses 1848–1922
(Alan Sutton 1987)
Edward VII's children (Alan Sutton 1989)
Princess Victoria Melita, Grand Duchess Cyril of Russia, 1876–1936
(Alan Sutton 1991)
George V's children (Alan Sutton 1991)

Music

Roxeventies: popular music in Britain 1970–79 (Kawabata 1982)
The Roy Wood story (A & F 1986)
Singles file: the story of the 45 r.p.m. record (A & F 1987)
Beyond the summertime: the Mungo Jerry story [with Derek Wadeson]
(A & F 1990)

GEORGE III'S CHILDREN

John Van der Kiste

ALAN SUTTON

First published in the United Kingdom in 1992
Alan Sutton Publishing Ltd · Phoenix Mill · Far Thrupp · Stroud
Gloucestershire

First published in the United States of America in 1992
Alan Sutton Publishing Inc · Wolfeboro Falls · NH 03896-0848

Reprinted 1995

British Library Cataloguing in Publication Data

Kiste, John Van der
George III's Children
I. Title
941.07092

ISBN 0-7509-0034-2

Library of Congress Cataloging in Publication Data applied for

Typeset in Ehrhardt 11/12.
Typesetting and origination by
Alan Sutton Publishing Limited.
Printed in Great Britain by
WBC, Bridgend, Mid Glam.

Contents

Illustrations

Nos. 4,10,11,14,17,19–21,22 and 27, from The Royal Collection, St James's Palace, and No. 61 appear by gracious permission of Her Majesty The Queen (copyright reserved). Thanks are also due to the following for kind permission to reproduce illustrations as above: Birmingham City Museums and Art Galleries (57); Brighton Museums and Art Gallery (31,36); Trustees of the British Museum (35,51,60); Commemorative Collectors Society, 25 Farndale Close, Long Eaton, Nottingham (24,28,29,38,41,43,52); Courtauld Institute of Art (26); Devon Library Services (37); Greater London Photograph Library (44,49,59); National Galleries of Scotland (1,2,39,42,55); National Monuments Record (5); National Portrait Gallery (18,22,32,47,50); Wallace Collection (6,15); The Board of Trustees of the Victoria & Albert Museum/Bridgeman Art Library (3). The remainder are from private collections.

Foreword

For many years, the Hanoverian kings and their families were ridicule personified. Such a process began with the Victorians, for Queen Victoria's first Prime Minister, Lord Melbourne, never ceased to impress on her what a foolish crowd her uncles (three of whom were still alive and in good health at her accession) had always been. The sons of King George III, 'the damnedest millstones round the neck of any government', in Wellington's impatient yet elegant phrase, received an almost uniformly bad press for nearly a century after the last one died in 1851.

Tentative efforts to help put the record straight began with the publication of Roger Fulford's *Royal Dukes* in 1933. He related in his Foreword that he produced his work on the advice of an unnamed contemporary who suggested he ought to write a book about 'those risible Dukes'. Yet, as he recognized, there was much clearing through the labyrinth of legend and rumour to be done.

In particular, Ernest, Duke of Cumberland and King of Hanover, stood out 'from the pages of history as a shapeless lump of filth, from which it is now almost impossible to scrape off the mud and see what manner of man it really concealed.' Largely through the efforts of Whig politicians, who were in power for much of the first forty years of the nineteenth century, Ernest became one of the most vilified characters in history since Attila the Hun. At various times he was reputed to have committed incest, rape, sodomy, and murder, and driven at least one cuckolded husband to suicide. Likewise King George IV, who was admittedly extravagant, untrustworthy, and behaved badly to his obnoxious wife, was thought to be the devil incarnate. His successor King William IV apparently spat at passers-by from his carriage window, and it was said that bets were placed on how long it would be before he went irrevocably insane like his father. This compounded the rather less than accurate supposition that King George III was mad, for it has been revealed comparatively recently that he suffered severely from porphyria, the symptoms of which were close to, but not completely consistent with, madness.

It suited the government, and the mentors of the young Queen Victoria and Prince Albert, to portray King George III's large family as something of an aberration. Comparisons may be drawn not unprofitably with Shakespeare's historical plays, produced partly to celebrate the glories of Tudor England and Queen Elizabeth I and to denigrate the last King of the preceding Yorkist dynasty, Richard III.

Had the politicians not made their contribution, the colourful distortions of contemporary diarists such as Greville and Princess Lieven would still have been sufficient to sustain the legends. Charles Cavendish Fulke Greville, Clerk to the

Privy Council and Secretary to the Island of Jamaica, was a Whig whose dislike of royalty did not prevent him from accepting well-paid posts from the sovereigns whom he so despised; his diaries, originally published in 1872 and described as 'indiscreet' by Queen Victoria, make entertaining but not altogether accurate reading. Princess Lieven, wife of the Russian Ambassador and an indefatigable source of political gossip, likewise had scant regard for the truth. It was the letters, diaries and memoirs of people such as these whose half-truths were long accepted as fact.

Only with the publication of selections from the private correspondence of Kings George III and IV, edited by Professor Aspinall, has a truer picture started to emerge. The surviving letters, inevitably, only tell part of the story. King George IV wrote little, partly as he suffered from a weakness of and twitching in his hands in middle and later life; and an ill-advised series of passionate love-letters to the actress Mary Robinson in his youth, which had to be bought back at enormous cost by his enraged father, can have done little to encourage him to commit his thoughts to paper thereafter.

A stream of biographies since 1960, notably Anthony Bird's *The damnable Duke of Cumberland* (which demolishes many of the more colourful myths pertaining to its subject and his family), volumes by John Brooke and Stanley Ayling on George III, by Olwen Hedley on Queen Charlotte, by Philip Ziegler on William IV, Christopher Hibbert's two-volume study of George IV, and studies of the Dukes of Kent and Sussex by Mollie Gillen, have had the benefit of these and of other material which had long been unavailable, and only at last are some of the legends being laid to rest. Perhaps it is significant, however, that the Duke of Cambridge, whose life of seventy-six years was never tainted by debt, scandal or parental disapproval, has yet to find a biographer of his own. To quote Lucille Iremonger, there is not much to be said of him, 'perhaps because he was the only son of George III to live above the age of four and keep all the commandments.'[1]

Over the years, the family have been frequently analyzed as individuals, though rarely as a group. The Princesses have been dealt with jointly by Dorothy M. Stuart, Lucille Iremonger (whose *Love and the Princess* purports to be a biography of Sophia, but is in effect a study of her sisters as well) and Morris Marples; but by and large their lives were so devoid of excitement that it would be idle to pretend that they merit biographies to themselves.

The concluding remarks of Percy Fitzgerald from his two-volume *Dukes and Princesses of the Family of George III*, published in 1882, can be scarcely improved on more than a century later. He admits with restraint that they were remarkable persons, but 'that in most of the members of the male family, with certain abilities, there was a strain of folly or eccentricity, owing a good deal to unrestrained self-indulgence and love of pleasure, which led to debt and difficulties; and which, in its turn, led to abandonment of principle, to strange shifts, and to careless oddities and recklessness.' The King of Hanover, he maintains, was the one gifted with most ability, but unlovable; that King George IV was clever, versatile, and accomplished, but selfish and self-indulgent; that the Duke of York was perhaps the best of the family, but his debts 'had the usual degrading effect'; that King William IV was straightforward and good-natured, but eccentric and wrong-headed; that the Duke of Kent was amiable, but unlucky: 'a long-suffering personage of a really affectionate disposition'; that the Duke of Cambridge had perhaps the most respectable career of all, as he was the least talked of; and that the Duke of Sussex 'had cultivated literary tastes, and his recorded observations, oral and written, show sound sense and study.'[2]

Fitzgerald was, however, writing at a time when little was known about them, and myths outnumbered fact. His remarks were both cautious and relatively accurate. All the same, the time seems right for an assessment of their lives as a family in the light of more recent research; and this I have endeavoured to do.

As ever, I am most grateful for the constant help, encouragement and advice during the writing of this book to my parents, Wing Commander Guy and Nancy Van der Kiste. I am also indebted to the staff of the Kensington and Chelsea Public Libraries, for a blissful morning of rummaging around in their superb biography collection; to Shirley Stapley, for the loan of material; to Steven Jackson, of the Commemorative Collectors Society, and all others who have lent illustrations; and last but not least, to Peter Clifford, Rosemary Aspinwall, and the rest of the editorial staff, for their work in bringing this long-cherished project to fruition.

John Van der Kiste

Prologue: King George III and Queen Charlotte

The Prince destined to become King George III was born on 4 June 1738, the second child of Frederick, Prince of Wales and Augusta, Princess of Saxony. It was an unfortunate tradition of the royal house of Hanover that father and son should dislike each other intensely. King George I, the first of the dynasty, had hated his son who succeeded him as King George II in 1727. The latter detested his eldest son Frederick, calling him 'the greatest villain that ever was born', and only public opinion persuaded him to allow the young man to come over to England from the ancestral home of Hanover. Frederick's mother, Queen Caroline, hated him as well, calling him 'such an ass that one cannot tell what he thinks,' while his sister Amelia remarked disdainfully that he would 'put one arm round anybody's neck to kiss them, and then stab them with the other if he can.'

In 1736 he married Princess Augusta of Saxe-Gotha, and during the next fourteen years she presented him with five sons and four daughters.

Frederick was an unfaithful husband, but Augusta took his infidelities as a matter of course. Something of a dilettante, he took more of an interest in music, theatre and sport than politics. His children were well educated, and by the age of eight Prince George could read and write English and German, as well as taking an interest in public events and issues. He was also taught French, history, mathematics, religion, music and dancing, and he was the first British king to study science, learning the fundamentals of physics and chemistry as a boy. In later life, however, the King would regret his isolation from boys of his own age during adolescence. Unhappily, the experience did not prevent him from making similar mistakes with his own sons.

Frederick was never strong, and while gardening at Kew one winter, he caught a chill from which he died on 20 March 1751. A month after his death, his eldest son was created Prince of Wales and Earl of Chester. He had automatically succeeded to his father's title of Duke of Edinburgh on the latter's death. Frederick's widow was aged only thirty-two, and with a son who would almost certainly be King before long, she expected to have some power over him when he came to the throne. In such a position, she was easy prey for favourites, and in her endeavours she was helped by her close friend (and lover, according to contemporary gossip) the Earl of Bute.

Unhappily, Augusta regarded it as a pious duty to her husband's memory to maintain the feud with her father-in-law. Friendly overtures from the King to his grandson and heir were firmly rebuffed, until the King remarked disdainfully that the lad was 'fit for nothing but to read the Bible to his mother.' Under her upbringing George became an immature, inexperienced young man, full of prejudices. She would complain that he was too childish, albeit honest and good-natured. In 1756 he was offered an independent establishment by the King, but refused it on the grounds that his mother's happiness depended upon their not being separated, and anything which affected or displeased his mother would make him uneasy.

On 25 October 1760 King George II died, and the next day his grandson was proclaimed King.

In his opening address to Parliament, King George III declared that he gloried 'in the name of Briton'. Throughout his eighty-one years, of which almost sixty were spent on the throne, he was unique among British sovereigns, before and since, in never setting foot outside England (or indeed north of Cheltenham). The first Hanoverian king, George I, was already an old man by the time he was called upon to succeed to the throne; he spent little time in England, and saw no point in attempting to learn the language. King George II learnt to speak it adequately for official purposes, though French remained the official language at court, as it was for most European courts, but he still regarded the ancestral home of Hanover with greater affection, and in private derided the House of Commons and the English as 'king-killers or republicans'. There would be no such divided loyalties in the heart of his grandson.

The bachelor King of twenty-two longed to marry, having no desire for a mistress or a series of passionate entanglements. During his youth, it was said, he had fallen madly in love with the Quakeress Hannah Lightfoot and contracted a secret marriage with her. More serious was his infatuation with Lady Sarah Lennox, the daughter of the Duke of Richmond, and a direct descendant of King Charles II, with whom he was besotted for a while. There would have been difficulties in court protocol if His Majesty was to marry a subject; and she was related by marriage to the ambitious parliamentarian, Henry Fox. There was no love lost between Fox and Lord Bute, and the Dowager Princess of Wales had no desire to see her son make a marriage which would surely set him against her closest friend. It was imperative that the King should have some eligible young Protestant German Princess as his bride, before his infatuation with Lady Sarah should reach the point of no return. As he was not only King of Great Britain but also Elector of Hanover, it was almost inevitable that his bride would be drawn from one of the German ruling houses. Matters were made easier by the fact that the unambitious Lady Sarah only liked him as a friend, and was in love with Lord Newbattle, the future Marquis of Lothian.

Colonel Graham was sent to Germany to report on eligible princesses, and his choice fell on seventeen-year-old Charlotte. She was well-educated, particularly in history, botany and theology, and spoke French fluently. She had no interest in politics, a great advantage for a potential Queen Consort. Mecklenburg-Strelitz, or as it was unkindly dubbed by contemporary wags, 'Muckleberg Strawlitter', was a small duchy in North Germany, about the size of Sussex, and the family were accustomed to a dull, frugal and uneventful life. To be chosen as Queen of Great Britain was a dazzling honour for one of the Duke's daughters.

Charlotte was small, thin and dark, with a nose tilted upward and a large mouth. Her hair was 'a pleasant shade of brown'; this, according to some observers, was her only redeeming physical feature. She was said to be exceptionally plain, though the daughter of one of her gentleman-pages commented on her 'slight, pretty figure,' and 'her eyes bright and sparkling with good humour and vivacity,' giving the lie to a legend that she was exceptionally ugly. Her wardrobe was meagre; she had only one proper gown, which was kept for Sunday best. When Mr Drummond, the English ambassador to Prussia, was sent to Strelitz to perform the betrothal ceremony, she was dazzled by the gifts of jewellery which he brought with him.

On 8 July 1761, the betrothal of His Majesty King George III and Princess Charlotte of Mecklenburg-Strelitz was announced. Two ladies from court, the Duchess of Ancaster and the Duchess of Hamilton, were sent out to the German Duchy to escort her and her servants to England.

The Princess set off for England aboard a ship, tactfully named the *Charlotte*. On their crossing she behaved in cheerful and friendly fashion, her spirits surviving the nine days they spent at sea, while her servants and the English Duchesses suffered agonies from sea-sickness. She chattered away, sang, and proved how well she had been educated for her destiny by thumping out English tunes on the harpsichord, it was said, so as to 'encourage her companions in their misery'. They were expected to sail up the Thames to be met by the King at Greenwich, but bad weather forced them to land at Harwich, and continue the journey by road.

The wedding was celebrated on 8 September, the evening of her arrival in London, at the Chapel Royal, St James's. After supper the Queen was helped into her wedding dress, of white and silver, with a purple velvet mantle laced with gold and lined with ermine, fastened on the shoulders with large tassels of pearls. She trembled with nerves as the King's brothers, the Duke of York and Prince William, led her up the aisle, the Duke comforting her with a gentle, 'Courage, Princess, courage!' Although she had ten maids-of-honour, including Lady Sarah Lennox, to carry her train, it was so heavy that as the evening passed it dragged down the neck of her gown, until 'the spectators knew as much of her upper half as the King himself.'[1] Apart from this, everything passed off satisfactorily, though one elderly peer had to be forcibly restrained from doing homage to Sarah as his new Queen.

Afterwards the Queen played the harpsichord and sang some songs while guests in the drawing-room awaited supper. She spoke a little French to them and German to the King, before excusing herself on account of tiredness, retiring to a private supper with him, and then to bed.

Out of consideration for her, the King dispensed with one of the less delicate wedding customs. It was tradition that the Queen should appear in her night-dress, to be 'bedded' beside her bridegroom before the whole Court, but King George decided to spare her this indignity.

A fortnight later, they were crowned at Westminster. There were some mishaps, particularly at the banquet in Westminster Hall afterwards. The principal diamond fell out of the crown, an apparent ill-omen which superstitious spectators would recall some years hence when the Americans declared

King George III, from the studio of Allan Ramsay, c. 1767

Queen Charlotte, from the studio of Allan Ramsay, c. 1763

their independence; the London aldermen found no table prepared for them at the banquet; and the Earl Marshal was reprimanded after the heralds had made a muddle about the order of procession. Overcome with nerves, he confessed that there had been much he would have wished otherwise, but he had taken care that the next Coronation would 'be regulated in the exactest manner possible.' Far from being offended by such intimations of his mortality, the King roared with laughter at this gaffe and made the poor man repeat it several times.

Still dominated by his mother, he was sometimes inconsiderate to his wife. Shortly before the wedding, he had warned her, 'Never be alone with my mother; she is an artful woman and will try to govern you.' None the less, their first year of married life was made unhappy by Augusta's selfish, often successful efforts to crush any signs of independence in this young Princess whose head must have been turned a little by what had seemed such a glittering prize. When she discovered that the Duchess of Mecklenburg-Strelitz had asked her daughter not to wear jewels when taking Communion, she insisted that the Queen should as it was expected of her. The Queen liked playing cards with her maids for relaxation; the Princess of Wales prohibited games of chance, as they were 'wicked'.

The King was too much in awe of his mother to defy her and stand up for his young wife. Neither did the rest of his family attempt to make her feel welcome, his unmarried sisters mocking her for her lack of sophistication. She was not encouraged to make friends among her husband's subjects; no English ladies were permitted to approach her without first obtaining permission from her German attendants. Whatever lively spirits this plain but apparently eager young woman had when she came to England must have been soon extinguished by such cruelty. She had no contact with society, remarked the diarist Walpole acidly, 'except for the Ladies of the Bedchamber for half an hour a week in a funereal circle, or a ceremonious Drawing Room.' Overruled, insulted, a stranger in her husband's kingdom, she resorted to defensive chilliness. It was hardly surprising that she became embittered and unpleasant, not to say cruel, to those under her control, particularly her adult daughters.

The King was the one sober and virtuous member of an otherwise raffish, self-indulgent family. Kind and considerate, others found him dull and on occasion mean. Any inclinations he had towards parsimony were reinforced by his Lord Steward, Lord Talbot, who had been responsible for the cheese-paring arrangements at the Coronation banquet. For example, the latter had issued no invitations to representatives of the citizens of London, and only when he was told firmly that they could hardly be expected to contribute £10,000 to provide a dinner for the King and have no share themselves, were seats hastily provided for them. Despite his ineptitude, he was put in charge of the staff of the royal household. Economy was his constant watchword. One of his first acts was to declare that in future no meals would be provided at the Palace for anybody other than Their Majesties, the maids of honour and the chaplains. The Queen's first party, to which about a dozen couples were invited, was described as a 'gingerbread affair'. The guests arrived at seven, and danced until after midnight, when they were sent home without any refreshments whatsoever.

As for the King and Queen, they usually dined off tough mutton and inferior claret. To them, though, this was no hardship, for they were abstemious by nature. The King drank little wine, and enjoyed simple food. As the satirist Peter Pindar put it, 'A leg of mutton and his wife, Were the chief pleasures of his life.' He was afraid of growing fat, and his careful diet, coupled with regular exercise, prevented him from the Hanoverian tendency to put on weight in middle age.

Members of the aristocracy did their best to avoid the Court, but Cabinet Ministers were obliged to wait in attendance regularly on the King. They were disgruntled to find that no refreshment was ever offered them either, but the local inns must have been grateful at the resulting increase in trade from hungry servants of the crown.

Humble country folk were more fortunate. The King liked to stroll into their cottages unannounced and talk to them about simple everyday matters. If he suspected that a cottage's tenants seemed lacking in creature comforts, he would spontaneously leave some money behind. When a committee was appointed to examine the state of his finances during one of his first major illnesses, it was found that nearly a quarter of his personal income was thus given away in charity.

As for relaxation, King George III loved the theatre, and he went once a week for much of his life. Sometimes leading actors and actresses of the day were invited to entertain at court, Sarah Siddons being a particular favourite with the King. Slapstick and pantomime always amused him, and were greatly preferred to Shakespeare's 'sad stuff.' He played the violin, flute and harpsichord, and enjoyed listening to music, particularly religious songs. Sometimes boys were invited from Eton to come to 'feasts', or long concerts of church music – although they too were sent away afterwards without refreshment. In the Chapel Royal, he would beat time enthusiastically with his music roll, and thump the heads of the pages with it if they began chatting among themselves.

During the first few years of his reign, King George was a zealous collector. In 1762 he acquired two excellent collections of Italian, Flemish and Dutch drawings and paintings. As his grandfather had presented the royal library formed by his predecessors to the British Museum in 1757, there was none in the palaces on his accession, so he began to form a new one. Within a few years it comprised several thousand volumes, and kept two cabinet makers in regular employment making bookcases and presses to keep up with new acquisitions. Medals and maps particularly fascinated him, but his greatest passion as a collector was for clocks and watches. He fully understood how they worked, and paid large sums for several very complicated and expensive timepieces, as well as barographs, telescopes and barometers.

Painting held less interest for him, although he played his part in encouraging the fine arts, particularly by assenting to the foundation of the Royal Academy in 1768, visiting its annual exhibitions and attending the banquet. Yet the work of Sir Joshua Reynolds, the Academy's first President, found little favour at court, and nor did the revolutionary paintings and drawings of William Blake. His favourite painters were Allan Ramsay, who was entrusted with executing the formal state portraits of King and Queen early in the reign, the expatriate American Benjamin West, who became the Academy's second President,

Thomas Gainsborough, who produced surely the most charming portraits of the family, including the famous oval portraits of parents and thirteen of the children in 1782, and the German-born Johann Zoffany.

His most famous nickname, 'Farmer George', was a result of his interest in agriculture. From time to time he sent letters on the subject to the 'Annals of Agriculture' under the pseudonym of Ralph Robinson. He regularly sent produce from the farm at Great Park, Windsor, to market and sold it at a profit, a practice not calculated to make him popular among his fellow-farmers.

Like the lack of hospitality offered to visitors, this indicated something of a mean spirit at the royal court, reputed to be the dullest in Europe. If a King and Queen live simply and economically, they are taken to task for being dull. If they are hedonists and spendthrifts, they are taken to task for gross extravagance while the poorest of their subjects starve (as were King George and Queen Charlotte's contemporaries at the court of Versailles, King Louis XVI and Queen Marie-Antoinette). How do they strike a satisfactory balance?

The answer, of course, is that they can not. As James Gillray's pair of savage caricatures published in 1792 showed, it was impossible to please everyone. The first, 'Temperance enjoying a frugal meal', mocked a miserly King George and Queen Charlotte at dinner. The second, 'A voluptuary under the horrors of digestion', portrayed their debauched eldest son recovering from a heavy meal, surrounded by gambling dice, unpaid bills, and patent cures for venereal disease. Similar comparisons may be made with the King's great-granddaughter, the widowed Queen Victoria, and her raffish, society-loving son Prince Albert Edward; according to the then (1870) Prime Minister W.E. Gladstone, the Queen was invisible and her heir not respected. As in the time of Queen Victoria and Prince Albert, the lack of fashion and fashionable vice in the head of society during King George III's reign disappointed if not shocked aristocracy, letter-writers and diarists alike. It was their opinions which passed into history, and suggested that such lack of vice made the sovereign and his wife unpopular. Dull, yes, and often objects of ridicule; but to suggest that they were hated for leading such a quiet, unpretentious life is surely exaggeration.

Such was the contrariness of human nature, though, that the children born to them would in time yearn to be everything that their stolid, staid, dutiful parents were not.

1 *'I never saw more lovely children'*

On 12 August 1762 Queen Charlotte gave birth to her first child. Twenty-one years later, to the week, the fifteenth and youngest was born. By any standards the family of King George III and Queen Charlotte was a large one, and it was unequalled in the annals of British royalty. Queen Anne had endured eighteen pregnancies, but only five babies were born alive, and of these only one lived long enough to celebrate an eleventh birthday. The unhappy overtaxed mother herself died at forty-nine, having been a virtual invalid for several years.

That Queen Charlotte lived into her seventies and her husband, a sickly seven-months infant, attained the age of eighty-one, is evidence that the line was comparatively healthy. Even more remarkably, most of their sons and daughters were physically robust, with boisterous spirits to match. The stamina of the elder ones did not extend to the younger, however. Of the first twelve, all but the Duke of Kent (who died of pneumonia at fifty-two) reached their sixties or seventies, and two (the Duke of Cumberland and the Duchess of Gloucester), like their father, lived into their ninth decade, but the last two sons died in infancy and the youngest daughter only lived into her twenties.

Some of the children, namely George, Frederick, Augustus, probably Edward and perhaps Sophia, suffered from the royal malady of porphyria. It was a complaint, not a fatal disease, but it does perhaps account for the chronic or regular bouts of ill-health from which they suffered, albeit far less severely than their father.*

When dignitaries gathered on the afternoon of 12 August while Queen Charlotte was in labour for the first time, no heir had been born to a reigning monarch for nearly three quarters of a century. The last occasion had been the arrival of King James II's son in 1688, when absence of credible eye-witnesses had led to suggestions that an infant had been brought into the royal chamber in a warming-pan. So that there should be no dispute in future, a custom was adopted whereby a group of eminent persons would be summoned to St James's Palace to testify that the newly-born heir to the throne was indisputably royal. They included the Archbishop of Canterbury, the First Lord of the Treasury, two Secretaries of State, and officers of the Privy Council and the Royal Household. The father-to-be remained within his own apartments at the palace,

---

* See Chapter 3, p. 35.

but despite his reputation for being careful with money, he had promised £500 to the bearer of news of a daughter, double that sum if it was a son.

At twenty-four minutes past seven, the child was born. The Earl of Huntingdon hurried to the King's rooms and informed him that he was the father of a baby girl. Whether he received his recompense or not was not recorded, but the King assured him with delight that he cared little for the child's sex as long as the Queen's health was not in jeopardy. Going straight to her, he discovered that the Earl had been incorrect; the child was 'a strong, large, pretty boy'.

Five days later, the royal infant was created Prince of Wales. A week later, members of the nobility were admitted, for two hours on six successive afternoons, filing into the room in groups of up to forty at a time, to see the heir. They gazed at him as he slept in a cot behind a latticework partition, or rested on a velvet cushion on the lap of his wet nurse, Mrs Margaret Scott. While doing so they were served with royal cake and caudle, a mixture of warm eggs and wine. On one day alone five hundred pounds of cake and eight gallons of caudle were consumed.

On 16 September the baby was baptized George Augustus Frederick, in an unpretentious domestic ceremony in the Queen's drawing-room at St James's.

Shortly after his marriage, King George III purchased Buckingham House, a few hundred yards from St James's, from Sir Charles Sheffield, a natural son of the Duke of Buckingham, for £28,000. Within two years he had spent considerably more on structural alteration, extensions and redecoration. The Queen's House, as it was known until further enlargement and partial rebuilding

Buckingham House from St James's Park, watercolour by Edward Dayes, 1790

some sixty years later, and then renamed Buckingham Palace, thus made an ideal royal residence within easy reach of the capital with its view down The Mall towards the cities of Westminster and London, and St Paul's Cathedral in the distance.

Here the royal couple and their children lived in relative privacy and simplicity, and used the Palace at St James's for more formal functions, such as drawing-rooms and levees.

On 16 August 1763, during a summer of intense heat and thunderstorms which caused some discomfort to the mother in labour, Prince Frederick was born at Buckingham House. At the age of seven months, he was created Bishop of Osnabruck in Hanover. There were considerable emoluments attached to the Bishopric, which was, alternately with the Holy Roman Emperor, in the gift of the Elector of Hanover, and King George III was anxious to keep it in the family when the right of appointment fell to him. Until created Duke of York, this second son was always known by his ecclesiastical title, and his first set of china, made specially for him by Josiah Wedgwood, was stamped with his mitre.

In 1764 the Queen had a miscarriage, but on 21 August 1765 she produced a third son, William. The first daughter, Charlotte, arrived on 29 September 1766, and on 2 November 1767 another son, Edward. He was born the day before his dissipated bachelor uncle Edward, Duke of York, was buried, and thus given the name in his memory. In later life, he would remark theatrically that the circumstances of his birth 'were ominous of the life of gloom and struggle which awaited me.'

Next came two daughters, Augusta, born on 8 November 1768, and Elizabeth, on 22 May 1770. On the morning of 5 June the following year, the experienced mother attended a reception, and gave birth in the afternoon after only fifteen minutes' labour to another son, Ernest. He was followed by two more boys, Augustus (27 January 1773), and Adolphus (24 February 1774). As if the royal nurseries were not full enough by this time, along came Mary (25 April 1776) and Sophia (3 November 1777), followed by the less healthy, short-lived Octavius (23 February 1779), Alfred (22 September 1780), and Amelia (7 August 1783).

The parents' efforts to show their children to some of their subjects were not well-received. In October 1769 some of the nobility were invited to an infants' drawing-room. At one end of the room was a dais on which stood the Prince of Wales, aged seven, in scarlet and gold, wearing the Order of the Garter, and the Bishop of Osnabruck, in blue and gold, attired in the Order of the Bath. The Princess Royal was seated on a sofa between William and two-year-old Edward, 'elegantly dressed in togas according to the Roman custom'. While the Princes may have received the fawning courtiers with 'the utmost grace and affability', and while such traditions were commonplace in the courts of Germany, in England the event was greeted with hilarity. In the press, caricatures were printed of outraged noblemen humbling themselves before a kite-flying Prince of Wales, a Bishop on his hobby-horse, William spinning a top, and a baby Princess receiving sustenance from a wet nurse behind a screen. The King and Queen were wise enough not to repeat the idea.

The Prince of Wales had been created a Knight of the Garter at the age of three and a half, and soon afterwards he would be invited to the Queen's 'drawing-rooms'. It was considered important to introduce the future King into such ceremonial functions at an early age. Extrovert by nature, he revelled in this, and when he was five, Lady Sarah Lennox commented with disdain that his father had 'made his brat the proudest little imp you ever saw.' Such an upbringing was not calculated to make him anything other than conceited, but endearing qualities were also evident. He had a great sense of humour and a pronounced gift of mimicry. As there was little for him to do in the often artificial life at court but to observe those around him, he soon sharpened his talent for imitating those around him to perfection.

George and Frederick were always close during childhood, and at Kew they were encouraged to cultivate a strip of land, although they did so without any of their father's enthusiasm. Despite the age difference, they attended the same classes for eight hours each day, and learned to ride and fence together.

The educational regime, supervised by their father, was strict. Lord Holderness was appointed the Prince of Wales's governor, and Dr Markham, the Bishop of Chester, their chief preceptor. The former resigned in 1776, and the latter was promoted to the Archbishopric of York, his place being taken by Dr Hurd, Bishop of Worcester. The boys rose at six o'clock and began lessons at seven, studying Latin, French, German, Italian; mathematics; religion and morals; history, government, and laws; natural philosophy or the 'liberal sciences'; and 'polite literature' (mainly Greek and Latin; the only English writers considered worthy of study were Shakespeare, Milton and Pope). Additional accomplishments, such as fencing, music, and landscape drawing, were also taught. To Dr Hurd, the King remarked that they all lived 'in unprincipled days, and no change can be expected but by an early attention to the rising generation.'[1] Yet the rising generation, at least as far as royalty was concerned, consisted of high-spirited boys who were difficult to control. One tutor, Mr Fairley, recalled in later life that there was 'something in the violence of their animal spirits that would make him accept no post to live with them.'

From an early age, the Prince of Wales irritated his father, thus giving some portents of the traditionally stormy relationship between King and heir. When shut out of his father's dressing-room one day, as a boy of ten, the Prince of Wales retaliated by shouting 'Wilkes and Liberty!' through the keyhole. To His Majesty, the radical journalist John Wilkes was the devil incarnate; but whether the King was infuriated by his son's impudence, or laughed it off 'with his accustomed good-humour', depends on whose version one reads. The boy particularly resented being made to wear a baby's cambric frock with lace cuffs, long after seeing other children of his age wearing more suitable clothes. To servants, he would complain in exasperation how his father treated him, seizing his lace collar and complaining bitterly that he was to be kept looking like a baby.

This mischievous child grew up to be a mischievous adult. When he was twelve, the King complained to Holderness that the Prince did not apply himself to his work; he showed 'duplicity' and had a 'bad habit . . . of not speaking the truth.' Naturally intelligent, he was inclined to be lazy, unlike the more honest, lively and industrious Frederick, whose conduct and progress pleased his father and tutors far more.

King George loved his children when they were small, but as they grew up he became less fond of them. As a parent, he was over-protective, attempting to teach his sons the virtues of rigorous simplicity, hard work and punctuality. The boys must be beaten at the first signs of laziness, and it distressed their sisters to see their two eldest brothers being held by their tutors and thrashed with a long whip.

The Princesses fared better under the eye of their mother and their much-loved governess Lady Charlotte Finch, who was appointed to the household in 1762 and stayed for thirty years. The King's drawing master, Joshua Kirby, was responsible for introducing Thomas Gainsborough, a close friend, to the royal family, and the latter taught the princesses the rudiments of painting and drawing. With his tutelage, and the art collection being formed by their parents, they had no shortage of inspiration or of fine pictures to copy. Charlotte and Elizabeth were the most active artists in the family, and several copies made by them survive in the Royal Collection. From copying drawings, perhaps tracing, Elizabeth progressed to become the most prolific of the sisters. Later she published lithographs, etchings and mezzotints, mainly of mythological scenes. She also designed, worked and supplied items of interior decoration at the Queen's House and later Frogmore, where she helped design garden buildings, and painted flower murals in the upper room of the Queen's Cottage at Kew. Sophia, an excellent horsewoman, preferred embroidery, and Amelia inherited her parents' love of music.

They were all strictly brought up, and the Queen insisted that the governesses must never 'pass any incivilities or lightness in their behaviour.' She lacked spontaneity with her children and was perhaps too stern with her daughters, for in later years they would complain about their mother, while always retaining great affection for their father. Mrs Harcourt thought that she kept them at 'too great a distance', and another lady at court doubted whether she had ever possessed any maternal feeling at all.

It was no wonder that they enjoyed breaks from family routine, when they were allowed to visit the houses of more indulgent hosts. Their indulgent great-aunt Amelia often invited them to her home at nearby Gunnersbury, where they played riotous games of skittles for hours on end.

There were also duty visits to various acquaintances of the elder generation, such as when the whole family were taken to Farnham to see Dr Thomas, Bishop of Winchester, on his eighty-second birthday. The Bishop's niece, Mrs Chapone, was particularly impressed with Prince William, then aged twelve. He was 'so sensible and engaging that he won the Bishop's heart,' staying to talk to the elderly gentleman while his brothers and sisters ran playing around the house.

Buckingham House was the family's main London residence, but the elder children were brought up mainly in the country, at first at Richmond Lodge. The Dowager Princess of Wales lived at the nearby White House, Kew. Soon after her death in February 1772, the growing family moved in, and Richmond Lodge was demolished.

As the family grew, it became necessary to set up additional establishments for the elder children. By 1773 the Prince of Wales and Prince Frederick had their

Queen Charlotte with George, Prince of Wales, and Prince Frederick, in her boudoir, Buckingham House, by Johann Zoffany, c. 1764

own apartments in the Dutch House at Kew (sometimes also known as the Prince of Wales's House), as well as at Buckingham House, and Princes William and Edward were 'boarded-out' in the house on the south side of the Green now known as Kew Palace. Their education was entrusted to two governors, General Budé, and Dr Majendie, a classical scholar who had taught Queen Charlotte English. Princes Ernest and Augustus, by then aged five and three respectively, were similarly settled in the smaller house next door accompanied by a staff of servants, including their own page, dresser, and governor.

All the children were expected to join their parents for breakfast at the Queen's House, taken punctually at nine o'clock, the youngest being brought in by the wet-nurse. They were given milk, or sometimes tea, and dry toast. The boys had already risen at six and spent two hours at their lessons, and after this refreshment, they would return to their houses for at least two hours of lessons, generally more, followed by a walk in the gardens, whatever the weather. Dinner was taken at about three o'clock, with 'soup if they choose it, when not very strong or heavy, and plain meat without fat, clear gravy and greens'. Fish was available, 'but without butter, using shrimps strained from the sauce or oil and vinegar', usually followed by 'the fruit of a tart without the crust'.[2] As a treat, on Thursdays and Saturdays they were allowed an ice of whatever flavour they wanted. Coffee was likewise available only twice a week, but they were normally permitted a glass of wine to finish the meal.

After dinner, all the children joined together in the garden for games. Cricket, hockey and football were the favourites, and Charlotte was particularly proud of her cricketing skills. They also had a model farm in which they were expected to work; one small field was set aside for them to sow and reap wheat, which they subsequently ground and used for making bread.

At five o'clock the children gathered again at their parents' apartments to read, write or 'make improving conversation'. The governesses were expected at six-thirty to take them off to bed, and a light supper was served except on Mondays.

As for clothes, each Prince had six suits of full-dress clothes a year and 'various common suits', new boots every spring and autumn, and new shoes once a fortnight.

The King and Queen set great store by their children's health. Two doctors were always kept in attendance. Bleeding and blistering were frequent remedies for childhood complaints, and all the youngsters suffered this with great regularity. They were vaccinated at an early age, a hazardous procedure in the days before Dr Jenner had substituted cowpox for inoculation with smallpox itself. When the four-year-old Prince of Wales had to stay in bed after his vaccination, he was asked whether he did not find it dull having to rest. 'Not at all,' he replied rather precociously; 'I lie and make reflections.'

The court at Kew enjoyed pleasantly rural surroundings, by no means cut off from their subjects. Many of the houses around the Green were residences for other members of the royal family, yet no attempt was made to keep the public out. The Botanical Gardens at Kew were open to the public on Thursdays, and Richmond Gardens on Sundays. Londoners would regularly come on Sunday afternoons in the hope of seeing a crocodile of neatly-paired royal infants taking a well-ordered walk across the lawns. The King himself would usually be seen setting a brisk pace at the head of this procession or, watering can in hand, directing operations among the flower beds.

Some fifty years later Charlotte Papendiek, daughter of one of the royal pages, recalled the summer of 1776 when she had been a girl of eleven, and Kew Green was covered with carriages on both days. Parties would travel up the river, with bands of music; 'The whole was a scene of enchantment and delight; Royalty living among their subjects to give pleasure and to do good.'[3]

Once they had moved to their own 'establishments', the princes and princesses seldom saw their parents, and never informally. Their Sunday afternoon walks were often the only time they met. During the season they were taken to London on Thursdays for the Drawing Rooms, and when they reached the age of ten, they were expected to attend evening parties for music and cards at Kew or Windsor, hardly the most lively occasions for these high-spirited youngsters. When summoned to be present at royal games of whist, they had to stand behind the Queen's chair, and sometimes fell asleep in that position. Unless offered a chair themselves, they were not allowed to sit

Kew Palace

down. When leaving their parents' presence, they had to walk backwards. Conversation was limited, as Queen Charlotte was particularly strict about the royal code that prevented children from speaking to their parents, unless spoken to first.

The King was happiest at Kew, where he could drive over to his Observatory, spend contented hours in the botanical gardens, and retire to the thatched cottage built for Queen Charlotte. There they would take tea, listen to their daughters playing the harpsichord or mandolin, and help them with their sketching.

He had always disliked Kensington Palace and Hampton Court, places which would ever be associated with the unhappier moments of his childhood. At Hampton he had once had his ears soundly boxed by King George II. Not until the second decade of his reign did the growing family make it necessary for him to consider living at Windsor Castle, largely neglected since the death of Queen Anne in 1714. Later the state apartments were brought back into commission, and in 1804 the royal family moved into the Castle, much to the chagrin of Queen Charlotte, who found it cold and inconvenient. King George intended to have further modifications made, but such plans were not put into effect before his final serious illness, and it was left to his eldest son and heir to complete the Castle's modern transformation.

In 1802, the White House at Kew was demolished and the King moved into the Dutch House* as a temporary measure, pending the building of a Gothic palace nearby. The Dutch House was small and inconvenient, with the Princesses' bedrooms on the top floor so tiny that they had to hang their dresses on the backs of the doors. As the King's health declined he visited Kew less, and left it in 1806 for the last time. The unfinished Gothic Palace was demolished in 1828.

While the children played and attended to their lessons at Kew, their father was engaged in promoting legislation which would have an adverse effect on several of them – the Royal Marriages Act. The virtuous King was almost exceptional by Hanoverian standards in making a successful and reasonably happy marriage which did not compromise family dignity. One of his sisters, Caroline Matilda, had been married at fifteen to the mentally-unbalanced, homosexual King Christian VII of Denmark; their unhappy union was dissolved after she took their court physician as a lover: he was executed for adultery, and she was sentenced to exile, ostracized by her family, dying at the age of twenty-three. Two of his brothers, the Dukes of Gloucester and Cumberland, made secret marriages with commoners, only informing him when it was too late to annul them. Determined that his children should not make such unsuitable matches, he brought his influence to bear on Parliament.

In order to maintain the dignity and purity of the British monarchy, he was determined that none of the direct descendants of King George II might marry before the age of twenty-five without the King's consent. After that, they could marry provided they gave a year's notice to the Privy Council, and as long as Parliament assented. He warned his Prime Minister, Lord North, that he expected 'every nerve to be strained to carry the Bill through both Houses with a becoming firmness;' as it did not relate to the government of the country, but personally to him, he had 'a right to expect a hearty support from everyone in my service and shall remember defaulters.'[4]

Several leading parliamentarians expressed their disgust at such an authoritarian measure, one prophesying with some foresight that it should be called 'An Act to encourage fornication and adultery in the descendants of George II'. Yet the King had his way, and by the end of March 1772 the Bill was law. It had thus been decreed that Protestant royalty could only marry other Protestant royalty, restricted the right of his sons to marry almost anyone who was not a German princess, and so limited the possibilities for his daughters that they were forced either into prolonged spinsterhood or secret liaisons.

During their adolescence, however, the cares of the future weighed less heavily on them. On 12 August 1778, the sixteenth birthday of the Prince of Wales, the royal family was expected to breakfast at Bulstrode Park (about nine miles from Windsor) with Queen Charlotte's friend Mrs Delany and the Dowager Duchess of Portland. Their hosts watched them coming up the drive, the King driving the Queen in a phaeton and pair, the Prince of Wales and

* The present 'Kew Palace'.

Prince Frederick trotting behind on horseback. In a post-chaise and four behind them came the Princess Royal, looking after their then youngest brother, Prince Adolphus. Following was a coach and six in which rode Princesses Augusta and Elizabeth, with Princes William and Edward. They all alighted and came clattering cheerfully into the hall. While the King showed the two eldest boys the pictures in the dining-room, the Queen and Mrs Delany talked about embroidery, and then the family came to admire the Duchess's collection of china, the young ones looking carefully and asking questions, the boys whistling and trying not to look too interested. They then sat down to breakfast with a hearty appetite.

Before leaving, the King invited his hosts to join them at Windsor the following evening, so they could meet all the family. In addition to the party which had come to Bulstrode, there were Princesses Mary and Sophia, aged two and one respectively, as well as Princes Ernest (seven) and Augustus (six). The royal family strolled on to the terrace so that eager sightseers might notice them, then the rooms were lighted up, tea was served, and music played. The children gave a display of dancing; with the two Princes performing a minuet, after which the Prince of Wales danced with the Princess Royal, though the latter did not keep very good time. Finally Princess Mary and Prince Adolphus took the floor and romped around 'in a dance of their own composing'. Returning home afterwards, Mrs Delany was charmed with the family, and felt far less tired than she had expected.

A similar picture of domestic bliss was provided by Mrs Delany at the time of the Princess Royal's thirteenth birthday in September 1779; 'The King carried about in his arms by turns Princess Sophia and the last prince, Octavius. I never saw more lovely children, nor a more pleasing sight than the King's fondness for them, and the Queen's; for they seem to have but one mind, and that is to make everything easy and happy about them.'[5]

2   'Fatherly admonitions'

This happy family life would not last for much longer. The Prince of Wales, frequently exhorted by his parents during boyhood to 'disdain all flattery', and generally behave as a paragon of virtue, found it impossible to live up to their exacting standards. 'Act uprightly and shew the anxious care I have had of you has not been misspent,' the King wrote to his two eldest sons in May 1778, 'and you will ever find me not only an affectionate father but a sincere friend.'[1]

Only human, the Prince confessed to being 'rather too fond of wine and women.' In the summer of 1779 he became infatuated with Mary Hamilton, one of the ladies at court, six years his senior. He wrote her sentimental letters almost every day for several weeks, expressing his undying affection, gave her trinkets, and perhaps offered marriage as well. Fortunately for both of them, she took at face value these outpourings of an excited youth who would doubtless transfer his extravagant affections elsewhere before long, insisting she could give him nothing but her friendship.

Within a few months, he had indeed lost his heart again. That autumn, he attended the theatre to see Shakespeare's *The Winter's Tale*. He was infatuated by the actress of twenty-one playing the part of Perdita, Mary Robinson. They arranged to meet secretly in the grounds at Kew, and he presented her with a locket with his portrait in miniature. '*Adieu, adieu, adieu, toujours chère.* Oh! Mrs Robinson,' he wrote to Mary Hamilton as he informed her that her place in his affections had been usurped.

If Mary Robinson was Perdita, then he would be Florizel, the son of King Polixenes in the play and Perdita's devoted lover; and in his rash correspondence, the Prince signed himself 'Florizel'. She had been married for five years, but she, her husband and their infant daughter had already seen the inside of a debtors' prison; not only was she flattered at finding herself the mistress of the heir to the throne, but also saw some financial security ahead of her. Without a thought for what trouble he might be causing himself in the future, the Prince sent her one passionate love letter after another, many promising gifts he would shower on her, including a bond of £20,000, when he came of age in August 1783, and was granted his own establishment.

The infatuation lasted for over a year, but by the spring of 1781, Florizel was tiring of his Perdita. Less scrupulous than Mary Hamilton, she had carefully preserved his correspondence with an eye to the future. Advised of the existence of 'a multitude of letters', the angry King agreed through the Prince's sub-Governor, Lieutenant-Colonel Hotham, to buy them back from her for £5,000, the money to be found by Lord North. Believing this was the end of the matter, he was further distressed to hear of the bond. This was only annulled

Mary 'Perdita' Robinson, by Thomas Gainsborough, 1781–2. Although painted after her affair with the Prince of Wales was over, she is shown holding a miniature of him

after much negotiation, conducted by Charles Fox, resulting in life annuities of £600 for Mrs Robinson and £200 for her young daughter.

Long before this, the King had determined to separate the eldest brothers, lest the corrupting influence of his first-born spread to those immediately below him. They idolized their eldest brother, evidently admiring him for his exploits, and the forthright way in which he dared to stand up to their father.

Already the King had decided what the fate of his three eldest should be. The reprobate Prince of Wales was born to be King; Frederick was going to become a soldier; and William would join the Navy. At thirteen years of age this third son was growing up an amiable but somewhat impressionable, undisciplined and hot-tempered Prince, shorter and less handsome than his brothers. William was given no say in the matter, but if, as he claimed in later life, nothing had made him happier than the decision to turn him into a sailor, it was indeed a fortunate choice.

On 15 June 1779, the Prince arrived at Spithead, accompanied by General Budé, to join the *Prince George* as a midshipman. As he had led such a sheltered existence, meeting new shipmates from a wider circle came as something of a shock to him, but his was not the quiet, retiring, sensitive nature which shrank from contact with others. Legend has it that, when being asked by his mates as to how they should address him, he replied that he was entered as Prince William Henry, 'but my father's name is Guelph and therefore if you please you may call me William Guelph for I am nothing more than a sailor like yourselves.'

Midshipmen who joined at a similar age were normally enrolled in the Royal Navy by their parents, and were drawn largely from the nobility, the landed gentry or professional classes, so there was nothing unusual about the Prince's introduction to the profession. They were billeted on board in the midshipmen's mess, and served with food which was almost inedible. Fortunately for William, his status ensured that he was often invited to dine at the Admiral's table, where the fare was better; and a cabin was set aside for him to pursue his studies with Dr Henry Majendie.

At this time, the country was virtually in a state of war. The American War of Independence had broken out in 1776, and the French and Spanish had since allied themselves with the Americans. The Navy therefore had to keep ships continuously at sea to supply the garrisons in America; fighting the French in the West Indies; supplying Gibraltar, currently besieged by the Spaniards; guarding the Channel, and endeavouring to keep the French fleet bottled up in their own ports. Soon after Prince William joined, the *Prince George* sailed to join the Channel fleet, which was charged with preventing the meeting of the French and Spanish fleets during the summer. It failed to do so, and the British fleet was obliged to withdraw to Plymouth before the combined might of the enemy. For a while there was the fear of invasion, but once the crisis was over, Prince William was granted leave, and spent the Christmas of 1779 at Windsor with his parents.

Back on board after about a week, the fleet under Admiral George Rodney captured a Spanish convoy and its escort. The Spanish flagship was occupied by British crew and named the *Prince William*, in respect of the Prince in whose presence the capture was effected. Continuing along the coast of Portugal, the fleet caught sight of the Spanish off Cape St Vincent, pursued them and battle

The British fleet off Cape St Vincent, in which Prince William Henry served under Admiral Rodney, 1779–80, and took part in action off Gibraltar with Don Juan de Langara

was joined. Although his ship was in some danger from enemy action, the Prince's hope that they would 'give these dons a sound thrashing' was fulfilled.

In high spirits, the victorious British ship sailed on to Gibraltar, where William visited the pubs, became involved in a brawl when he overheard a group of soldiers insulting the navy, and was clapped in prison, but set free after the Admiral's urgent intervention. On their journey back to England, the ship intercepted a French convoy, and captured it. Returning to London, the Prince was charged with handing the captured Spanish flags over to his father. It was not only his parents who, for perhaps the only time in their life, were proud of and delighted with the conduct of their third son. He was treated as a virtual hero by the public, who acted as if the Prince of fourteen had personally won the battle, with a little assistance from Rodney. When the King and Queen took him to Drury Lane to watch a performance of *The Tempest*, the audience cheered him so loudly as he stepped to the front of the royal box that the curtain for the start of the play was delayed for quarter of an hour, and in the excitement several people narrowly escaped asphyxiation in the rush to take a look at him.

This hero-worship was short-lived. Within a few weeks he was at sea again, engaged in the more mundane business of cruising in the Channel without seeing anything of excitement, interspersed with periods of leave at Kew and Windsor. The novelty of going to sea had worn off, and he was frustrated by his parents' letters bemoaning his bad temper, thoughtlessness, and his reluctance to accept criticism. 'I love you so well, that I cannot bear the idea of Your being only Mediocre,' wrote Queen Charlotte. 'Perfection is the thing you should aim at.'[2]

Christmas 1780 was spent with his parents again, and during this holiday it was observed that Prince William, like his eldest brother, had seemingly fallen in love. At a ball a St James's Palace given in honour of the Queen's birthday, he danced with Miss Julia Fortescue, who lived with her parents at Green Park. Less-than-secret assignations in the park, and possible suggestions of marriage, soon reached his parents. Before he could entangle himself further, he was sent back to his ship. Meanwhile, the King was determined that service on waters close to home provided too much scope for amorous liaisons, particularly with the Prince of Wales and his baneful influence close to hand. A more remote posting was the obvious solution.

It was not safe to leave Prince Frederick at home to be contaminated either. The decision to send him abroad must have caused the King some heart-searching, as he was clearly still the favourite of the elder children. Soon after Christmas 1780 he was sent to Hanover, under the care of his supervisor Colonel Greville, and a few servants. A curious crowd at Colchester came to gape at the Royal Arms on his carriage and another crowd saw him embark at Harwich. Compared with such an unceremonious send-off, he received quite a regal welcome in the ancestral home. As the citizens of Hanover had not seen their Elector since the days of George II, they came to give the present Elector's second son a jubilant welcome. Deputations of citizens, members of the government, and ministers from foreign countries, flocked to pay their respects to the Prince-Bishop of Osnabruck.

After spending a few months at Hanover, he went on to Brunswick as the guest of the Duke. The latter had married Princess Augusta, King George III's elder sister. It was not a happy match, for the Duke was coarse and brutal, treated his submissive wife badly, and was openly unfaithful. The first child was born insane, the second blind. However, Prince Frederick enjoyed his uncle's company, even though the latter's attempts to interest his nephew in his daughter Caroline bore little fruit. Had it been otherwise, Prince Frederick would have spared his elder brother the ordeal of having to marry this wayward and unfeminine cousin himself.

One of the King's motives in sending Frederick to Hanover was to give him some military training. The Duke introduced his nephew to Frederick the Great, King of Prussia, who took a fancy to the young Prince. Every autumn he attended the Prussian reviews, and a state ball and dinner were given to mark his visits to Berlin. Prince Frederick was impressed with the Prussian military machine, its efficient marching, drilling and formation.

He pursued his military studies with some application, although it was not surprising that he entered into the social life of Hanover with far more enthusiasm. Like his eldest brother, he was anything but immune to the charms of women and the heady delights of wine, and the thrill of gambling. At the cloistered courts of Kew and Windsor, these had been forbidden fruits to the young man; in Hanover, no obstacles were put in his way. As his parents and tutors had noticed approvingly, Frederick was always an enthusiastic lad; and his approach to the pleasures of good living was marked by the same enthusiasm which he had applied to his lessons as a small boy.

The Prince of Wales had had brief affairs with several other women in succession, most of them married and older than himself. There were regular reports of his wild behaviour, riding 'like a madman' in Hyde Park, mixing with profligate company, and drinking himself insensible. The contrast with the industrious Prince Frederick was acute. 'I wish to live with you as a friend, but then by your behaviour you must deserve it,' the King appealed to him. 'When you read this carefully over, you will find an affectionate father trying to save his son from perdition.'[3] Frederick added his own entreaty to his elder brother, warning him that 'you cannot stand this kind of life.'

Meanwhile, William was serving under Admiral Digby, in command of the American station. In August 1781, the week of his sixteenth birthday, he arrived in New York, the last stronghold of loyalist America. The citizens felt that King George III had sent his son there to soften the hearts of the rebels, and perhaps his presence would end the war.

Prince William found it a dull city, although it was briefly enlivened by talk of a conspiracy by the American rebels to capture the Prince and the Admiral, as they would surely be a useful bargaining counter when the time came to make peace with Britain. However, the British authorities learnt of the plot, and placed an extra guard on the Admiral's house.

In April 1782 the Prince was transferred to the *Barfleur* under the command of Sir Samuel Hood, who was asked to keep a strict eye on him. As the ship sailed for Jamaica, William heard with disappointment that peace had been concluded with all combatants in the American war, and any more chances he might have had of covering himself with glory in combat were therefore over. In addition, both the Prince and Hood quarrelled with Captain Napier, who was chosen to be his supervisor. 'William was ever violent when controlled,' wrote the King, who was angry when he heard of the quarrels. 'I had hoped that by this time he would have been conscious of his own levity.'[4]

It was soon evident that the King's sons would prove as troublesome as his own brothers had been. The primness and restrictions of his own early life, and the fact that he had been deprived of the companionship of others at an early age, made it difficult for him to sympathize with his sons as young men. Having taken only a sporadic interest in their education and left them to the care of often unsuitable attendants, he must have hoped for the best; if so, he was bitterly disappointed when he saw the results.

The Prince of Wales's love of good living had already caused friction between father and son. In time their relations might have improved, had the Prince's maturity not coincided with the unsettled political situation and England's loss of the American colonies in the 1780s. His emergence into society came at the time of a period of acute political rivalry. Opposition politicians, hopeful of future office, had made it their practice with the coming of the Hanoverian dynasty to patronize the heir to the throne. The Tories had been long in power, and it was inevitable that the Prince should find himself fawned upon by the Whigs in Parliament. In particular he found a kindred spirit in the charismatic Charles James Fox, who was introduced to him by his uncle the Duke of Cumberland. A warning to the Prince from one of his equerries, Colonel Gerard Lake, that he should guard against becoming a 'party man', and allowing his 'great good nature . . . to be imposed upon by people who have not the smallest pretensions to your civility', was disregarded.

In 1782 Lord North resigned as prime minister, after the British defeat in the American war of independence, and for a few months the country was governed by a Whig administration under the Marquess of Rockingham. The following year, a coalition of Whigs, supporters of Fox, and the discredited Lord North came to power.

Fox and his followers had pledged themselves to argue for generous provisions for the heir to the throne on his coming of age in August 1783, and the Cabinet agreed that he should be granted £100,000 a year, of which £12,000 would come from the revenues of the Duchy of Cornwall and the rest from an annual grant approved by Parliament. At the same time, the King would be asked to settle his extravagant son's outstanding debts, already totalling about £30,000. These proposals filled the King 'with indignation and astonishment'. He readily pointed out that he had managed with half this allowance at a similar age, and when his subjects were taxed so highly, he could see no justification for 'a shameful squandering of public money' to gratify his son's passions. A compromise was reached by which the Prince would receive £62,000 a year, of which £50,000 would be provided by the King from the Civil List, and the remainder from the Duchy of Cornwall. Parliament would be asked to find the £30,000 to settle his debts, and a similar sum for fitting out Carlton House.

A dilapidated mansion a few hundred yards from St James's Palace, left uninhabited since the death of his grandmother, the Dowager Princess of Wales, the Prince set about transforming Carlton House into a testament to fashionable, gracious living. While the King remarked optimistically that it merely needed a touch of paint and 'handsome furniture where necessary', the Prince and his architect Henry Holland transformed it into a splendid building with

Carlton House, the south front

Corinthian porticos, an Ionic colonnade, and a temple paved in Italian marble, among other less modest home improvements. He moved in early in 1784.

By now the large family was almost complete. Queen Charlotte suffered particularly from depression during her fourteenth pregnancy, giving birth in September 1780 to the invalid Prince Alfred. In the summer of 1782 Lady Charlotte Finch took him to Deal 'to make use of the salt waters', but he did not improve. By the time they returned to Windsor they had given up hope, and three weeks later, on 20 August, he died within a month of what would have been his second birthday. As the sorrowing parents took one last look at him, they took comfort in the knowledge that had he lived he would have led 'a life of pain'. Queen Charlotte, commented some contemporaries, had become 'a proper mother' by losing one of her children.

'I am very sorry for Alfred,' the King noted, 'but if it had been Octavius, I should have died too.' Octavius, the second youngest son, was a particularly appealing child on whom his parents lavished much affection. Yet he was struck down by illness after being vaccinated for smallpox, an ordeal from which the elder children had soon recovered, and he followed Alfred to the grave in May 1783, aged four. At first the King was inconsolable; 'Heaven will be no heaven to me if Octavius is not there.' Yet despite these two infant mortalities, by the standards of the day, the parents were certainly fortunate to see so many of their children survive childhood.

At the time, the Queen was carrying her last child. A daughter was born on 7 August 1783, and christened Amelia after her great-aunt. Her eldest brother, now approaching twenty-one, was her godfather. Amelia was to become her father's favourite. Two years later, Mrs Delany wrote with enthusiasm of spending evenings at the Queen's Lodge 'with no other company than their own most lovely family,' sitting round a large table, 'whilst the younger part of the family are drawing and working, the beautiful babe Princess Amelia bearing her part in the entertainment, sometimes in one of her sisters' laps, sometimes playing with the King on the carpet.'[5]

In the summer of 1783, the Prince of Wales made his first visit to the Sussex seaside town of Brighton, for a short recuperative course of sea-bathing to relieve his swollen neck glands. Brighton had long been recommended as a fashionable 'cure', as the sea water contained a greater percentage of salt than any other watering-place in England, owing to its remoteness from a river mouth. Splendid views of the Downs, and its air of general informality, charmed the Prince. The following year, he leased Grove House, some six hundred yards from the seafront, for ten weeks. While staying there he rode on the Downs and went shooting at nearby Falmer, as well as swimming. Racing and shooting parties helped to establish some conviviality in what had been for centuries the quiet little cobbled town of Brighthelmstone, and the Prince so enjoyed himself that he decided to establish his own personal residence in the town. On his fourth visit he employed the architect Henry Holland to convert an old farmhouse by the sea into what would become the Pavilion, and in 1787 he moved into the partially refurbished building.

While the Prince of Wales amused himself on the south coast, his next two brothers were at Hanover. William had returned from sea in June 1783. After spending several years in the Navy, he lacked the polish and *savoir-faire* so cherished by society, particularly his more sophisticated eldest brother. Practical jokes in the midshipman's mess were more his style. Even so he was a good-hearted, companionable young man with an outgoing manner. Horace Walpole, who never considered himself 'apt to be intoxicated with royalty', found him 'lively, cheerful, talkative, manly, well-bred, sensible, and exceedingly proper in his replies', as well as 'in great spirits all day'. Taking to London society at once, he convinced the King that he, too, should be removed from the corrupting influences of London and his eldest brother without delay. Accordingly he was sent to Hanover, where the King fondly hoped he might emerge 'the Prince, the gentleman and the officer'.

He was accompanied by the genial Captain William Merrick, and General Budé. The latter's presence was unwelcome to the Prince, who associated him with his childhood days and resented this apparent refusal to acknowledge that he was virtually an adult.

King George was confident that his loyal, dutiful and affectionate second son would keep William in the paths of righteousness. On one matter the King and Frederick were in complete agreement: the young midshipman sailor was too fond of practical jokes, and 'so excessively rough and rude that there was no bearing it.'[6] If the father hoped that such criticism would prove that Frederick was to be trusted to make a gentleman out of him, disillusion would soon come. The brothers were pleased to see each other again, and Frederick introduced him to the world of gambling. He was a poor card-player, and lost money heavily, losses which he hated to make good. William was no more competent, though more conscientious in paying his debts.

An annual allowance of £100 was insufficient to cover his cost of living, clothing and gambling, and within a year of moving to Hanover he was heavily in debt. Budé asked the King for permission to settle his losses, and the King agreed with a heavy heart; reproaching his son at the same time that 'if you permit yourself to indulge every foolish idea you must be wretched all your life, for with thirteen children I can but with the greatest care make both ends meet and am not in a situation to be paying their debts if they contract any,' and that vanity, 'which has been too predominant in your character has occasioned this, but I hope for the future you will be wiser.'[7]

Despite such diversions, life in Hanover proved extremely tedious for the naval Prince. He was no horseman, and found routine daily inspections of the royal stables boring. An attempt to take up boar-hunting was abandoned when he discovered that the recoil of the gun hurt his shoulder. Visits to the theatre were a chore, as he found it difficult to follow the German satisfactorily. Above all, he disliked the arid, formal society life of Hanover, preferring the company of naval officers and whores.

Although he patronized the brothels from time to time, he had a couple of brief affairs. First, there was a fling with his cousin Princess Charlotte of Mecklenburg-Strelitz. This attachment to her namesake niece did not alarm the Queen in England, or indeed surprise her, 'as you are of an age when young men are apt to fancy themselves in love with every sprightly young woman they see or are allowed to keep company with.'[8] For a time he also courted Maria Schindbach, a merchant's daughter. It was rumoured that he made a secret marriage with Caroline von Linsingen, daughter of a General in the Hanoverian infantry, and had a son by her. Subsequent research, however, proved that he was in England on the days that he was supposed to have initially met and later married her.

Attempts to broaden his mind educationally misfired. At Göttingen he attended a lecture by the historian Michaelis, which turned out to be less a lecture, more an impromptu harangue on the sovereignty of the people. Rather naively, William reported on it approvingly to his father and suggested it be translated into English. King George was horrified at the thought of his impressionable son being fed such subversive ideas, and Michaelis was dismissed from his post.

By the spring of 1785, William was desperate to leave the tedium of Hanover. Prince Frederick, who had been created Duke of York the previous year, came to his assistance, though his motives perhaps came less from a desire to help his brother than from the fact that he was tired of his presence in Germany. Whatever his reasons, in April he wrote to the King, suggesting rather sanctimoniously that 'there can never be any real alteration for the better in him [William] till he has been kept for some time under severe discipline, which alone can be done on board of ship, for his natural inclination for all kinds of dissipation will make him, either here or indeed in any place by land, run into society where he can form to himself only an idea of pleasure.'[9] Reluctantly the King recalled William, who was delighted to return, but his joy was short-lived. The Prince of Wales was holding a fête at Carlton House on the evening of his arrival, and naturally wanted his brother to attend. The King insisted that William should stay quietly at Kew with his parents, ostensibly on the grounds that he wanted to know how things were at Hanover, but really as he wanted to keep the brothers apart.

William was promoted to the rank of Lieutenant in June 1785 and sent back to sea without further delay.

The Prince of Wales was proving a sore trial to the King and Queen. His championship of Charles Fox was an irritation; but worse still were the heir's amorous adventures. In the spring of 1784, he became friendly with Maria Fitzherbert, a twice-widowed Roman Catholic of twenty-eight. Soon he was infatuated with her, but much as she loved him, she told him that her religious scruples would never allow her to become merely his mistress. On the other hand, marriage to her would directly contravene the Royal Marriages Act.

After pursuing her passionately, he tried to make her relent with a dramatic suicide attempt at Carlton House, pretending to stab himself, and thereby tricking her into joining him. She accepted a ring from him and promptly fled to France, either to escape any further attentions, or perhaps in the hope that he would join her for a secret marriage. He requested permission from his father to live abroad, on the grounds that he intended to economize. Rumours went around society that he intended to sell his jewels and go to start a new life with

Maria Fitzherbert, by Richard Cosway

Mrs Fitzherbert in America. Alarmed at the prospect of losing his royal patron, Fox begged him to give up all thoughts of marrying her. The Prince assured him that he had indeed done so, although he had already sent her a letter of more than six thousand words, begging 'Maria my beloved wife (for such you really are)' to return to England, where they could marry in secret.

In December 1785 she returned to her house in Mayfair. An Anglican priest, the Reverend Robert Butt, was released from a debtors' prison on payment of £500 to settle his liabilities, considerably less than those of the Prince of Wales. In return for the promise of a bishopric when the Prince ascended the throne, he agreed to perform a marriage ceremony according to the rites of the Church of England at her house. On 15 December the Prince and Mrs Fitzherbert were quietly married at her house, with her uncle and brother as witnesses.*

---

* Mrs Fitzherbert kept most of her letters from the Prince of Wales until after his death. In 1833, four years before she died, she consented to the destruction of most, but insisted on keeping a few. These, including some which established the truth of her marriage to the Prince, were preserved by Messrs Coutts until 1905, when they were transferred to the Royal Archives. The Duke of Wellington had been determined to prevent their publication as the Prince, by marrying a Catholic, had forfeited the Crown; and it was largely owing to the Duke's insistence on secrecy that the marriage did not become public knowledge until some years after his death in 1852.

Over Christmas and the New Year, there was speculation that Mrs Fitzherbert would be created a Duchess and move into a wing of Carlton House. However she continued to live quietly in her house at Park Street. A few people suspected that they had gone through a form of marriage, but most of the Prince's friends refused to believe that he would have behaved so foolishly after he had given Fox his word that marriage was out of the question. Though the King and Queen heard rumours before long, they preferred simply to ignore Mrs Fitzherbert's existence.

It has since been alleged that children were born to Mrs Fitzherbert and the Prince, among them three sons, one of whom was educated in America, and a daughter, more commonly supposed to have been the illegitimate child of her brother, John Smythe. No conclusive evidence, however, exists in the case of either.[10]

Meanwhile the Prince's debts continued to mount dramatically. In April 1786, he was forced to appeal to his father for assistance in his 'very difficult situation.' The King demanded a full written statement of his son's liabilities and some guarantee that in future his expenditure would be contained within the annual grant awarded to him on his coming of age. In desperation the Prince closed down Carlton House in July 1786, dismissing his servants and reducing the size of his household, selling his stud and most of his carriages, and driving off to Brighton with Mrs Fitzherbert in a hired chaise. He was determined to show his father and critics that he could live well within his means if he so tried, although he must have known that such a dramatic display of economy would bring sympathy from his friends and supporters in Parliament.

By now the fourth royal Prince, Edward, had joined the Duke of York in Germany. He left home with little regret, for from childhood he was the son liked least by his parents. The King was always ready to find fault with him, while the Queen would treat their eldest son's lapses indulgently but regard Edward as the epitome of 'imprudence and extravagance.'

As the *Morning Chronicle* remarked on 18 May 1785, 'There was a time when the English would not be pleased to see their Princes go in such numbers to reside out of the country; and much less so since the accession of the reigning family to see them live in Germany; but now that they have a native Prince on their throne the English are not afraid of foreign attachments, which during the reigns of the last two monarchs, influenced the Councils of the nation much more than a regard to its real interests.'

The King had intended to send him to Göttingen, but the Duke of York advised against it, as the young men all lived separately there, 'and the Professors have very little more than a nominal authority over them, so that there does not pass a day without some very great excess or other being committed.' It was not right, he went on, for a sheltered young man to go to such a place 'where he shall hear every day of these excesses and where he will in a manner be obliged to keep company with the very people who commit them.'[11]

The Prince settled at the royal palace in Luneburg, Hanover, at the start of his military training, accompanied by his tutor, Baron Wangenheim. He applied himself diligently to his studies, writing to the King of spending four hours a morning studying German, law, artillery and history, as well as one hour every evening, three times a week on religious subjects, and three times a week the classics. In his leisure time he enjoyed shooting, dancing, dining and music. However, he complained bitterly of the miserable allowance he was granted to live on, 'one guinea and a half per week, sometimes melted down by military forfeits to twenty-two shillings'. After a year at Luneburg he moved to Hanover, but was irked at the system of espionage carried out; 'my letters were intercepted; several never reached the King; he was displeased at my apparently undutiful silence; false representations were made to him respecting my conduct; I was described to him as recklessly extravagant; I had the means of being so, undoubtedly, on a guinea and a half a week!'[12]

In time-honoured fashion, he soon fell into debt. The Duke of York interceded on his behalf, telling the King that it was absurd for people to lead him into temptation by offering him credit to any amount that he pleased. Wearily the King paid his debts after Edward apologized for his 'disobedience to your express commands.'

That same year, three more brothers came out to Germany. There seems something strange in this most British, least-travelled of kings making such efforts to Germanize his sons from an early age, and it can only be explained by his determination to keep them as far away from their eldest brother's evil influence as possible. In the summer of 1786 Ernest, Augustus and Adolphus were sent to the University at Göttingen. Despite the Duke of York's strictures in the case of Edward, the King must have felt that three boys of a more tender age, if adequately supervised, would be safe enough from life's little temptations. With a household headed by Colonel Carl von Malortie, they arrived at Göttingen on 6 July, and a few days later they were formally matriculated into the University. On their father's orders they were to conform to all the usual university regulations; their establishment was to be run on military lines; and familiarity with their fellow students was to be kept within careful limits. They were granted a sum of 600 crowns a week for table expenses, including 'two grand institution dinners' to which they were expected to invite their professors and some of their fellow-students.

The King had wished to attach an English clergyman to the establishment, but he was persuaded that the boys would make better progress in German if they had no Englishman to talk to. They were expected to master the German tongue. The language was never heard at the King's court, and seldom in his domestic life. While they were still learning, they attempted to communicate with their tutors in Latin, as only one of their tutors at the university spoke fluent English, but this was a failure as the English and German pronunciations of Latin were so different. Eventually French had to be used until they had a sufficient command of German. Before the end of the year, the King gave orders that German was to be the exclusive language of the household, and any of his sons who broke this rule at table should be punished. In Ernest's case, this bilingual upbringing made for an oddly Germanized turn of phrase in his letters home. He would tell his parents that 'Here do I lead a very happy life,' and 'every week have we public concerts, assemblies and balls where nothing but joy reigns.'[13]

Princesses Charlotte, Augusta and Elizabeth, by Thomas Gainsborough, 1784

All three Princes were natural students. For the first year, they were tutored in private, but once their German was good enough, they attended lectures with the other students on advanced mathematics and physics, natural history, politics, religion, law and theology. So as not to lose touch with English, they read journals regularly including the *Spectator* and the *Guardian*. Augustus enjoyed theology, and his correspondence home prompted King George to write in December 1786 that 'your letters contain such religious sentiments that I do not doubt but your conduct will ever be agreeable to them.'[14]

Ernest was particularly fond of music, and took lessons on the flute, 'the only instrument that I could play for I am able to be as near the notes as I like.' Already he was particularly short-sighted, in an age when young men did not wear spectacles in public. He was also different from his brothers in that he never showed the same tendency to plumpness. While he was not alone among them in growing to be over six foot, he remained slender throughout his long life. As an adolescent he was much more quiet, less inclined to chatter and make small talk than they were. Yet he had a quick mind, was a shrewd judge of character, and his sharp tongue would sometimes get the better of him. Many years later his brother William remarked that Ernest was a very good fellow, 'but if anyone has a corn he is sure to tread on it.'

Another characteristic which marked Ernest out from his brothers was his refusal to 'indulge in gush'. From time to time, their letters to other members of the family were couched in extravagant language which may strike readers in a more reserved age as somewhat overdone, and none more so than those of the Prince of Wales. No such over-affectionate phraseology ever permeated Ernest's dry, matter-of-fact correspondence. In his youth he was often thought to be lacking in warmth and human affection, though his marriage, contracted in middle age, was to be one of the most successful.

Göttingen was delighted by its royal patronage, and treated the Princes with unnecessary fulsome deference and respect. Shopkeepers were always ready to supply goods on credit, and the local notabilities feted and entertained the youths as much as Malortie would allow. As their elder brothers had discovered, the willingness of others to lend them money soon put them in debt.

In August 1787 the Duke of York returned home. He had been deliberately kept in Germany for several years in order to escape the influence of his eldest brother, but the King was impatient to see him again. There had been many changes in the family since he had left, not least the death of two young brothers, one of whom was not even born when he was last at home, and the arrival of his youngest sister. It must have been an emotional reunion between father and son. Describing the Duke's homecoming, the diarist Fanny Burney wrote glowingly of 'The joy of his excellent father! Oh that there is no describing.' Piously, she echoed the King's hope that he might 'but escape the contagion of surrounding example.'

'The contagion' himself, however, could not resist the opportunity to join in the family welcome, and lost no time in renewing his acquaintance with his long-absent brother. Wine, women, gambling and running up enormous debts had been something of a way of life for both young men on opposite sides of the North Sea. Now they became inseparable companions, and the King angrily if unfairly blamed the Prince of Wales for leading the Duke astray. By the end of the year, the latter had ceased to visit the family at Windsor.

A kindred spirit was about to join them. Since being sent back to sea, Prince William had been promoted to Captain of the frigate *Pegasus*, and served in the North American stations and the West Indies. During this time he celebrated his twenty-first birthday riotously on board ship at Newfoundland, and gave away the bride at the wedding of Captain Nelson, with whom he had made friends on a Caribbean cruise some years earlier. In the autumn of 1787, there was a risk of war between Britain and Holland over the issue of navigation of the Scheldt, and he was ordered to proceed secretly to Ireland, ready to serve in any action which might ensue. The dispute was settled by the time William had crossed the Atlantic, but the King, outraged by regular reports of his son's dissipation and debts abroad, still insisted on his recall to England.

Gloomily, William wrote to the Prince of Wales on 27 December on the prospect of a confrontation with the King; 'There can be no great pleasure in going, with a certainty that my Christmas box or New Year's gift will be a family lecture for immorality, vice, dissipation and expence, and that I shall meet with the appellation of the prodigal son.'[15] However, the King had no wish to see him, and when *Pegasus* docked at Plymouth on 27 December, instructions were received from the Admiralty that he was to remain in port until further notice.

Hearing of their brother's disgrace, the Prince of Wales and the Duke of York decided to come to Plymouth and cheer him up. Arriving on 8 January 1788, the merry trio devoted themselves to two days of dinners, balls and miscellaneous inspections. Their visit, short though it was, whetted his appetite for society life, and taught him to worry less about their father's regular admonitions. Light-heartedly, he wrote to the Prince of Wales in February that 'the old boy is exceeding out of humour,' and that 'fatherly admonitions at our time of life are very unpleasant and of no use; it is a pity he should expend his breath or his time in such fruitless labour.'[16]

When his brothers were gone, he sought consolation in the arms of Sally Wynne, the daughter of a merchant in Plymouth who hoped that by currying royal favour in such a way he might fulfil his ambition of becoming Agent Victualler to the Navy. Although the King could hardly have been surprised, he was angry to hear of his son's latest amorous entanglement; 'What, William playing the fool again!' He ordered that his son should be posted to America once more. By August, a bored and lovesick William was at Halifax, under the command of Captain Charles Sandys, a vulgar, drunken dolt. With no active service, the men led an aimless, tedious existence, enlivened only by the customary distractions of drinking and whoring.

3 'Sincerely do I love this good and worthy man'

In June 1788, a few days after his fiftieth birthday, the King fell seriously ill. It began with a series of severe abdominal spasms lasting from three in the morning to eight at evening, followed by a 'bilious attack' lasting for a couple of days.

The illness of George III has since been diagnosed as 'acute intermittent porphyria'. It is a rare inborn metabolic disorder, usually starting as a persistent cold and cough, followed by symptoms including colic, nausea, constipation, acute chest pains and cramps. More severe attacks include a very fast pulse, with fever and sweating, and sometimes delirium; gabbling speech, followed by hoarseness or loss of voice; insomnia, irritability, and inability to taste. In the worst cases there is mental aberration, hallucinations and delusions, and the patient may become violent. The disease is named from the discoloured urine, described as blood-red, purple, or the colour of port wine, hence 'porphyria'. As already noted, four or five of King George's children were also afflicted to some degree, albeit less severely, and probably the King's granddaughter Princess Charlotte of Wales, who died in giving birth to a stillborn son at the age of twenty-one.

His recovery was slow, and it was suggested that he should spend a period of convalescence away from the cares of state. Lord Fauconberg, one of his Lords of the Bedchamber, offered the use of his house at Cheltenham, Bay's Hill Lodge.

Accordingly, a small party including the King and Queen and the Princesses Charlotte, Augusta and Elizabeth, set off from Windsor at five o'clock one morning, and completed the journey to Cheltenham in one day. Although their lodgings were cramped, they were all delighted with Cheltenham and the surrounding countryside. In particular the Princesses, it was said, were in high health and spirits. It was the furthest they – and their father – had yet been from home. The King found the waters 'salutary', and insisted that with these, with good mutton, and plenty of exercise, he would soon become well again.

The King had a 'flow of spirits quite unequalled' – perhaps the first sign of the 'hurry and flurry' which would later be a characteristic of his recurring illness. He and the Queen retired to bed late and rose early, as he had suddenly developed an insatiable appetite for sight-seeing. Large crowds gathered to see him wherever he went, and were quick to spread gossip afterwards. At Cheltenham, some said, His Majesty ran a race with a horse.

News came that the Duke of York wanted to see them, but there was no room at the house. Determined to show his favourite son every hospitality, the King noticed a small wooden house on the outskirts of Cheltenham. At his request the entire building was removed to a site beside Bay's Hill Lodge, and after five days' work it was ready for the Duke's arrival. Even so, the Duke declared that he could stay for only one night, as military business demanded his imminent return to London. The King's disappointment was evident, so as a compromise the Duke delayed his journey back (presumably to rejoin the Prince of Wales), so that his father could at least have one extra day of his company.

After five weeks the King and Queen returned to Windsor and Buckingham House. He was delighted with his apparent recovery, and Lady Harcourt remarked that she had never seen him 'in better health or spirits'. All the same, his swings of mood – irritable one moment, over-affectionate the next – were disconcerting to those around him. His volleys of questions, and his rapid, stumbling speech, punctuated with numerous 'Whats' and 'Heys', had always given an impression of eccentricity; now it became more marked.

By mid-October he was clearly unwell again. One morning he sent for his physician Sir George Baker, who arrived to find him in bed suffering from acute stomach pain and difficulty in breathing. None of the medical treatments prescribed for him seemed to produce any satisfactory effect. By a great effort of will, he roused himself to appear at a levee on the 24th of the month, in order to calm public apprehensions about his health. As he still looked ill, it had the opposite effect.

Next day he travelled to Windsor, still suffering from painful swollen feet, an abnormally fast pulse, and his manner still a little odd. Those whom he stopped to talk to about his health were alarmed by his voluble, hoarse voice, marked by an 'extreme quickness of speech and manner that belongs to fever.'

The family were frightened by a strange scene at chapel that weekend. The King suddenly started up from his pew, embraced his wife and daughters, and then burst into tears. 'You know what it is to be nervous,' he said to Princess Elizabeth, 'but was you ever so bad as this?' 'Yes,' she said firmly, recognizing the importance of humouring him.

Temporarily chastened by these reports, the Duke of York came to visit the King later that week, and found him in 'a violent degree of agitation'. He had complained to his doctor of being unable to sleep – or when he did so, sleep was disturbed and often delirious – and that his hearing and vision were affected. To Frederick he confided sadly, 'I wish to God I might die, for I am going to be mad.'

Unfortunately, the Duke of York was not long affected by this unhappy episode. Instead of staying at Windsor or Buckingham House to give moral support to his mother and sisters, on whom the strain was acute, he was to be seen night after night drinking and gambling at his club, telling the secrets of the sickroom and mimicking his father. In particular the Queen was close to despair at times.

On 5 November, the Prince of Wales arrived from Brighton to see for himself, and stayed to dinner. The King was no longer well enough to ride, and instead he had been for a drive in his chaise earlier that day. Although he seemed in good humour, he gave so many contradictory orders to the servants, and got in and out of his seat so many times, that they began to fear the worst. At dinner the Prince and the Duke of York sat down to eat with the King. According to Fanny Burney (who was not present), the King assured the Duke excitedly that he loved him so much, he could refuse him nothing. As for the Prince of Wales, he had behaved very badly, but he was still his son and he still loved him. The embarrassed brothers fell silent. Then the King became delirious, the Queen had hysterics, the Princesses burst into tears and the Prince of Wales was so upset that Princess Elizabeth had to bathe his temples with Hungary water. Later the Prince claimed rather dramatically that his father had grabbed him by the collar and thrust him violently against the wall.

That night the King chattered deliriously, his hoarse, weak voice heard by servants through the door. Baker, he repeated endlessly, told him lies, and he declared that 'I am not ill, but I am nervous. If you would know what the matter is with me, I am nervous.'

As he became worse, the family feared that he would die or become incurably deranged. The Prince of Wales, said Fanny Burney, 'took the government of the house into his own hands. Nothing was done but by his orders, and he was applied to in every difficulty. The Queen interfered not in anything; she lived entirely in her two new rooms, and spent the whole day in patient sorrow and retirement with her daughters.'[1]

The Queen was probably the one most shaken by her husband's state of mind. She was so upset, and so unable to control her feelings, that the doctors forbade her into the sickroom lest her state would only increase the King's agitation and make him worse. Consequently she did not see him at all for another five weeks. During this time she fiercely resented the way in which the Prince of Wales had assumed command and taken charge of events.

Later that month, the Queen agreed that her husband should be moved to Kew, on condition that she and her daughters went too. Gradually he recovered, despite a plethora of doctors each insisting on their own special cures, strait-jacket restraints and the like. Meanwhile, Parliament discussed the need for a Regency. William Pitt, the Prime Minister, knew that should the Prince of Wales be declared Prince Regent, the royal prerogative of creating ministers would pass into his hands, and a Whig administration would soon be formed. Wisely, Pitt played for time, and Fox (who had as much to gain as anyone from his friend becoming Regent) clumsily declared that a Regency was the Prince's by right, and not subject to parliamentary restrictions. In the ensuing debate, allusions were made 'with respect to a certain lady', thereby suggesting that with regard to the secrecy over his marriage the Prince of Wales could not be trusted; and there were references to his extravagance over the Royal Pavilion at Brighton. The press sided with Pitt, and offered sympathy for the King. By mid-February 1789 he was recovering; the Lord Chancellor informed Parliament that His Majesty was convalescent, and the Regency Bill was therefore dead.

Some of his trusted political confidantes came to acquaint him tactfully with business transacted during his illness. He may have been given some forthright remarks about the conduct of his eldest sons, for the Prince of Wales and the

Frederick, Duke of York, in Garter robes, by Sir Joshua Reynolds

Duke of York were only permitted to see him for half an hour, and in the presence of the Queen, and on the understanding that they must not talk to him of politics. They were angry that ministers had daily access to him, while they were denied any opportunity to exculpate themselves. The Prince of Wales felt privately that his mother 'had much to answer for'. That she was keeping them away from their father could hardly be denied, but she felt herself responsible for keeping a sufficient distance between him and those who might 'agitate' him too much. However, she made her attitude clear at the first royal Drawing Room following his recovery, by making herself conspicuously pleasant to the 'loyal' and cold-shouldering the 'disloyal'. While she had invitations to parties at Buckingham House sent to the Prince and the Duke, she wrote to them explaining that their friends must not expect to be asked.

On 23 April, St George's Day, the family attended a service of thanksgiving for the King's recovery in St Paul's Cathedral. The two eldest Princes made their feelings clear by chattering to each other and to their uncles throughout the service, and eating biscuits during the sermon. When White's Club held a thanksgiving fête at the Pantheon, they allowed their complimentary tickets to be offered for sale in Bond Street.

Prince William had been in the West Indies when he heard of his father's illness, and wrote back sympathetically to the Prince of Wales in January, 'Sincerely do I love this good and worthy man and long may he yet with his usual firmness reign over us. The poor Queen: what a situation for her.'[2] It was fortunate that he was not at home at the time, otherwise he would have probably sided with his elder brothers, and risked his father's alienation. Indeed, he congratulated his brothers on their united stand against the Queen and ministers, adding that 'I only hope to be admitted of the party.'

Like them, he had experienced the perpetual nagging of his father's letters, expecting him to be the paragon of virtue that he had been at a similar age. Moreover, when he had been in disgrace at Plymouth, his brothers had stood by him. If it came to taking sides in the family divisions, he would feel morally obliged to stand with his brothers. It had rankled when his name was suggested for the Council of Regency, should one need to be declared, but the Queen contemptuously refused to consider him. Although an inexperienced and often headstrong young man, he had served with distinction in the Navy, and seen far more of the world than any other member of the family, and his mother's rejection seemed a sorry gesture after all he had done.

On 29 April 1789 his ship *Andromeda* arrived at Spithead, and three days later he was at Windsor. When he saw the father whom he had so recently expected never to meet again, he confessed afterwards that he was so overcome by emotion that he could hardly stand.

Within a week of his return, however, it was announced that HRH Prince William Henry had decided to offer himself for election to the House of Commons and would stand for the vacant seat of Totnes, Devon, as a protest against the delay in granting him his dukedom. As a mere prince he was dependent on his father's bounty, but as a Duke he would receive a parliamentary grant of around £12,000 a year. Had a title been conferred on him at the age of twenty-one, as in the case of Prince Frederick, he would have been at least £30,000 richer. Though any such election would have probably been declared invalid, the protest was effective. Fearful of the prospect of his son attempting to play the orator and enlisting the sympathy of the South Devon electorate, the King signed the patent on 16 May creating him Duke of Clarence and St Andrews and Earl of Munster, gloomily commenting that he knew it was another vote added to the Opposition. With this act, the Prince's active naval career virtually ceased.

On 1 June, the new Duke gave a party at Willis's Subscription Rooms to celebrate his title. As guests wandered through the rooms, they were allowed to look through an open door into a room where their host sat beside the Prince of Wales and the Duke of York. On the wall behind them was a transparency of their arms, and underneath in huge letters, 'UNITED FOR EVER'. Thus did the Duke of Clarence inform the world that he was supporting his brothers against the King.

Yet he was at heart more good-natured and more loyal than his brothers. At Windsor he still showed affection for his father and respect for his mother, and remained on excellent terms with his sisters. When he saw Princess Mary again he pretended not to recognize her, as she had grown so much, and jokingly asked if she was one of the Queen's new ladies-in-waiting.

However the lustre of Carlton House soon faded for him. The Prince of Wales never ceased to surround himself with witty, sophisticated company, and partisans such as Fox and Sheridan, a member of parliament and playwright, found much to make fun of in the bluff and ignorant sailor who had spent so much time abroad.

Preferring his own quiet hearth to Carlton House, that autumn he took a house, Ivy Lodge, on Richmond Hill. Here he settled down with Miss Polly Finch, a courtesan from Berkeley Square whose craving for society ill-accorded with the Duke's yearning for quiet domesticity. The affair did not long endure. He had taken to reading history, particularly naval history, with some relish, and evidently thought that his mistress should share his new interest. With reluctance she submitted to his reading aloud volume one of *Lives of the Admirals*, but when she realized that there were more to come, she packed her belongings and retreated to Berkeley Square. Before Christmas, he left Ivy Lodge, and lived for a few months in his apartments at St James's. Afterwards he purchased Petersham Lodge, Roehampton, where he spent a considerable sum in embellishments and renamed it Clarence Lodge.

It was a cosier existence than that led by his elder brothers. In May Colonel Charles Lennox, cousin to the Lady Sarah to whom the bachelor King had been so attached, was with some friends when they met the Prince of Wales and the Duke of York. The Colonel made some insulting remark, and the Duke of York challenged him to a duel. Without telling his eldest brother, the Duke crept quietly out of his suite at Carlton House one morning, drove in a hired post chaise to Wimbledon Common, and met the Colonel to take up the challenge. The ground was measured at twelve paces, the Colonel fired first and, according to Fox, shot away one of the Duke's curls. The Duke refused to fire, saying that he had merely come to give satisfaction to Colonel Lennox.

Although he could scarcely have approved of such behaviour, the King was so overcome at Frederick's escape that on their next meeting he took him in his arms and wept from emotion. The Queen was less sympathetic. Not only did she ignore a request from the Prince of Wales not to receive Colonel Lennox, but she treated him with particular courtesy when he next presented himself at court, and cold-shouldered the Prince, holding him responsible for the whole affair.

At the time of his father's illness the fourth brother, Prince Edward, was in Geneva, the 'dullest and most insufferable' place, chafing under the control of Baron Wangenheim. The town held sad memories for him, for a brief affair with a French actress, Adelaide Dubus, had resulted in the birth of a daughter on 15 December 1789, christened Adelaide Victoire, and the mother's death in childbirth. On her death she left the baby in the custody of her sister, and the father arranged for her to receive a life pension. All pleas to his father to let him return to England had been ignored, as the King had no desire to add a fourth adult brother to the rebellious trinity already at home. During the winter of 1789 he made good his escape, and set off secretly for London, arriving back unexpectedly one night in January 1790, and finding a bed at a hotel off St James's Street. As soon as they heard of his arrival, along came his two eldest brothers, eager to find another brother united in rebellion, and invited him back to Carlton House.

The King was furious at this breach of discipline. A military posting to Gibraltar was promptly arranged for him within less than a fortnight's notice, and the King only grudgingly permitted him an interview of ten minutes' length before he was due to set out. It was a harsh way of dealing with him, but the posting had its bright side, for Prince Edward had been appointed to the command of a regiment, no mean promotion for a man of twenty-two. £500 was advanced to his governor, General Crawford, for his expenditure to set himself up at Gibraltar. In addition he was granted an officer's pay of £5,000 per year, in order to enable him to 'maintain an appearance before his brother officers'.

Nevertheless he sailed from England with some bitterness. The Duke of York had been permitted to stay in London with a huge grant from Parliament, doing no work at all, while he had been sent to one of the outposts of empire. Once at Gibraltar, he threw himself heart and soul into his work as Colonel of the Royal Fusiliers. He rose from his bed early to inspect, drill his men, and to order floggings. His severe sense of discipline made him unpopular among the soldiers, and unlike his brothers he was a light drinker; being drunk, he maintained, entrenched on his dignity. A human failing such as occasional over-indulgence might have endeared him a little more to his troops. News filtered back to London that the troops in Gibraltar were discontented, and in May 1791 the Prince and his regiment were ordered to Canada. By this time he was obliged to give bonds to his creditors, redeemable in seven years, for the sum of £20,000.

By now the student princes at Göttingen were nearing the end of their education. In June 1790, when the Prussian army mobilized, Prince Ernest wrote to his father for permission to join his elder brother and train with the Prussian forces. The King ignored the request for three months before replying, through Colonel von Malortie, that Ernest was not to join the Prussian army, but should leave university at the end of the year and undergo intensive military training with his own Hanoverian forces.

The Princes left Göttingen in January 1791. One of their first duties was to write formal letters of thanks to the university. Ernest remarked in a letter to his father that he left with genuine regret, as everyone behaved with such kindness to him that 'I should be one of the most ungrateful of men if ever I was forgetful of all I owe to Göttingen & its professors.'[3]

The asthmatic Augustus was too delicate to join the army. Apart from the Duke of Clarence, he was the only surviving son of King George III not to become a soldier. The King had planned a naval career for him, but soon after his enrolment as a student, his health began to give cause for concern. Suffering from what was diagnosed as a 'pleuritic complaint', he was often absent from lessons with attacks of chest pain. Admonitions about 'too good an appetite and too little walking' were not enough, as Augustus became fat through illness and subsequent lack of exercise. Yet he was resilient and cheerful between attacks, and his stoic endurance brought him respect from family and friends alike.

Ernest and Adolphus settled in a small palace at Hanover, and their military education was supervised by the Hanoverian commander Field Marshal von Freytag. Three times a week Ernest rode the few miles to Isernhagen, to learn cavalry drill and tactics under Captain von Linsingen of the Queen's Light Dragoons. He continued to study with Major Hogreve, and was still reading modern history with Georg Tatter and French with a M. Fleury. His days at Isernhagen were divided between riding with the dragoons, exercising them as a trooper, and then, for the last hour or so of the day, acting the part of junior officer in command of small parties. Already an excellent horseman, he also became a very good shot despite his short sight. After only two months, von Freytag was so impressed that he gave him a place with the cavalry as Captain, and in March 1792 he was officially commissioned with the rank of Colonel, though merely acting as a Captain.

In addition to the practical cavalry training he was placed under Major von Drechsel of the Footguards for infantry training, which he enjoyed much less. He appealed to the King to let him remain in the cavalry, and King George, impressed with his son's progress, granted his request. There was, however, ample time for Ernest to experience some degree of social life. Hanover's main social centre was a billiards club, and he took the game up as an ideal means of relaxing and meeting people. Although he wrote accounts in his letters of 'galavanting' with young women, no breath of scandal was attached to his name.

As a young man, Ernest was typical of the privileged army officer class. 'I cannot conceive how the common people have so great a dislike to serve,' he wrote, 'for in my opinion a soldier's life is the best & first in the world.'[4]

In June 1791 Prince Edward reached Quebec. Discipline was still his god, and he demanded that his soldiers should parade as soon as it was light. He himself rose while it was still dark, fortifying himself with a cup of coffee. The men grumbled at his harsh standards, and some of the officers suggested a lightening of the regime, but he would not listen. When a deserter – one of many – was caught, the Prince sentenced him to the maximum 999 lashes allowed by the regulations.

At length, a group of soldiers decided to seize him and put him to death. The secret was badly kept, and the ringleaders were court-martialled. One, Private Draper, was sentenced to death; the others were ordered lashes of varying numbers. The Prince marched at the head of the company on the day fixed for the execution; behind the soldiers marched Draper, in grave clothes, following his coffin, and the regimental band playing funeral dirges beside him. When they reached the gallows, the Prince walked towards the condemned man and pardoned him. As the son of his sovereign whose greatest prerogative was the dispensation of mercy, he said, he was fortunate in being able to exercise clemency; as his Colonel, the indispensable laws of military discipline would have rendered it impossible otherwise.

Although disliked by his soldiers, the Prince became popular with the civilian population of Canada. There was more relaxation and social life there than at Gibraltar. When he reached Quebec, in reply to the citizens' address of welcome, he announced that he hoped to 'find the opportunity of being personally serviceable' to them. One evening each week, his house was put at the service of an amateur society of musicians which he had organized. He became one of the leaders of Canadian Freemasonry, and founded Sunday free schools in Quebec. Perhaps his greatest triumph was when one night there was a serious outbreak of fire, and the citizens watched the massive figure of the Prince, black and sweaty, leading the improvised fire brigade. When elections were held in Canada and the disappointed, defeated French Canadians rioted after the results were known, the Prince personally visited the scene of the disorders. Mounting a chair in the street, he called out to the rioters: 'Let me hear no more of these odious distinctions of French and English. You are all his Britannic Majesty's beloved Canadian subjects.'

Shortly before leaving Gibraltar, he had acquired a mistress, Therese-Bernardine Mongenet, known as Madame Julie de St Laurent. Although he made no attempt to follow his eldest brother's example by contracting an unofficial marriage with her, they lived together in a state of virtual domestic bliss for nearly thirty years. She was intelligent and good-tempered, shared his literary and musical tastes, and added a touch of gaiety and lightness to his character which had so far been somewhat lacking.

It was a source of some consolation to the King that his beloved second son should be about to obey the Royal Marriages Act by choosing a suitable bride. Domestic bliss, thought the King, was the perfect antidote to boredom and idleness in his sons, and polite suggestions to Frederick that he should go to Germany and seek a suitable consort had their effect.

A few years earlier, the Duke of York had met the small and plain but vivacious Princess Frederica, eldest daughter of King Frederick William II of

Prussia. Baron Christian von Stockmar, who came over to England with Prince Leopold of Saxe-Coburg several years later, described her as 'a little animated woman, (who) talks immensely, and laughs still more. No beauty, mouth and teeth bad. She disfigures herself still more by distorting her mouth and blinking her eyes.'[5] She was happy to accept the Duke's hand in marriage, and as she had reached the age of twenty-four without anybody else showing much interest in her, her parents were relieved that she had found a suitor. After a short betrothal, they were married at Berlin on 29 September 1791.

On 17 October they left for England, having their first experience on the journey of revolutionary France, whose citizens had deposed King Louis XVI two years earlier. As they passed through Lille, a mob surrounded their carriage, and refused to let them pass unless they removed the royal arms from the side of their vehicle. Reaching England in mid-November, they were remarried on the 19th at Buckingham House, a second ceremony being required as the Archbishop had no authority to grant a licence for the solemnization of marriage in Prussia. A grant of £40,000 was settled on the Duke.

Shortly before his marriage, the Duke had sold Allerton Mauleverer, an estate in Yorkshire purchased for him by the King from revenues accruing from the Duke's income as Bishop of Osnabruck during his minority. With the proceeds, the Duke bought the palace of Oatlands Park, three miles from Weybridge. Previously lived in by King Henry VIII and King Charles I, it had later been bought and largely rebuilt by the Duke of Newcastle. Shortly after the Duke of York bought it, it was largely destroyed by fire and he built a mansion on the site, overlooking the Thames Valley and the North Downs. Later he added to his estate by buying the neighbouring manors of Byfleet and Brooklands.

The marriage was not a success. The Duke of York was unfaithful, but like his grandfather, he had at least chosen a wife who accepted such behaviour as natural. Less fortunate was her inability to bear children. Once it was evident that the marriage always would be childless, they spent much of their lives under separate roofs. Yet relations between them remained amicable enough, and never caused any scandal; and the censorious Queen Charlotte never refused to receive them at court, as she was to do with a future daughter-in-law, the woman who would marry Prince Ernest.

The modest, self-effacing Duchess was never drawn to the glitter of London society or the pettiness of quarrels between her in-laws, all of whom (except the Prince of Wales, who resented her remaining aloof from Mrs Fitzherbert) liked and respected her. A phlegmatic, kind-hearted woman, she contented herself at Weybridge with attending church every Sunday, taking an interest in educating the poor, and giving to the needy.

A better example of domestic (albeit unmarried) bliss was provided by the Duke of Clarence. In the spring of 1790, he became infatuated with the actress Dorothy Jordan, who had established herself a reputation as a distinguished comic player on the London stage for five years. She was already a friend of the Prince of Wales, and her acting skills were much admired by the royal family.

Her personal life had been an unsettled one. Born Dorothy Bland in 1761, the

Dorothy Jordan

illegitimate child of an actress, her father (the disinherited son of an Irish judge) abandoned the family when she was thirteen, and when her mother died four years later, she went on the stage in Dublin to support herself. She became involved with a stage manager, but by the time she was carrying his child, the affair had ended, and she fled to England, changing her name to Mrs Jordan in view of her condition. There was plenty of work for her as an actress, and soon she was established as one of the most popular players on the London stage. By now she had set up home with the son of a physician, by whom she had two daughters, but when he refused to marry her, she agreed to move in with her ardent and devoted royal admirer.

Being the mistress of a Prince who was so close to the succession did not solve Dorothy's financial problems, any more than sharing his hearth with a celebrated actress alleviated those of the Duke. Every quarter he made out to her a payment of 200 guineas, while she continued to earn her living on the stage. Both were extremely generous to those around them, reluctant to discharge servants, and they regularly entertained on a lavish scale. As their family of ten FitzClarences grew, five boys and five girls, so did their debts. Still, it proved a happy existence for nearly twenty years. Although he can scarcely have been expected to approve of the relationship, King George was reported to have joked with his son about Mrs Jordan on occasion, and continued to attend her performances at the theatre. Initially they divided their time between

Bushey Park

Clarence Lodge and his apartments in St James's Palace, until his appointment in 1797 as Ranger of Bushey Park gave them Bushey House, a mile from Hampton Court.

For the last two years, Prince Augustus had borne his illness with great courage. In the summer of 1790, he was confined to his room for five weeks, during two of which he was unable to lie down. Blooded and blistered by the doctors, he could not sleep in a bed again until November. 'His patience passes all description, he never frets, he is always in good humour,'[6] Ernest commented admiringly. Anxious letters flew between brothers, sisters and parents, all desperately concerned for his health.

On medical advice, he went south for the winter, and arrived in Nice in December 1790. Visiting places in southern France and Italy, he saw and observed much and thus made good some of the gaps in his education. Visits to a Carthusian convent near Pavia, Roman ruins, the countryside around Innsbruck, and various churches all inspired enthusiastic letters home. He was also pleasantly surprised that the journey through France was not as dangerous as he had feared. Having been led to believe that the country was unsafe for strangers, he assured friends and family that 'every Foreigner seems to be looked upon kindly, and has nothing to fear from any one as soon as he submits to have his passport frequently examined.'[7] This foreign travel broadened his horizons, as did acquaintances, including a fellow student from Göttingen, Josiah Dornford, a Londoner and son of a man active in prison reform. His liberal views influenced the Prince, who was already starting to show some sympathy with radical opinion as a result of his reading. Such political leanings would find little favour with the rest of his family, apart from his brother Edward.

In August 1791, Augustus decided that he would like to enter the church, as his health ruled out any idea of joining the navy, or indeed any active kind of life. He wrote to the King, pointing out that he had discussed the pros and cons with others, and given the matter much thought; 'at a moment when in some measure the Church of England is attacked, nothing can give it more strength than your Majesty's giving one of your sons a place in it.'[8] He intended to remain abroad for another eighteen months to allow his health, 'which is greatly recovered, time to be completely settled,' then come to talk things over with his father, and enrol at university in England. Unhappily months went by with no word from the King. As he had always expressed affection for his son, it was strange that he should have kept silent for so long. So Augustus was left to wander aimlessly and disconsolately throughout Europe, growing ever more restless under his governors' supervision. The Queen continued to write letters full of gossip about people and family at home, but there was no word from the King.

In November 1792 he went to Rome. Several members of English society lived there at the time, and naturally Prince Augustus was drawn to their company. Among them were the Countess of Dunmore and her young unmarried daughter, Lady Augusta Murray. One day he arrived at the church of St Giacomo just as the Countess and her daughters were leaving. He noticed that the lace of Lady Augusta's shoe was undone, and stopped to tie it up.

From this humble beginning, the affair gained momentum. Although she was several years older than the Prince, he fell ardently in love with her, and notwithstanding the Royal Marriages Act, offered her his hand without the rest of his family's knowledge. He was bored and frustrated with no direction in life. Another letter to his father in January 1793, written against the background of revolution and disturbances in Rome, with attacks on and by the French population of Rome, stating that 'should your Majesty think my presence of any use at this moment in England you have only to order,'[9] met with silence yet again.

Although Lady Augusta adored him equally, she refused his proposal, and showed him the disadvantage at which he was placing himself. This, the Prince wrote later, 'instead of checking my endeavours, served only to add new fuel to a passion which already no earthly power could make me resign.'[10] A written promise of marriage, oaths sworn upon the Bible, and endless entreaties, were not enough. Oaths unsanctioned in church were worthless to her, and she insisted on a proper ceremony of marriage.

On 4 April 1793 he obtained the services on an English clergyman, the Reverend William Gunn, with whom he had become friendly. That evening, shortly before eight o'clock, Lady Dunmore's carriage rolled out of the courtyard of their hotel, to attend a party at the Venetian Ambassador's. In her absence, the Prince and Mr Gunn slipped into the hotel. With no witnesses, a ceremony of marriage was performed. Gunn read the necessary office, and made out a certificate. All three swore to keep it secret, and in return Prince Augustus later honoured a promise to make Gunn his senior chaplain.

Lady Dunmore apparently accepted the situation, and made no attempt to stand in their way. In the summer, she and her daughters moved to Florence, and the Prince followed them. In August he was recalled to England as his governor had hinted to the royal family that he was forming a dangerous attachment, although he had not guessed the true situation. Lady Dunmore and her daughters followed him to England, and lived together in a house in Lower Berkeley Street, where the Prince continually visited them. By now, he knew that he would soon be a father.

On three consecutive Sundays that autumn, the congregation at St George's, Hanover Square, heard the banns of marriage read out between a Mr Augustus Frederick and a Miss Augusta Murray. Neither the clergyman nor his congregation attached any interest or suspicion to these names, especially as several families named Frederick lived in the parish. On 5 December, another wedding ceremony was performed, the heavily pregnant bride explaining her condition by saying that she had married him in Italy when he was under age so she wished to be remarried in England.

On 13 January she gave birth to a son, named Augustus Frederick. Two days later, the proud father called to see his child, and on the following day left the country. The King, mindful of rumours about his son's liaison, had ordered him out, ostensibly for health reasons – the 'agitation' had played havoc with the Prince's health and asthma, and he was only sleeping 'one night out of six' – but chiefly to separate him from his wife. Once he was on his way to Italy, an application was made to the ecclesiastical courts, that the marriage should be set aside on the ground that the King's consent had never been obtained in accordance with the terms of the Royal Marriages Act. The marriage ceremony at St George's was officially annulled, and Gunn's performance in Rome was dismissed as 'a show and effigy of marriage.'

Although he had to make every pretence of obeying his sovereign lord and father, the lovesick Prince was too much of a gentleman to jettison his wife and child. The extent of the King's intention to punish him still had not fully dawned on him, or the realization that the King intended to keep them apart permanently. Once he was back in Rome, he waited for Augusta to join him, but the King did his best to prevent her from leaving England.

Augustus was shocked that the government was not content with having broken up his marriage 'in so cruel and unprecedented a measure as they did'. That such efforts should now be made to keep him and his wife apart made him more miserable still. To the Prince of Wales, he expressed his sole desire '*now was* to bury myself in some remote corner of the Continent and there to occupy myself about the happiness of her whose misfortunes I am solely the cause of, and the education of my boy.'[11] He considered surrendering his royal rights and defying the royal edict, but as his health was so delicate and as he was untrained for any profession, it was uncertain as to what he could do. He asked the Archbishop of Canterbury to propose to the King, as Elector of Hanover, that the marriage might be acknowledged as a left-handed (or morganatic) one in Germany, but to no avail.

After living alternately in Rome and Naples, he moved to Berlin. The change of climate brought on a severe asthmatic attack, and in August 1799 Lady Augusta, travelling under the name Mrs Ford, joined him. She had heard alarming reports of his state of health, and exaggerated rumours that he might be dying. Their son was brought over to Berlin a few days later, and the Prince soon recovered. For several years they lived quietly and happily in the German capital.

4 'If you fall all must fall'

By the end of 1792, Britain was on the verge of war, and it was only to be expected that at least one of the royal family should be actively involved in the fighting. The new revolutionary republic of France was at war with the invincible central European alliance of Austria and Prussia. After a campaign in 1792 France took possession of the Austrian Netherlands and prepared to attack Holland. The Dutch could not defend themselves, and the Stadtholder requested the British to come to their aid. It was not in the interests of British foreign policy to let the mouth of the Rhine fall into the hands of a strong hostile power, and a British force was sent out to Holland. France therefore declared war on Britain and Holland on 1 February 1793.

King George III wished the British troops to be commanded by the Duke of York, now aged twenty-nine, and a Major-General. Having already seen much military training in Prussia during the previous decade, the Duke was quietly confident in his new role, and glad to be given a chance to prove himself. His dissipation in London and disloyalty to his father had been born mainly out of frustration at not having a proper job to do, and being unable to serve his country properly. Here at last was the role after which he had hankered.

The Prince of Wales also longed to make an active contribution, and readily declared his willingness to serve under his brother. It was, however, deemed inexpedient for both of the King's eldest sons to expose themselves simultaneously to the risks of war against a foreign power. As consolation, the Prince of Wales was commissioned as Colonel Commandant of the Tenth Light Dragoons ('the Prince of Wales' Own') by the King. Resplendent in uniform, he and the King rode down the Mall early one foggy morning in February 1793 to review the three battalions of Guards drawn up on the Horse Guards' Parade under the Duke of York's command, before they set out for the Netherlands. After the review was completed, the Duke of York led the soldiers on a march to Greenwich, the King, the Queen, the Duke of Clarence and the Princesses behind in carriages. As the soldiers embarked, they passed the King and his family. The ever-delicate Sophia fainted with emotion, nine-year-old Amelia bawled loudly in her distress, and Mary choked as she heard one man say: 'Who would not die for them?'

As a Commander-in-Chief, the Duke of York would later make an able administrator. Modelling his ideas on what he had already seen for himself, he would eventually make great improvements in the commissariat and transport departments. As a General in the field, however, he was less able; inexperience and youth told against him. He was frustrated that the government had made his appointment conditional on three other generals, with whom he was to consult at all times, being attached to the Duke's staff; and that the general campaign was to be directed by the inept Secretary of State for War at Whitehall, Henry Dundas. The Duke would therefore be responsible in the eyes of his country at least for commanding the force, while four senior officers, who could not agree among themselves, controlled all that he did. As inevitably happens in time of war, the various commanders of the allied armies were given to quarrelling among themselves and countermanding each others' orders.

Prince Ernest was already a Colonel in the Hanoverian Dragoons. From Germany they marched through Antwerp to Tournai where they arrived in April 1793. The Duke of York had already set up his headquarters at Tournai, and he was delighted to hear that his younger brother would soon be there, and in addition to ordering that the Light Dragoons should be quartered inside the town, he ordered a celebration dinner to be prepared to which his brother, Field Marshal von Freytag, and the Second in Command, General von dem Bussche, should all be invited. Whether due to a genuine misunderstanding or a refusal to accept orders from an officer of such tender years was responsible, it is not known, but the septuagenarian Freytag took the rumours of an imminent French attack (which never materialized) as the pretext for countermanding the orders about quartering the dragoons in the town, and absented himself from the dinner. It was only the first in a series of petty squabbles that made the Duke of York's position a frustrating one.

None the less, allied forces successfully kept the French at bay. On 7 August they attacked the French forces near Tournai; in the ensuing battle Prince Ernest was thrown from his horse, and his head was cut open by a sabre. After the victory which followed, the defeated French were at a low ebb, and the moment would have been right for the allied Anglo-Hanoverian-Austrian forces to march on to Paris with very little resistance. However the forces no longer appeared to act in concert, and they lost the advantage which might have prevented the war from lasting sporadically for another twenty-two years. Dundas and the British Government ordered the Duke of York and his force to capture Dunkirk, and after failing to do so the British army retreated to the Netherlands.

In January 1794 Ernest, now fully recovered, was promoted to the rank of Colonel of the Heavy Dragoons. For the next few months there was little military activity at Tournai, but plenty of social life. Lady Harcourt, wife of an officer, remarked that the more she saw of the Prince, the more she liked him, and that 'in good hands he might be made a charming young man.' She did however notice his tendency to tease and make offensive jokes. After a visit to a convent, he kissed the Abbess, and would 'talk nonsense to all the poor nuns.' She feared that he was 'too wild for England.'

In mid-April, the campaign began again. The Anglo-Hanoverian forces kept the French army in check, and the regiment lost a few men in a skirmish later that month. More serious fighting took place on 10 May when Prince Ernest came under heavy artillery fire. One cannon ball hit and killed the horse ridden by his orderly immediately behind him, and Ernest himself was struck on the left arm. In the heat of battle he put it down to imagination at first, but next day his arm was very painful and he could not even hold a fork in his hand. By the end of

Prince Ernest, by Sir William Beechey

the month his arm had to be set and immobilized. At the same time, he found the sight of his left eye becoming clouded. It was apparent that a cannon ball had narrowly missed him, but the blast had still been strong enough to affect him.

Forced to rest for a while, he chafed at being kept inactive, not resuming his duties till June. Lady Harcourt thought him foolish to ride to Lille with his arm in a sling, unable to see clearly ten yards in front. He was given leave to convalesce, and arrived in England on 30 June.

On his return home, he found in effect two courts. At St James's, the Queen's House, Windsor, and Kew, the King, Queen and their unmarried daughters continued to lead their dull, formal and retiring existence. Surrounded by court officials, they were shunned by the fashionable upper class.

The latter flocked to the Prince of Wales's lively court at Carlton House. As he approached his thirties, the Prince was still good-looking; easy living and illness had not yet made him the bloated monster of popular legend. Charming and kind to his friends, he was still inclined to selfishness and could not always be trusted – as Fox had seen, the denial of his intentions of marriage to Mrs Fitzherbert was an example – and would lie to avoid unpleasantness. Well-read, witty, an excellent mimic, as a patron of the fine arts, painting, music and literature, he was without parallel in the annals of contemporary royalty. Though it was not appreciated by the masses at the time, much of his debts sprang from his expenditure on art, particularly the acquisition of Dutch paintings and French furniture, thus building up a collection for which twentieth-century art historians have forgiven him much. Still inclined to debauchery and heavy drinking, he had apparently learnt his lesson and now stopped short of excess; anybody who had given themselves so completely to self-indulgence in those days would have hardly survived to the age of sixty-seven.

Like the next bearer of the title Prince of Wales, the eldest son and heir of his niece (the future Queen Victoria), Prince George was a *bon viveur* whose reputation was greatly exaggerated by gossip. It might be noted at the same time that the future King Edward VII was likewise frustrated in many ways in a desire to serve his country, although he was able to use his personal skills as an unofficial diplomat in the courts of Europe; and, like George IV, he too ascended the throne in his late fifties, at an age when his health and zest for life were diminishing.

Many of the Prince of Wales's problems might have been avoided if he had been given a job to do. His parents distrusted him, not so much because of his debauched behaviour, more because of the political company he kept. The Tories, supporters of the King, had been in power for several years, and the Whigs had assiduously cultivated his heir. They therefore expected to be summoned to power in the event of the Prince of Wales's succession to the throne, and the indecent haste with which they had begun to prepare themselves for government when a Regency looked likely in 1789, a prospect which had been viewed with delight by the Prince himself, only widened the rift between father and son.

While three brothers were serving abroad in the army and one had travelled widely on naval service, the Prince of Wales was thrown back on a life of idleness at home. A love of racing at York and Newmarket, and entertaining at Carlton

House and Brighton, was supplemented by other pastimes, such as a short-lived devotion to the 'manly exercise' of cricket.

Yet he was concerned by events in France, and personally welcomed parties of French refugees as they arrived at Brighton to escape the revolutionaries' wrath. Many of the aristocrats who were killed in the Terror had been close friends, and had often been guests at Sussex in happier times past. His hatred of the 'damnable doctrines of the hell-begotten Jacobins', as he referred to them in a letter to Queen Charlotte, tempered his enthusiasm for Whig doctrines, if not his admiration for their leader, Fox.

The ball held at Windsor on his twenty-ninth birthday, 12 August 1791, had marked a demonstration of family reconciliation, *The Times* noting effusively that no heir to the throne since Edward the Black Prince had 'been more generously admired for his amiable manner.' A three-minute maiden speech in the House of Lords on 31 May 1792, in which he supported a proclamation against seditious writings and declared his devotion to the existing form of the constitution, was further proof that their son had apparently outgrown his contrary ways.

Kept from active service, the Prince of Wales still took his duties as seriously as matters permitted. That summer he wrote to the heads of allied command, the Duke of Saxe-Coburg, and Francis II, Holy Roman Emperor, requesting

George, Prince of Wales, by John Hoppner, 1792

54

permission to serve under them. Nothing came of this, as the King would not permit it, beyond a civil exchange of courtesies, and he was left to his Light Dragoons. In August he marched his regiment through the Sussex town of Lewes to establish a camp at Hove. For the next month he conducted military exercises and manoeuvres with his men on the South Downs. His enthusiasm for the art of soldiering did not extend to sharing his men's privations, for the Colonel's tent was a large marquee emblazoned with the Prince of Wales's feathers, containing a luxurious divan bed and chairs. In any case, the Light Dragoons were rarely more than two hours' ride from the Brighton Pavilion. Yet he became acquainted with the tactics and problems of military drill, and for the rest of his life he retained a detailed knowledge of uniforms. As the weather became colder, and as he was disappointed not to be promoted to the rank of full General, his military enthusiasm soon waned and he returned to Carlton House.

In February 1795, the Duke of York was appointed Field-Marshal and Commander-in-Chief in succession to the elderly Lord Amherst. In the light of his recent experiences in the field, he was well suited to the task. He had seen for himself in the Holland campaigns how much the British army suffered from poor, outdated organization and inefficient officers. Many of the soldiers had been sent out to Europe in 1793 in slop clothing – a linen jacket and trousers, without waistcoats or stockings. Money and intrigue were the only channels to promotion. Determined to improve conditions under which private soldiers had to serve, he made great efforts to make their living conditions more comfortable. In order to improve the training and efficiency of officers, he founded the Royal Military College at Woolwich, and two years later a military school at High Wycombe which would be the forerunner of Sandhurst. Both were established with the purpose of giving officers a genuine chance to learn their profession and earn promotion on merit rather than by money or nepotism. Thanks to reforms such as these, a considerably better-trained army would face the French only a few years hence.

Prince Ernest appreciated the tactical wisdom of keeping on friendly terms with his parents and eldest brother at the same time. He found life at Windsor and Kew as tedious as his spinster sisters did, and to relieve the tedium he busied himself in planning and drawing fortifications as much as his weak sight would allow. Dutifully he accompanied them in the summer of 1794 to Weymouth, which the King and Queen had established as a part of their annual routine, for the medicinal benefits of sea bathing. The people of Weymouth were so moved by patriotic zeal that they provided a band to strike up the National Anthem, and other patriotic songs every time His Majesty walked into the waters. The Princesses, however, found Weymouth tedious beyond words, especially in wet weather, when the theatre was their only diversion.

When the court returned from Weymouth in September 1794, Ernest went to Carlton House, and stayed there for the next month. During this period, he first acted as emissary between his brother and Mrs Fitzherbert, whose relationship had deteriorated, and brought her the letter from her husband telling her that they would have to separate. The Prince of Wales was finding her increasingly temperamental and difficult to live with, while she feared for her safety with the raffish, drunken companions he regularly brought round to her house. She also

Frances, Countess of Jersey

viewed with alarm his infatuation with Lady Jersey, a friend of the Queen, and a grandmother nine years older than the Prince himself.

There was another major cause of a breakdown in relations between the couple. The Prince now realized that the pressures on him to contract a valid marriage could no longer be resisted. Despite regular intentions of economizing, his liabilities continued to mount, until by 1795 they exceeded £60,000, or one twenty-fifth of the country's entire annual budget at the outbreak of war.[1] Declaring that 'the choice of wife was indeed a lottery', it was with relief that he had welcomed the Duke of York's marriage, but dismayed as it became evident that the Duchess would have no children. It was to fulfil his dynastic obligations, and to alleviate his debts, that the Prince resigned himself to the prospect of matrimony.

The Court of Privileges had recently ruled that Prince Augustus's marriage to Lady Augusta Murray was null and void. As Maria Fitzherbert saw, if the marriage of a Prince to a Protestant who could count King Henry VII of England and other European monarchs among her ancestors was unacceptable, what hope was there for a Roman Catholic who was a commoner?

Had the Prince decided sooner, he might have been able to marry perhaps the only eligible German princess with sufficient beauty and strength of character to be the making of him, Princess Louise of Mecklenburg-Strelitz. Instead, she had married the Crown Prince of Prussia. Muttering gloomily that 'one damned German Frau is as good as another,' he left the bride-searching to be done by others. The Duke of York had long thought that their cousin Caroline, youngest daughter of the Duke and Duchess of Brunswick, would be right for his brother, although the choice was extremely limited and she therefore had little competition. The King was prepared to trust Frederick's judgment that she was 'a very fine girl', but not so the Queen.

She had never liked the Duchess of Brunswick, who as the King's eldest (and only surviving) sister, the sharp-tongued Princess Augusta, had caused much mischief at court during the early years of their own married life. Moreover she had heard that the daughter was even worse, notorious for 'making an exhibition of herself by indecent conversations with men,' and regarded by her parents as being badly behaved to the point of mental instability. Had she made her objections known, the Queen might have helped to prevent the marriage which was to bring such misery to the family; but she lived in dread of the King's violent recurring illness, and she was not prepared to risk it by opposing a scheme of which he approved so strongly.

Such rumours about his prospective bride seemed to make no difference to the Prince of Wales. Marriage to any officially-approved Princess, and the settlement of his debts, was all that mattered to him. His own parents' marriage had been arranged, and they had never seen each other until just before the wedding ceremony; so there was no reason to suppose that his would be any the less successful. Parliament voted an increase in his annual grant from £60,000 to £125,000, though part of this sum, plus the whole of the Duchy of Cornwall revenues for the next twenty-five years, would be held to meet repayment of his debts and the interest arising.

In November 1794 Sir James Harris, who had long been a friend of the Prince, was sent to Germany to complete the legal pre-marriage formalities and bring the bride to England. He was alternately amused and repelled by this cheerful but noisy, giggling Princess of twenty-six, whose language was indelicate, even by the standards of the age; who wore coarse underclothing and did not change it often enough, or wash herself properly; who was startled when he told her that if she encouraged anyone other than her husband to make love to her, she would be guilty of high treason; and who asked one of the pages to send the Prince a tooth which she had just had extracted. Her appearance was equally unprepossessing; she was short, stocky, and plain, her only redeeming characteristic being a fine head of thick hair. Though he knew that formalities and negotiations had probably gone too far to call the marriage off, he never thought to warn the royal family in England just what kind of princess was about to become the Queen Consort-in-waiting, and for this the Prince of Wales never forgave him.

The journey of the Princess, her mother and Harris to England was delayed by French military action at Hanover, and they did not reach Greenwich until

5 April 1795. With extraordinary lack of tact, Lady Jersey had been assigned to her as a lady-in-waiting. Caroline had already heard, either from Harris or from her own mother, that this woman was her prospective husband's mistress, and it was a bad start when this same Lady Jersey was prominent among those who welcomed her to England. The Prince of Wales was not present, and a detachment of the Light Dragoons escorted them into London. The Princess arrived at St James's Palace, her temper not improved by Lady Jersey's heavy-handed criticism of her clothes.

When the Prince was introduced to her, he greeted her politely, but could not conceal his disappointment at the sight of her. Turning to Harris, he remarked that he was not well, and wanted a glass of brandy. After he had left, Caroline asked her attendants with horror if the Prince was always like that, adding that he was not nearly so handsome as his portrait. However, she was marrying the most eligible bachelor in Europe, and she appeared less downcast at this inauspicious beginning than he was. By dinner that evening, she had recovered her high spirits. Her conversation, 'flippant, rattling, affecting raillery and wit,' dwelt with much coarse detail on Lady Jersey's relations with the Prince. The latter, everyone else (but not Caroline herself) noticed, was horrified.

Three days later, the wedding took place at St James's Chapel. The

The wedding of George, Prince of Wales, and Princess Caroline of Brunswick, by Henry Singleton, 1795. The King and Queen are seated on the left and right of the couple; behind the King are (probably) the Dukes of Kent, Gloucester and York

Archbishop paused a long time at the 'just cause or impediment' clause, and looked searchingly at both groom and monarch, before pronouncing the Prince and Princess husband and wife. The Prince was moist-eyed, confused, and unsteady on his feet, less from emotion than from the fortifying effects of the brandy which he had taken to get him through the ceremony. The optimistic King, who gave the bride away, was in high spirits throughout and apparently paid no heed to his son's discomfiture.

The first few days of the honeymoon were spent at Windsor, after which the couple went to Kempshott House, near Basingstoke. According to the bride (whose embittered later recollections were doubtless exaggerated), her husband spent most of the bridal night in the fireplace, where he had fallen in a drunken stupor, and did not climb into bed with her until the morning.

Contrary to popular belief, the mutual antipathy did not start from their first meeting. Twice during the summer the Prince wrote to his mother, who was prepared to give her daughter-in-law a fair chance, of Caroline's good health and high spirits, and the pleasure she was gaining from their residence at Brighton. That a child was on the way was further cause for celebration.

Princess Elizabeth, who was particularly devoted to her eldest brother, was anxious that the marriage should be happy. With nothing but unkindness from Lady Jersey, Caroline appreciated this conciliatory sister-in-law, and sent Elizabeth good wishes on her birthday in May. Writing soothingly to her brother, Elizabeth said that the Princess of Wales 'spoke very openly to all parties concerning her present happiness . . . & having the appearance of perfect good temper I flatter myself that you will have her turn out a very comfortable little wife.'[2]

While the Prince of Wales was struggling, albeit briefly, to make the best of an unpromising marriage, he was increasingly concerned at the 'nunnery', as his frustrated sisters described themselves to friends. At home with his family, King George III frequently burst into tears, walked around the room, and kissed his daughters affectionately, thanking God for giving him them as a comfort for the misdeeds of his sons. The Princesses were 'variously agitated, and sometimes so much as to go into fits.' When he was not present, the days were tedious indeed. 'Mama sits in a very small green room which she is very fond of, reads, writes, and Botanizes,' Elizabeth wrote from Frogmore in July 1791. 'Augusta and me remain in the room next hers across a passage and employ ourselves much in the same way. Of a Saturday my younger sisters have no master, so they also come down.'[3]

The politician and poet James Bland Burges, who saw much of the family at this time, remarked sadly that there was probably not 'a more unhappy family in England than that of our good King.' The Princess Royal was especially miserable, 'convinced that she now has no chance of ever altering her condition; afraid of receiving any impressions of tenderness or affection; reserved and studious; tenderly loving her brothers and feeling strongly every unpleasant circumstance attending them, she is fallen into a kind of quiet, desperate state, without hope and open to every fear.'[4] Her only salvation, he believed, was to let her marry.

In 1795 the Princess was twenty-nine years of age, and the least good-looking of the sisters. She was clumsy, gauche, and painfully shy, particularly in the presence of her mother, but away from the Queen she was more lively and animated.

She was also an embittered tell-tale. Although she and her mother were not on good terms, her younger sisters blamed her for stirring up trouble at home, and Princess Sophia recorded some unpleasantness, 'and now I have heard many a story that Princess Royal has repeated to the Queen.' One summer at Weymouth, the governesses noted that the younger Princesses seemed more cheerful after the eldest had departed.

The Princess Royal's lack of good looks and repressed character, however, did not alter the fact that as the King of England's eldest daughter, she was particularly eligible as regards marriage. Over the last fourteen years, various prospective husbands had been suggested for her, including the Emperor of Austria, the Crown Prince of Denmark (notwithstanding Queen Caroline Matilda's tragic fate), Prince Frederick of Orange, and the King of Sweden's brother, the Duke of Ostrogothland.

The King doted on his daughters, but was too possessive to agree readily to his beloved eldest one marrying a foreign prince. (Marriage with a member of the English aristocracy would be equally out of the question, even if it meant that she was not leaving home for distant shores). After his recovery from illness in 1789, some of the family were even more hesitant about raising issues which might disturb his mental balance again, but others decided that the question could not be deferred indefinitely.

Always ready to help his sisters, the Prince of Wales took the initiative in the summer of 1795 in enlisting the aid of his maternal uncle, Prince Ernest of Mecklenburg-Strelitz, in trying to arrange a marriage between his sister and the Duke of Oldenburg. The Princess Royal was enthusiastic, declaring that 'could it be brought about, it would be the properest situation.' Princess Elizabeth rather prematurely began referring to her in letters to the Prince of Wales as the Duchess of Oldenburg, adding that 'her maiden-blush cheek is turned into a Damask Rose whenever the Duke's name is mentioned.'[5] Nothing came of the negotiations, although the disappointed Princess Royal was soon to find marriage with another member of the Oldenburg family.

Spinsterhood and excessive protection were not the only crosses the Princesses had to bear. Burges noted in November 1794 that, out of their allowances of £2,000 a year, they had to provide themselves with clothes, servants' wages, and jewels, of which neither the King nor Queen gave them any. Charlotte and Augusta managed to live within their means, but Elizabeth found it as difficult as her brothers; she was 'a bad economist, and, as she says herself, must go to gaol very soon.'[6] On at least one occasion she was obliged to ask the Prince of Wales discreetly to lend her a three-figure sum to discharge her debts, a plea which the fond brother could never refuse. Compared with his own debts, Elizabeth's requests for sums like £600 were indeed trifling.

The Prince of Wales was always kind and thoughtful towards his sisters, and as they relied on him for help and support, they were devoted to him. Though any family rifts were always a cause for concern, the Princesses' attitude towards the other brothers often depended to some extent on how they stood in the Prince's estimation at the time.

As the new year of 1796 dawned, the whole family anxiously awaited the news from Carlton House of an heir in the next generation. Elizabeth wrote excitedly to the Prince of Wales how the door bell made her 'jump and fly to the window, in hopes of being the person to bring news of the happy event to Mama, who thinks much of you, for we are sure you are upon the *high fidgets*, walking about the room, pulling your fingers and very anxious.'[7]

For two nights the agitated father-to-be was unable to sleep. On 7 January he wrote to his family that the Princess, 'after a terrible hard labour for about twelve hours, is this instant brought to bed of an *immense Girl*, & I assure you notwithstanding we might have wish'd for a Boy, I receive her with all the affection possible.'[8]

Diplomatically the delighted King said that he had 'always wished' first for a granddaughter; there was plenty of time for brothers and sisters to join her. Princess Elizabeth told how he talked of nothing but his grandchild; that evening he drank her health at dinner, and went into the equerries' room, inviting them to drink to the infant princess as well. The Queen was likewise full of 'the little beauty,' who was destined to be named Charlotte after her. 'Thank God you are now happy,' Elizabeth wrote to her brother.

Little did she know the true state of his feelings. Three days after the baby was born, he sat down at Carlton House and made a long 'last will and testament'. In this document, he bequeathed his possessions to Maria Fitzherbert, his 'true and real wife'. 'To her who is called the Princess of Wales,' he wrote, 'I leave one shilling', but not the jewels she wore, which were his, 'having been bought with my own money.' Maybe he was once again well fortified with brandy when he wrote this, and by the end of January he had apparently recovered his equilibrium. Yet he never destroyed the will. Three copies were made – one for his papers, one for his executor, and one under seal for the King. One of these eventually passed into Mrs Fitzherbert's hands.

To the outside world, the Prince of Wales gave the impression, albeit briefly, of trying to make an impossible marriage work. On 15 March, husband and wife went to the opera together, and were seen to be on terms of almost affectionate cordiality. Yet only later that week, he sent for Harris to discuss ways in which it might be possible for the Princess to be given a separate establishment. They could continue to reside in Carlton House, with their own apartments, and only meet on formal occasions. Contact would be maintained by exchange of notes when necessary, as had been done by the King and the bachelor Prince when both had lived at the Queen's House.

At the end of April, he wrote to Caroline to discuss the terms on which they could each maintain 'tranquil and comfortable society' by avoiding each others' company. Caroline was not prepared to accept this, and insisted on raising the matter with the King. She was particularly aggrieved at the retention of Lady Jersey in her household. Tactfully, the King attempted to see matters from everyone's point of view. To his son, he admitted that the Princess had not 'been happy in the choice of conduct she has adopted . . . if you had attempted to guide her, she might have avoided those errors that her uncommon want of experience and perhaps some defects of temper may have given rise to.'[9] He knew that the Princess of Wales had her shortcomings, but that she was more sinned against than sinning. His own son's faults, he recognized, were considerably greater, and on him devolved the responsibility of keeping up appearances and doing his best to accommodate his wife. As the King pointed out, the public would certainly not be prejudiced in the Prince's favour.

Even Princess Elizabeth, deeply concerned that her brother's relations should not be ruptured beyond repair, and anxious at the effect that his trouble was having on the Queen, told him diplomatically that Lady Jersey's resignation had to 'take place for the sake of the *country* and the whole Royal Family, for if you *fall* all must fall.'[10] Lady Jersey did indeed resign at the King's insistence, and the Princess left Carlton House to set up her own establishment at Charlton, then a village in Kent beside the Thames.

After the Princess Royal's premature hopes of freedom, a husband was found for her. He was Frederick, Hereditary Prince of Württemberg. Like the plump, thirty-year-old Princess herself, he was no catch. Aged forty, he was a widower, his late wife Augusta having been the Princess of Wales's sister. She had been sent away from her husband and children for flagrant infidelity, but no divorce took place; rather too conveniently, she had not long been at her prison fortress before she died of a fever, or haemorrhage in such a manner that immediate burial was necessary. King George was so discomfited at the rumours that she had been poisoned that he initially refused his consent to the match. Only persistent entreaties by the houses of Russia, Brunswick, and officials in England including the foreign secretary, Lord Grenville, persuaded him, and he gave his assent in July 1796.

In August, the Prince informed Lord Grenville that he would be ready to embark at Hamburg early in December, but had to postpone his journey because of stormy weather. In March 1797 the King instructed his home secretary, the Duke of Portland, to draw up the marriage treaty, following as closely as possible a similar marriage settlement concluded in 1766 between the Duke of Brunswick and Princess Augusta, when an annuity of £5,000 was settled out of His Majesty's Irish revenues.

When the Prince crossed the North Sea in April, the weather was no better than it had been in December, and he looked much the worse for wear after a very bad crossing on his arrival at Harwich on 10 April. He was given time to recover before coming to London, and advised by the King to remain incognito for a time, 'in order to obviate the inconveniences which would otherwise be felt by both parties by a prolonged ceremonial.'[11]

The marriage treaty was signed in May. Among its conditions were that the children of the marriage were to be brought up in Württemberg, but could not marry without the consent of the King of England or his successors; and that if the Princess Royal's husband should predecease her, she should be at liberty to return to England, bringing all her jewellery, including any obtained during her

Charlotte,
Princess Royal,
from a cameo
attributed to
Peter Rouw

marriage; and that her English attendants should leave her at Hanover, where the German ones should join her, but she should be free to celebrate divine service according to the rites of the English church. With her trousseau were included two sets of children's clothes, one for a boy and one for a girl. Sadly they were never needed, and sold unused after her death.

Neither bride nor groom were particularly attractive. The Princess Royal, a careless and slovenly dresser, was the least clothes-conscious of her family; unlike her mother and sisters, it was said of her that she never took the slightest notice as to whether her friends were wearing old or new gowns. She was almost as portly as her husband-to-be, nicknamed by wags, 'The Great Belly-gerent'. Napoleon Bonaparte later remarked that God had created the Prince to demonstrate the utmost extent to which the human skin could be stretched without bursting.

The Princess was 'very fussy and agitated' as soon as she was told that her betrothed was in England, but according to Fanny Burney, she was 'almost dead with terror and agitation and affright at their first meeting.' She could not speak a word, and the Queen had to answer for her. Tactfully, the Prince said he hoped this first would be the last disturbance his presence would ever occasion her; but, after her initial shyness, she recovered and joined in the conversation. He made a good impression on his future sisters-in-law, who were all happy to welcome him into the family; and at length she was 'quite revived in her spirits again, now this tremendous opening sight is over.'[12]

The marriage was celebrated on 18 May 1797 at St James's Palace, the bride dressed becomingly in white satin with a train of rich crimson velvet with fur trimming. She was rather upstaged by the bridegroom, observers maintained, with his suit of silk, shot with gold and silver richly embroidered, and resplendent in Russian and German insigniae.

After a rough sea crossing, they reached Germany, and made their home at the palace of Ludwigsburg, surrounded by long avenues of chestnut and limes. At a dinner party on their first night, a band played the English National Anthem in her honour; and she wrote to her father that she 'required all the Strength in my power not to burst into Tears.'[13] She was charmed with her new home, especially when her husband took her on a short tour of the more mountainous districts of the duchy, telling her that there were no mountains in England. Having seen little of England apart from flat pasture land around Isleworth, he could have been forgiven this misconception.

Princess Charlotte was glad to have escaped from the 'nunnery', and was horrified when her husband had a severe fall from his horse in August, breaking his arm. He was particularly anxious that his wife should not be unduly affected, for by then she was expecting a child. In December he succeeded his father as Duke, and Charlotte was Duchess. Unhappily, after a long and difficult labour, she gave birth to a stillborn daughter. Charles Arbuthnot, English Minister at Stuttgart, informed the Prince of Wales that her situation was at first extremely critical, 'for having been delivered of a dead child, and having suffered very greatly in her lying-in, so much fever ensued that for a short time the physicians were apprehensive of her safety.'[14]

A week later, she wrote to the King: 'I trust that I feel this as a Christian, and submit with resignation to the will of the Almighty, but Nature must ever make me regret the loss of the little thing I had built such happiness on.'[15] Her recovery was slow, and early in June she was still to weak to walk, but spent most of her day convalescing in a little flower garden the Duke had tenderly made for her.

She found consolation in needlework, and upholstering chairs with velvet. Another artistic venture was painting flowers and animals onto porcelain, for which she later had her own kiln in the palace grounds, where she could fire her work. A number of plates, cups and saucers, and flower vases were produced, many signed with her initials, and much treasured as family gifts.

5 'More wretched than I can express'

In North America, Prince Edward looked on family events with some impatience. He felt his isolation keenly, while two younger brothers were fighting the French. Meanwhile, he had the rather less prestigious task of helping to defend territories and capture the French islands in the West Indies. Yet he stuck to his post in the hope that he would be appointed Commander-in-Chief of the British Army in North America, but when the post fell vacant in 1795, the septuagenarian General Prescott was chosen and sent out from England instead. Weary of the Duke's excessive discipline, the officers began to whisper that they would soon be free of him. He wrote to the King asking permission to return home, but this was refused. Resigning himself to an indefinite stay, he set about building a small house in Halifax.

Edward regarded himself as a child of misfortune. His brothers Frederick and William had received their dukedoms and parliamentary grants at the ages of twenty-three and twenty-four respectively, and he calculated that had he been thus favoured at a similar age, he would have been at least £60,000 better off by this time. Adding to his debts were the expenses incurred in replacing his 'outfits'. As an army officer serving abroad, he needed to take an outfit – plate, glasses, linen, china, furniture, wine and books – as well as any other articles, equipment and uniform required. During his Canadian service he was unlucky enough to lose no less than six outfits. Three were captured by the enemy during the war with France and her allies; one, packed on sledges for transport during the bitter Canadian winter, disappeared through the ice before his eyes; and two more were wrecked, one of which included a personal library of 5,000 books. The total loss on all these outfits was estimated in excess of £25,000.

One day in October 1798, he was returning from a field day on horseback, when a few planks that had been put over a stream gave way under him, and he was thrown heavily. Despite prompt medical attention, his recovery was slow, and the doctor recommended his return home to take the waters at Bath. He reached England just before Christmas, and was cordially welcomed by the family.

In March 1799, he was at last awarded his grant of £12,000 a year, and in April he was raised to the peerage as Duke of Kent and Strathearn and Earl of Dublin. Now aged thirty-one, he had been expecting these distinctions for some time, as his elder brothers had received their titles and grants at a younger age; but it was thought that reports of his harshness had found their way to England and prejudiced the King against him. It certainly seemed a little unfair that

Ernest was created Duke of Cumberland and Teviotdale and Earl of Armagh at the same time. Yet he was comforted by the news that he was to be appointed Commander-in-Chief in British North America in succession to Prescott. Accordingly he set sail for Halifax with Madame de St Laurent in July.

The Duke of Kent was quite open about his liaison with Madame, as was the Duke of Clarence about Mrs Jordan. They were thus spared the frustrations of their youngest surviving brother Adolphus. The latter had been his parents' favourite, partly – as asserted by historians and biographers – as the King was less involved in politics and the machinations of the Whigs when his younger children were at their most attractive and least troublesome; and partly as he was a good-natured child whose natural affection towards his parents did not lessen as he grew up. He seemed to lack the contrariness and rebellious spirit of his elder brothers.

For several years he lived in Hanover, and at the age of twenty-one he visited the Prussian court for the first time. He became fond of Princess Frederica of Mecklenburg-Strelitz, who had been married at fifteen to Prince Frederick Louis of Prussia and widowed at eighteen with three children, one of which died a few weeks after his father. Soon after her husband's death, she began a liaison with Adolphus, and he proposed marriage. Contemporaries doubted whether she was really in love with him, or whether she merely admired him and regarded him as a friend, moreover one who would provide her children with another father.

Early in 1798 Adolphus approached his father for permission to marry. The King did not refuse, but insisted that he must wait until war was over. The Prince, it was believed, may have offered to release her from her engagement, and though they continued to exchange letters – albeit less frequently and ardently – the affair soon ran its course. Some of the royal family, particularly Queen Charlotte, thought indignantly that the Princess had jilted him. Any lingering doubts that she was prepared to wait for him were dispelled by the summer when she became involved with Prince Frederick of Solms-Braunfels, became pregnant by him, and married him in January 1799, barely three months before the child was born.

The Prince of Wales, having fallen out with Lady Jersey, had gone back to Maria Fitzherbert – and a succession of mistresses, some of whom may have borne him children. However, he yearned to patch up his differences with Maria, and at length she decided to seek the advice of her confessor, who appealed to Rome for guidance. Was Mrs Fitzherbert genuinely the wife of the Prince of Wales in the eyes of the church or not? In May 1800, Pope Pius VII gave his judgment that if the Prince was truly penitent for his sins, and sincere in his promise of amendment, she might rejoin her husband.

For the next few years, they lived together as husband and wife. Mutual acquaintances saw how she mellowed his uncertain temper as well as her own; she reduced his drinking, and nursed him back to health after he fell seriously ill with inflammation of the stomach.

In December 1800 Princess Sophia wrote Lady Harcourt a rather cryptic letter, bemoaning her loneliness, and adding that 'the excessive kindness of your

Princess Elizabeth, by Sir William Beechey

Princess Mary, by Sir William Beechey

manner has, I assure you, greatly soothed my distressed and unhappy days & hours.' It went on to thank her for her kind concern; 'but you will allow, I am sure, that I require time to recover my Spirits, which have met with so severe a blow ... It is grievous to think what a little trifle will *slur a young woman's character for ever.*'[1]

The 'little trifle' apparently referred to the Princess's liaison with Major-General Garth, one of the King's equerries, who slept at Windsor in the room directly over hers. Thomas Garth was aged fifty-six, with a face disfigured by a large purple birthmark. His age and ugliness put him at no disadvantage, for Princess Sophia and her spinster sisters were so secluded from the world, and allowed to mix with so few people, that it was said they were more than ready to fall into the arms of the first man outside the family who looked at them. The affair began when Sophia, who repeatedly suffered from 'cramps', 'spasms', and recurrent attacks of pain in the side, was moved from the Lower Lodge at Windsor, where she lived with her sisters, to the Upper Lodge, so she could be with her parents. One night the King and Queen had to go to London, and she was left behind.

The Princess may have gone though a form of marriage with Garth, but whether she did or not, she was so infatuated with him that 'she could not contain herself in his presence.' Her inability to contain herself apparently resulted in the birth of a son, also named Thomas, at Weymouth later that year. All the same, she never lived openly with him, and he remained a bachelor to all outward appearances until his death in 1829 at the age of eighty-five.

According to his equerry, Robert Fulke Greville, the King never knew of his daughter's pregnancy. 'She was said to be dropsical, and suddenly recovered. They told the old King that she had been cured by roast beef, and this he swallowed, and used to tell it to people, all of whom knew the truth, as "a very extraordinary thing."'[2] It was not so naive of the King as might be supposed. Not only was his eyesight failing, but Sophia was ill so often that it was easy to explain her sudden return to a normal figure in this way after the baby was born. Dropsy was in turn to afflict and ultimately contribute to the deaths of her mother and eldest sister. Garth acknowledged the boy as his own, and Sophia seems to have visited him from time to time at the house of Sir Herbert Taylor, later the King's Private Secretary, in Weymouth.

Within a few years, it was rumoured that young Thomas was the product of an incestuous union between the Princess and her brother the Duke of Cumberland. It either originated with Princess Lieven, wife of the Russian Ambassador, notorious for her love of gossip, or possibly with the Princess of Wales. The embittered Caroline had no reason to bear a grudge against her brother-in-law, but she was believed to be showing signs of mental instability, and she always found perverse pleasure in shocking her guests.

Sophia's persistent ill-health was probably psychosomatic. She was pampered by regular visits, presents, and constant sympathy from the Prince of Wales, and seemed to take a peculiar pleasure in enjoying her invalidism. Although she became blind late in life, she outlived all her sisters but one.

The more lively Princess Augusta, who had played cricket and football with her brothers and been regarded as something of a tomboy, also found an outlet

Princess Sophia, by Sir
William Beechey

for her affections in secret liaisons. Forbidden to marry an eligible prince while the Princess Royal was still unmarried, it seemed possible at one stage that a marriage might be arranged between her and the Prince Royal of Denmark. The sad fate of his sister Caroline Matilda, however, had been sufficient reason in itself for the King to reject any further alliances with the Danish house. She exchanged long letters so frequently with one of her father's doctors, Sir Henry Halford, that some suspected an illicit affair between them, but Halford was a married man and the relationship was probably innocent enough. Later she became passionately fond of one of the royal equerries, Major-General Sir Brent Spencer. She confided in the Prince of Wales what they felt for each other, but they had to content themselves with keeping their relationship as secret as possible. Even so, gossips at court suspected that they had gone through some private form of marriage.

Though Prince Augustus and his wife had been reunited in Berlin, he was still depressed and frustrated by events. In 1800 he celebrated his twenty-seventh birthday, and was thus past the age when the Dukes of York and Clarence had received their establishments and titles. In direct contradiction of the King's statement that provision for his remaining sons could not be considered till peace had been declared, Augustus read in the papers a few months later that his brothers Edward and Ernest had been given their dukedoms, and he was outraged. Further appeals to his father for useful employment fell on deaf ears, and he threatened to stand for Parliament as a candidate for Liverpool. Queen Charlotte regretted her husband's inflexibility, writing that she was sure her son's return to England and 'one conversation between him and the King might do more than millions of letters.'[3]

In May 1800 the Prince, travelling as Mr Ford, crossed the Channel and joined Lady Augusta, who had returned to her home in Hertford Street, London, several months previously. He still hoped that the King would give him some form of employment, and as his hopes faded he made preparations to winter abroad. In December 1800 he set out for Lisbon, and from on board ship he wrote enthusiastically about Brownsea Island, off Poole, which they could rent for £250 a year, and which he thought would suit them very well. He was confident that the Dorsetshire air would cure his asthma. He wrote to his son for the latter's seventh birthday, addressing the letter to 'the Prince Augustus Frederick'. A little later he wrote to Lady Augusta, 'to leave you I must not only be the most infamous wretch in the universe, but also the greatest fool existing.' All their difficulties he attributed to the interference of his eldest brother.

By the beginning of 1801, Lady Augusta knew she was expecting another child, and on 9 August she gave birth to a daughter, named Augusta Emma. But the liaison was almost over by now; quite why has never been satisfactorily

Augustus, Duke of Sussex, by Guy Head, 1798

established. The Prince, it was thought, may have been told that she had been unfaithful to him; she may have precipitated a quarrel with him by taunting him with desertion; either of these, or a combination of both, may have made a frustrated, disappointed, frequently sick man unable to resist parental pressure any longer, particularly if his invalid marriage was the only barrier to a dukedom and regular allowance.

At the end of the year he was given his parliamentary grant of £12,000 (which would be raised to £18,000 in 1806) and created Duke of Sussex, Earl of Inverness and Baron of Arklow. On separation, he agreed to pay Lady Augusta maintenance of £4,000 a year and grant her custody of the children.

The youngest surviving Prince, Adolphus, now aged twenty-six, still gave his parents no anxiety whatsoever. An Englishwoman travelling abroad in 1800, Mrs Trench, noted that 'His manners bear that stamp of real goodness which no art can imitate, no other charm replace; and though he presents himself with suitable dignity, his address immediately inspires ease and confidence. His conversation is fluent, various, and entertaining.' This most filial of sons 'never had done, and never would do, anything to give the King, his father, a moment's uneasiness. He cannot speak of his father without tears in his eyes.'[4]

On his return to England after studying at university, his political partisanship had been sought by the Prince of Wales, Fox and others, who hoped to find another royal ally for the Whigs. Though he showed some interest in liberalism, he placed loyalty to his father above all else, and became a firm supporter of Pitt. He served with distinction in the army, attaining the rank of Colonel in 1794 and of Lieutenant General four years later. Rising regularly at six in the morning, he set some time aside from military duties for scientific studies and practising his violin. In 1801, he was created Duke of Cambridge, Earl of Tipperary and Baron Culloden.

When the Duke of Kent returned to England in September 1800, he made a point of paying his respects to his father at Weymouth. He stayed there for three weeks, taking hot sea baths for his rheumatism, and then returned to Madame de St Laurent in London, where they settled into a house in Knightsbridge. Nominally a bachelor, he had apartments in Kensington Palace, but it was not deemed proper for him and Madame to live there together. He was careful not to do anything to offend his father. When the King was ill in 1801, he wrote that he and Madame 'consequently abstain from any amusement whatever.'

Early in 1802, he was offered the Governorship of Gibraltar. He was rather disappointed when the King warned him, as they bade each other goodbye, not to 'make such a trade of it as when you went to Halifax.' He reached the Rock on 10 May, eleven years after he had been removed from there by the government because of the mutterings of the soldiers at his severity. Since 1791, the discipline of the Gibraltar garrison had been deteriorating, until the Government felt that the abuses which had developed in all ranks must be put down, even at the risk of discontent. At the same time the Duke of Kent, whose name was a byword for strict discipline, was in need of an appointment. Without a second thought, the authorities offered him the post.

The Duke of York had his doubts, and warned his brother that some exertion would be necessary 'to establish a due degree of discipline among the troops; and which I trust you will be able gradually to accomplish by a moderate exercise of the power vested in you.'[5] However, the Duke of Kent had not learnt from his experiences. Schooled in the German tradition of savage, pedantic military discipline, disappointments had hardened his character.

He had barely landed on Gibraltar before he was complaining that the Guard of Honour lacked steadiness, and objecting to the men's drunkenness. Unhappily they had little else to occupy their leisure time. The rock of Gibraltar, two and a half miles in length and at most only three quarters of a mile wide, had ninety wine houses at the time. Drunkenness was not technically an offence among the soldiers, provided they were off duty; it was more an occupational hazard, for there was virtually no other recreation available. The town had one main, narrow street with a servicemen's recreation room, stocked with 'ancient English periodicals'; off this street were a few squalid guest houses; no communication with Spain was permitted in time of war, so food had to be brought in by sea from the coast of Africa; plague often cut off communication there, and the garrison had to rely on salt meat, and there was always a scarcity of water. Poor food, lack of water, boredom, and easy access to unlimited alcohol, could have but one result.

All the same, the Duke was disgusted at the lack of discipline and consequent breakdown of law and order. Gibraltar was notoriously unsafe, particularly at night, and when two visiting Spanish ladies were raped, he felt matters had gone too far. Attributing the trouble to drunkenness, he closed fifty wine shops.

By Christmas 1802, an elaborate code of orders had been drawn up, regulating barrack life, discipline on parade, and ordering the men to rise at 3.30 a.m. in summer, 4.30 in autumn, and 5.30 in winter. Strict requirements were laid down about clothing, and the length of officers' soldiers' hair. Sergeants were forbidden to drink with corporals or mix with them, and corporals could not fraternize with private soldiers. Above all, no soldier was allowed to enter a wine shop. He could buy wine at the regimental canteen, or beer at three specified houses permitted to sell malt liquor. On Christmas Eve and saints' days, they were to be cautioned by their commanding officers against entertaining the idea that the next day might be considered privileged for intemperance and indiscipline.

On Christmas Eve, 1802, patience snapped in the ranks. The second battalion of the Royals, the Duke's own corps, broke out from barracks, and tried in vain to persuade the other regiments to join them. On Christmas Day the Duke spoke severely to them about their wilful behaviour, but perhaps even he realized that punishment in this case was uncalled for. Two days later, a group of soldiers from the 25th Regiment attacked the Royals' quarters; some lives were lost and several more wounded before order was restored. It later emerged that this regiment and the Royals had agreed to lead a joint mutiny on Christmas Eve, but the regiment, not having received their pay, were too sober to join the high-spirited Royals. Taunted with cowardice, the 25th Regiment had their money two days later, got drunk on the proceeds, and went on to avenge the insult. Three of the ringleaders were sentenced to death and others were given the lash.

The Duke of Kent's draconian sense of discipline was held to have been responsible, and if the officers did not actually organize the disturbance, they were at least passive sympathizers. Major-General Barnett, second in command at the garrison, remarked that the Christmas mutiny was the best thing that could have happened; 'now we shall get rid of him.' The Duke was fortunate in that the mutiny was swiftly contained, before it could spread to other disaffected regiments, who might have been tempted to murder him.

Exaggerated rumours of the trouble soon reached England, and not until the end of January 1803 was the Duke of Kent's own official report received. He maintained that the cabinet and government were divided as to the cause of the mutiny, and that his recall was entirely at the insistence of the Duke of York. When Frederick's secretary, Captain Dodd, reached Gibraltar with the letters of recall, the Duke of Kent was surprised and angry. He was ordered to return immediately and hand over command to Barnett, whom he had always disliked and suspected of disloyalty. Instead he defied orders, insisting he would stay until the arrival of his officially-designated successor, Sir Thomas Trigge. Being unaware of the situation, Trigge was astonished on sailing into Gibraltar to see the Royal Standard still flying, and wrote to the government that the Duke had presented him with a copy of his orders, and dwelt much on the quiet state of the garrison. Trigge added that the standing orders were certain to produce disaffection in the officers and men, and thought that the quiet state of things could be dated from the day when the Duke announced his departure.

Though the Duke only had himself to blame, he was justified in feeling ill-used. He had been ordered by the government to restore discipline at Gibraltar, which had become exceedingly lax since his departure. His brother Frederick, he was convinced, was responsible for his recall. Had he done nothing, it was said, but 'winked at the drunkenness and the unsteadiness of the men,' there would have been no trouble. Barely had he arrived home before he was writing abusive letters to the Duke of York, attempting to appeal to the cabinet over his head, and demanding a court-martial, but in vain. Realizing that to surrender his post would be a tacit admission of guilt or failure, he did not resign, and no resignation was demanded by the King.

Fortunately he had other domestic diversions. In 1800 he bought an estate at Ealing, Castle Hill Lodge, from Maria Fitzherbert. This would be his country residence until his death, and here he would spend some of his happiest hours with Madame. Heavy debts did not prevent him from engaging a builder who could bring the house up to a state of elegance to satisfy his personal tastes.

For at least six months every year, the Duke lived at Ealing as a country squire, with Madame acting as gracious hostess to his guests. The lodge stood in over thirty acres of park land on Castlebar Hill, with extensive views of the surrounding countryside. Every comfort imaginable, including six patent water closets, was provided, with a library on both floors. Apart from the standard works of English literature, he had a military library with numerous maps and plans, as well as books on politics and contemporary issues. On the upper floor were a thirty-foot music room and billiards room of equal size. The house was filled with cages of artificial singing birds, organs with dancing horses, and musical clocks. Beneath the house, arched vaults and cellars stored coal, beer and ale, and a dairy house. There were a fire-engine house, stable and coach yard, and extensive domestic living and working apartments for staff in the main building were provided.

Though the Duke of York forbade him to return to Gibraltar, or issue any public defence of his conduct, he was consoled to some extent in September 1805 by his appointment as Ranger of Hampton Court Park, and promotion to the rank of Field-Marshal. Yet the former, although it carried a small salary, involved little work, and the latter was merely a nominal post which did nothing to disabuse him of the feeling that his military career was now over.

In another corner of Europe, the Duke of Cambridge was also experiencing thwarted military ambitions, though for an entirely different reason. In the spring of 1803, before war had officially broken out again between England and France, the French threatened Hanover with a small force under General Mortier, and declared that any Hanoverians found in the service of the King of England would be regarded as enemies of France. The Duke of Cambridge was appointed to command a combined Anglo-Hanoverian force, fourteen thousand strong, to resist this French attack, and he made valiant efforts to recruit the civil population in defence of the country.

But the placid Hanoverians had no stomach for further hostilities. First, they declared that the state should be neutral territory; when placards displayed on their borders to this effect, in French, failed to pacify the invaders, they made it known that, notwithstanding their numerical superiority, they would gladly accede to any reasonable peace terms the French might offer. Restrained with difficulty from conducting a reckless assault on the French, the Duke reluctantly returned to England, to lead a quiet life in his apartments at St James's Palace and at Windsor. In recognition of his services, he was raised to the rank of General in September 1803, and two years later he was appointed Colonel of the Coldstream Guards.

Until the age of fifteen, Princess Amelia had enjoyed good health. By then she was as tall as her eldest sister. Madame d'Arblay wrote of her 'innocence, an Hebe blush, an air of modest candour, and a gentleness so caressingly inviting of voice and eye, that I have seldom seen a more captivating young creature.'[6] Yet there was always a sense of melancholy about her. Each summer she went to Worthing with the King's equerry, General Goldsworthy, and his sister, and her nurse Mrs Cheveley, for the benefit of sea baths. Worthing was regarded as more suitable, for Weymouth had attracted so many people anxious to catch a sight of the royal family each summer that it was noisy and lacked privacy; not only was Worthing more peaceful, but it was closer to Brighton. The Prince of Wales was his youngest sister's godfather, and they were devoted to each other. From Weymouth in September 1797 she wrote to him affectionately, enclosing a

Princess Amelia

small purse which she had made for him, and also mentioning a strange complaint which was perhaps an early sign of her deteriorating health: 'I wish the wind would go down. It hurts the Drumsticks of my Ears.'

Princess Mary sympathized with her sister's being confined to Worthing, telling the Prince of Wales next year that 'was it not for her own very heavenly disposition nothing can be more dull than Worthing, or the life she must lead wherever she is, from being quite confined to the couch and suffering so much pain.'[7] That year Amelia was diagnosed as suffering from tubercular trouble in the knee, and from that time, she was never really well again.

When she was about eighteen, she was left behind one summer at Weymouth after the rest of the family had returned to Windsor, with a few equerries. Among them was General Charles FitzRoy. By 1803 Miss Gomm, who had helped Miss Goldsworthy to look after the Princesses when they were small, was anxious and warned the Queen of the situation. The Queen asked for her cooperation in turning a blind eye to it, so long as unpleasantness could be avoided. Most important of all, nothing must be said to the King, lest it unbalance his mind. The Queen regretted that Amelia should have spoken about it to her sisters, and asked her 'neither directly or indirectly to name a word of this unpleasant business' to her brothers. How she can have imagined that it would remain a secret from them is hard to imagine.

For by 1804, the family were once again alarmed about the King's mental condition. Amelia's love for a man whom she could not marry under the terms of her father's Act, and the state of anxiety which hung over the family, depressed the ailing Princess. 'God knows I am more wretched than I can express,' she wrote to the Prince of Wales on 19 August, 'and could an Extinguisher fall upon the whole family I think as things are it would be a mercy.'[8]

Yet she continued to hope. Studying the Act carefully, she realized that once she attained the age of twenty-five, she could marry FitzRoy legally, if she could obtain the consent of the Privy Council and if Parliament made no objection. From November 1804, she took to signing her letters AFR (Amelia FitzRoy), and had the monogram engraved on her silver. It was believed that she may have gone through some form of unofficial ceremony with him in anticipation of a formal union later. Should the King die, she knew her eldest brother and godfather – and, by then, sovereign – would surely never withhold his assent to their marriage.

When the Duke of Sussex returned from Lisbon, he formed a particularly strong rapport with his youngest sister, of whom he had yet seen but little. He thought her a 'lovely creature', while she told the Prince of Wales that Augustus was 'a good soul & possesses a most excellent heart. His fate as well as many others in this family has been a hard one.'[9]

The Prince of Wales also had reason to bemoan his fate at this time. When a French invasion appeared imminent in 1803, he asked for a military command so he could set an example which would 'excite the loyal energies of the nation,' and no longer remain 'an idle, a lifeless spectator of the mischief which threatens us.' His supporters in the House of Commons pressed his case, and he begged the King 'to be allowed to display the best energies of my character, to shed the last drop of my blood in support of Your Majesty's person, crown and dignity.'

Much as the King appreciated his patriotic zeal, he privately informed his son that he expected him to stand at his side in the field should the French invaders land, but there could be no question of promotion or a command, and no further mention should be made to him on the subject. As four of his younger brothers held high military rank, the Prince was aggrieved at having held the junior post of a Colonel of Dragoons for ten years. He appealed to the Duke of York, in his capacity as Commander-in-Chief, but the Duke sided with their father.

In exasperation, bent on proving his loyalty to the public, the Prince had the exchange of letters with the King published in the *Morning Chronicle* and two other papers on 7 December 1803. *The Times* was offered them as well, but declined on account of 'the delicacy of the subject'. The King was furious with 'the publisher of *my* letters,' and refused to speak to him for several weeks. Queen Charlotte and the Princesses had been trying to placate father and son; with this latest episode, the breach was as wide as ever. The public proved to be less sympathetic to the heir's plight than he had hoped, he had merely made himself look foolish, and provided the satirists with more ammunition.

To add insult to injury, the Prince's regiment was later withdrawn from its front-line encampment by the Sussex coast, where the French were expected to attempt invasion, and sent inland of Guildford. It was an indignity which he could not ignore. The Duke of Clarence recognized that it would 'produce an irreparable breach for ever' between his elder brothers. The Prince threatened that he would never speak to the Duke of York again, and the latter presented himself several times at Carlton House to explain his matters, but was sent away without being invited indoors. Princess Sophia regretted to her eldest brother how she was 'lamenting in silence that any coolness should subsist *between two* I do *dearly love*.'[10] Yet it was some time before the brothers were on speaking terms again.

By the autumn of 1804, the King's sole recognized grandchild, Princess Charlotte, was eight years old. The King felt that the Prince of Wales could not be trusted to supervise the child's education. He proposed that Charlotte should come to Windsor and be brought up in the family circle by her grandmother and spinster aunts. At the same time, he wanted the child's mother to see more of her, and in November he informed his 'dearest daughter-in-law and niece' of this.

The Prince angrily hastened to see his father for the first time since their argument about the publication of their letters. He threatened to break off

George, Prince of Wales, from a Wedgwood portrait medallion

negotiations, and not until the beginning of the following year was it arranged that the young Princess would live in Carlton House, or one of the adjoining houses in the Mall, while her father was in London; and when he was away, her governesses would bring her to her grandparents at Windsor or Kew.

By this time the King was ageing fast, and his attacks of illness were becoming more frequent. The Queen and their daughters had persuaded him that there was some justification for reducing the influence of the Princess of Wales on the young girl whom they all expected to succeed her father on the throne in due course.

During the previous year Sir John Douglas, an officer in the Marines, and a friend of the Duke of Kent, and his wife, a friend of the Princess of Wales, had received a letter accompanied by an indecent drawing, explaining that Lady Douglas had admitted another gentleman to her bed. The Douglases were certain that this had come from the Princess of Wales, and they showed it to the Duke of Kent. The latter recognized his sister-in-law's handwriting, remarked merely that it was 'unfortunate' and begged Sir John to forget it. Sir John was not inclined to do so; although persuaded not to take the Princess to court, he indignantly told his friends what had happened.

At length it reached the Duke of Sussex, who decided to go straight to Carlton House to tell the Prince of Wales. A little tactlessly, he added that their brother Edward had known about it for a year. The Prince angrily sent for the Duke of Kent and asked why he had kept to himself a matter which so closely concerned the honour of the royal family. The Duke explained that he had kept it to himself in order to try and avoid scandal, and also any further misunderstandings between the King and his eldest son. Though apparently mollified by this explanation, the Prince of Wales was inwardly furious at such a delicate matter being kept from him, and at what he saw as the indignity of having to learn about it from others. Ever afterwards, he complained of his brother Edward's treachery, and mockingly referred to him as 'Joseph Surface' or 'Simon Pure'.

At all events, something had to be done. It had been rumoured that in 1802 the Princess had given birth to a second child, and as she had lived apart from her husband for several years, there was no question of his being the father. Lady Charlotte Douglas testified that three years previously Caroline had taken her into her confidence and had admitted that she was the mother of a son, named William Austin. Although the King must have grown impatient with his son's continual complaints against his wife, he saw that the dignity of crown and family was at stake, and that this child might one day challenge the succession; for even if he was the illegitimate son of the Princess of Wales, he might put himself forward as another Perkin Warbeck, or another Duke of Monmouth.

The King consulted Lord Grenville, recently appointed Prime Minister, and a Royal Commission was established to examine all allegations into the Princess of Wales's conduct and report back to the King. The commissioners entrusted with what was to be known as the 'Delicate Investigation' were Grenville himself, the Lord Chancellor, the Lord Chief Justice and the Home Secretary.

They completed their work by midsummer, concluding that Her Royal Highness was innocent of the gravest charge that could have been brought against her. William Austin was not her son, but that of an impoverished labourer and his wife, who had happened to knock on the Princess's door to ask if she could help find work for her husband. She accordingly adopted the child as an act of charity, not realizing what a foolish and dangerous undertaking it was for somebody in her position. That she had repeatedly told Lady Douglas she was pregnant, describing her physical symptoms in detail, was evidently part of her delight in shocking people. Perhaps it also confirmed some of the family's suspicions about her mental balance.

Nevertheless, during their investigations they found her behaviour had been liable to 'very unfavourable interpretations'. Several people who had been invited to her house were repelled by her personal habits – her sitting on the floor and talking scandal with her ladies, and her regular diet of ale and raw onions – and were convinced that she was either more or less insane, or 'if not mad, she was a very worthless woman.' She had flirted (if not more) with several illustrious personages, including Admiral Sydney Smith, and the portrait painter Thomas Lawrence. While no proof of adultery was established, it could not be ruled out, especially in view of her boasting that she took 'a bedfellow' whenever she liked, and that she claimed to have been pregnant again. As a contemporary put it discreetly, she was 'of that lively vivacity that she makes herself familiar with gentlemen.'[11] In any other woman, her behaviour would have given rise to scandal; for the wife of the heir to the throne, it was extremely foolish of her.

The report was serious enough to lose the Princess her best friend and strongest protector in England, as well as her only champion in the royal family – the King. If it had been one attachment or indiscretion, he said sadly, he would have screened her if he could have done it with safety to the Crown; but in the face of such overwhelming evidence as to her moral instability, she was not worth the screening. No longer could the Princess be received as 'an Intimate' in his family; henceforth, relations between them would be restricted to 'outward marks of civility.'

6 'Do not grieve for me'

In 1802, Duke Frederick of Württemberg assumed the title of Elector, and in 1806 that of King. Though cut off from her homeland, the former Princess Royal of England was nominally a British ally; but after the battle of Austerlitz, with Württemberg a not unwilling puppet state of Napoleon, she was obliged to be technically her father's enemy. After her elevation to the throne, she mischievously sent her mother a letter addressed, *'Ma très chère Mère et Soeur.'* It was received with such coldness that the King insisted none of his family should refer to his eldest daughter as Queen of Württemberg.

In England, her relations began to wonder where her true loyalties lay. Was she following her husband's lead out of duty, or with genuine enthusiasm? Napoleon regarded her as a true ally of his cause, and was grateful when she helped to bring about a marriage between his youngest brother Jerome and her stepdaughter Caroline, to whom she was devoted.

Shortly after their separation, the Duke of Sussex brought an action restraining his estranged wife from using the Royal Arms and calling herself Duchess of Sussex. For a while she persisted in her claims, but in 1806, an agreement was made to settle her debts if she agreed to renounce all claims to royal style. She was granted the title Countess d'Ameland, and the children were known as Augustus and Mademoiselle d'Este, after a common ancestor of the Duke and Lady Augusta. They lived with the Duke, and he was a kind and affectionate father to them.

The Duke had been granted the use of apartments in Kensington Palace, where he spent the rest of his life. His main interest was a fine collection of books, including several hundred Bibles, in virtually all known languages, and a unique collection of Italian opera manuscripts. His library was his greatest extravagance, and by the time of his death it comprised some 50,000 volumes. In building this up, he was helped considerably by Dr Thomas Pettigrew, who was introduced to him by the Duke of Kent and initially became his surgeon. After his talent for organization, his literary associations with scholars throughout Europe, and diverse interests became known to the Duke, he made him his librarian. Pettigrew arranged and catalogued the collection, regularly visiting public and private book and manuscript sales on the Duke's behalf with such zeal that the latter was often obliged to ask him to keep his enthusiasm and 'this terrible book account' in check. As the Duke pored through his volumes, he would sketch in an elaborate hand pointing to any passage with which he particularly agreed or disagreed, often adding comments such as 'A most mischievous argument', or 'I don't believe a word of it'.

By now he had accepted that no official employment was ever likely to come his way. He had had high hopes of being appointed governor of Jamaica, or of the Cape of Good Hope, both positions being about to fall vacant. Such employment would allow him to live in a warm climate, and the salary would make a useful addition to his allowance. Although the Prince of Wales supported his claims and tried to persuade the government, the ministers were reluctant to appoint someone so sickly and inexperienced. In September 1806 this despondency, coupled with a severe recurrence of his chronic asthmatic complaint, seriously alarmed the family, particularly the Duke of Kent, who held him in high regard.

He found a chance to be of use, however, in presiding over and assisting with charities. With his radical views and sympathy for the underprivileged, as well as his poor health (not helped by heavy smoking), he was keen to help the blind, maimed and elderly. In 1809 he became chairman of the Bayswater Hospital Committee, and persuaded his mother to become its patron. It was renamed the Queen Charlotte Lying-in Hospital (later Queen Charlotte's Maternity Hospital), and minutes of the committee meetings showed a long record of changes and improvements that could be attributed to the Duke's supervision.

Over the next twenty-five years, it was estimated that he presided over seventy charitable institutions, chiefly hospitals and convalescent homes. 'His comprehensive benevolence demanded large subscriptions,' it was noted. Fund raising dinners and balls benefited from his attendance and patronage; he was ever ready to give generous financial contributions, and encourage members of the royal family and other titled patrons to do likewise.

Seven years later, he was elected President of the Society of Arts, despite a nomination for the Earl of Liverpool submitted the day before, probably by a government supporter as a half-hearted gesture against the Duke's liberal views. He was re-elected every year, unopposed save for one occasion, serving in this capacity until his death. The body, whose full title was Society for the Encouragement of Arts, Commerce and Manufactures, annually awarded premiums and medals for important achievements in all branches of practical knowledge. Among recipients were his equerry, Colonel Thomas Wildman, for planting five hundred acres of waste land with forest; the Australian explorer, Gregory Blaxland, for wine from his vineyard in New South Wales; and William Cobbett, for his discovery of British grasses for the manufacture of ladies' bonnets in imitation of Leghorn, which had to be imported from Europe.[1]

Meanwhile, Princess Amelia's passion for General FitzRoy continued unabated. Misses Goldsworthy and Gomm once again warned the Queen, as they were worried lest they should be blamed for what was happening. They were particularly upset by an anonymous letter accusing them of conniving at Amelia's love affair. A family argument resulted, 'a sad row', as the Duke of York called it, but the Queen still cared more for keeping up family appearances than her ailing daughter's happiness. In April 1807, she wrote to Amelia that, as she was 'beginning to enter into years of discretion,' she would see 'how necessary it is to *subdue* at once every Passion in the beginning, and to consider

Kensington Palace

the impropriety of indulging any impression which must make you miserable, and be a disgrace to yourself and a misery to all who love you.'[2]

Princess Elizabeth had longed for marriage, but whenever she brought up the idea in front of her mother, she was told that it was not a fit subject to be raised 'at the moment'. The Queen's refusal to hear of any further marriages among her daughters was partly down to maternal possessiveness, but partly no doubt as she feared for the consequences it would have on the King's frail mental state. Any crossing of his will was liable to unleash his reason once again.

Elizabeth assuaged her longing for children by looking after those belonging to others – though in a more intelligent fashion than her sister-in-law had done – and in charitable works for local orphanages. Though resenting her mother's possessiveness, she made the best of a bad job, writing letters for her, producing numerous engravings and collecting porcelain. She took up farming and kept a set of Chinese pigs at Frogmore.

To the family she was always Fatima, because of her hearty Hanoverian appetite. 'I was taken exceedingly ill in the night, violently sick,' she boasted once to her brother, 'and so swelled that they think I must have been poisoned, and that owing to a remarkable large lobster which I had eat of at supper.'[3] Self-conscious about her figure, she went for long walks early in the morning. Anxious not to become undesirable to prospective suitors, she drank sugar melted in water at night as she was told it would keep her temper sweet.

In the autumn of 1808, she learnt through one of her brothers that a most eligible offer of marriage had been made for her – by the Duke of Orleans. Although she was desperate for the offer to be considered, his religion (Roman Catholicism) added further strength to the automatic resistance of the King and

Queen. The Duke of Kent was apparently responsible, and she entreated the Prince of Wales in a letter of 25 September not to 'dash the Cup of Happiness from my lips.'[4] As she knew, the Prince of Wales would support her in any efforts she made to find a husband, but inevitably they came up against Queen Charlotte's vehement refusal to hear any more of it.

Queen Charlotte's reactions were predictable; but the Prince of Wales did not intend to wait, if he could help it. Alone of the children, he had some influence over his mother, and sometimes he could persuade her to change her mind. The negotiations continued for several weeks. On 2 October 1808 the Princess wrote gratefully to her brother; 'No words can ever express what I feel towards you for your unbounded goodness to me – you have eased my mind beyond belief.' Their sisters were sympathetic to her; Mary had 'been most angelical, but Augusta has really stood forward nobly for me, in short, I cannot say enough *for all*. Sophy also, for the state I was in made them see I was all but wild, and they have behaved so very amiably that I hope You will express your approbation. The reason why not a word has been said to the youngest was from delicacy . . .'[5] Later that month she was asking her brother regarding her suitor's anxiety concerning the legal status of any children that might be born to them.

The correspondence continued till March the following year, by when it seemed Elizabeth had given up hope of becoming the Duchess of Orleans. With Napoleon Bonaparte firmly in power, chances of a Bourbon restoration to the French throne seemed remote. Louis Philippe, Duke of Orleans, married Princess Marie Amelie of Sicily later in 1809; twenty-one years later, he ascended the French throne.

For some years the Duke of York and his mistress, Mary Anne Clarke, had lived in Gloucester Place. Though officially resident at Oatlands, he and the Duchess still showed themselves to the world at large as good companions, though they hardly bothered to keep up appearances, and it was evident that the marriage now only existed in name.

Mrs Clarke had first place in his affections, and as he could hardly bear to be away from her even for a weekend, he took a house for her at Weybridge so she could be close to Oatlands. One Sunday morning she crept in, uninvited, to Weybridge Church, watching the Duke and Duchess at prayers together. The Duke was embarrassed; the Duchess held her tongue, but wrote privately to William Pitt (of whom, as Prime Minister, all the royal Dukes and Princes stood in awe as he controlled their parliamentary grants), insisting that such a thing must never happen again.

At length, the Duke and Mrs Clarke tired of each other, and he lost his heart to a Mrs Cary. The people of Fulham (where she lived) and Chelsea became used to seeing the Duke riding through the streets in his carriage to visit her.

Feeling that she had been shabbily treated by her penny-pinching royal lover, Mrs Clarke bided her time. In 1808, Major Dodd, the Duke of Kent's military secretary, was supplying the press with private details about the Duke of York, who was privately blamed by the Duke of Kent for many of his misfortunes. Colonel Irving Wardle, member of parliament for Okehampton, an ambitious member of the opposition, scenting corruption in high places, became intrigued. He was more interested still when Mrs Clarke came to him with further details.

In January 1809, Wardle asked in the House that 'a Committee be appointed to investigate the conduct of His Royal Highness the Duke of York, in his capacity of Commander-in-Chief, with regard to appointments, promotions, exchanges, the raising of new levies and the general state of the Army.' Encouraged by loud cheers, he went on to say that unless corruption was attacked, the country would soon fall easy prey to its enemies.

The Tory government undertook to defend the Duke. Spencer Perceval, Chancellor of the Exchequer and Leader of the House of Commons in the Duke of Portland's government, took the responsibility. An official inquiry took place before the whole house, and proceedings lasted for seven weeks. It proved beyond doubt that Mrs Clarke had taken money to influence promotions in the army, but as far as could be ascertained, none of the money found its way into the Duke's pocket. Though it was proved that promotions had taken place after the money had been paid to Mrs Clarke, the government could produce documents from the War Office, and call officials who had charge of the promotions, to prove that the cases mentioned by the opposition had all taken place in the ordinary course of events, and there was therefore no evidence of corruption. During her examination in the witness-box, Mrs Clarke was caught out in several obvious falsehoods.

Saddened by his favourite son's disgrace, King George never doubted his innocence. Much as he deplored the Duke's connection with 'so abandoned a woman' as Mrs Clarke, he never allowed himself 'to doubt for one moment the Duke of York's perfect integrity and his conscientious attention to his public duty, or to believe that in the discharge of it he has ever submitted to undue influence', and was relieved to hear from Mr Perceval 'that if justice is done to the Duke of York there is no evidence which ought to convince any fair and unbiased mind that the Duke of York knew anything of Mrs Clarke's nefarious practices.'[6]

A verdict on the Duke's innocence was put to the vote, with a government majority of 82. Though exonerated from the gravest charges against him, and acquitted of knowledge, corruption and connivance at Mrs Clarke's practices, the fact that such a large minority in the House apparently believed in his guilt meant that he was in no position to continue as Commander-in-Chief.

Accepting his son's resignation, the King wrote to Perceval on 18 March that he must 'ever regret any circumstances that have deprived him of the service of the Duke of York in a situation in which his able, zealous and impartial conduct during so many years have secured to him His Majesty's entire approbation.'[7] In the previous fourteen years the Duke had done much to reduce the amount of political jobbery in army appointments, and had played his part in helping to build an army which was on the point of proving itself in Spain and Portugal.

His favourite son's disgrace was a sore trial to the King, now aged seventy and nearly blind; but worse was to come. After a severe attack of measles in 1808 Amelia had failed to rally, and before long pulmonary tuberculosis was diagnosed. Within the year, the doctors' treatment had failed to alleviate persistent discomfort, and they wondered whether moving her down to Weymouth might not give her a better chance. She would be far removed from FitzRoy, and was therefore reluctant to leave Windsor, but now she was too weak to resist. Princess Mary told the Prince of Wales that Dr Milman said, 'everything depends on her being kept as *quiet* as possible, and she ought to be *considered* in everything to make her as comfortable and happy as possible – must be *worried* about nothing, which, Entre Nous, in our House is very difficult, and with such a fine creature as she is, who possesses such very strong feelings, it requires great care to manage her well.'[8]

Whether Amelia would be 'happy as possible' away from FitzRoy was doubtful; but by this time, the King's deteriorating health and the Queen's coldness to her family had made the atmosphere at Windsor miserable indeed. It was no place for the depressed invalid, who believed her unsympathetic mother was waiting for her to die. The King insisted that no effort should be spared to try and restore his adored youngest child's health; he was adamant that she should go to Weymouth, and asked Princess Mary to keep her company. Mary was an affectionate, kind-hearted young woman. More self-contained than her sisters, she was the most protective of Amelia, for whom she had always felt sorry, and she willingly took on the task of acting as her companion and comforter.

Three days after their arrival, Mary wrote to the King that for the first time since settling in, Amelia had passed a night without moaning in her sleep. Bad nights had been a constantly recurring symptom, and she often dreamed that she was in prison. A bathing-machine formerly used by the King was turned into a 'parlour on wheels', with a couch from the royal yacht inside, and a green canvas curtain over the door to keep off the glare of the sea. Amelia was carried straight into it from her room, and drawn into the sea, 'as if she was going to bathe', staying in until the motion of the sea made her feel faint. On calm days she was taken out to sea in a small boat, and hauled up from shore in a slung chair, climbing seven steps to the pier. After a few days at Weymouth, she appeared alternately languid and cheerful. Though she could not cross a room without coughing, she found 'great comfort in resting quiet all day and not speaking.'[9]

Much as she appreciated her sister Mary's solicitude, she still could not unburden herself about the subject dearest to her heart, FitzRoy, to her sister. Only in a few others, including her friends the Hon. George Villiers and his wife, and the Prince of Wales, could she confide freely. After a visit from the Prince of Wales in September, she wrote to him; 'I always loved you better than any of my brothers, I knew, and now very much more. I shan't mind the Queen's ill and cross looks now, or Fatima's.'[10]

Elizabeth was accused of being particularly harsh to her youngest sister. The Princess of Wales's comments that Mary and Sophia were devoted to her, while 'Princess E. treats her with the most cruel unkindness and ill-temper'[11] could perhaps be disregarded, was it not for Amelia's own bitterness. To the Prince of Wales, she wrote, 'Don't tell the Queen that I can feel any pleasure in seeing her, for I can't, and Eliza some day or other shall *hear my mind*'.[12] She evidently regarded Elizabeth as the Queen's ally and confidante.

Queen Charlotte, by Sir William Beechey

On 21 October, Mary wrote to the King to complain of the Queen's attitude. 'I am the last person that have any right to complain myself, as nothing can be kinder or more Affe than all the letters wrote to me but upon one subject, which is my being absent from home and making myself so necessary to Amelia, which is not thought right, and considered so selfish of Amelia. If that is ever said to Amelia you must perfectly understand it will half kill her, who really, poor soul, never thinks of herself, and only wishes to give us all as little trouble as possible.'[13] In replying, the King answered that he had 'taken care to have it understood that you are not to be separated from her.'

Although he had often quarrelled with his father, the Prince of Wales was gravely concerned that he did not realize the seriousness of his daughter's illness. 'I assure you the dear King does not deceive himself about Amelia,' Sophia wrote optimistically to her brother.

A few days later, the sisters made their gentle journey back to Windsor. Amelia herself had wished to go to Kew, but the Queen would not agree, and as a compromise they settled on Augusta Lodge, Windsor, formerly occupied by one of the King's physicians. Princess Mary welcomed the idea, as Amelia would find it 'the greatest relief and comfort' to be near the King. His letters, she assured them, had acted 'like magic upon her, and calm and revive her for hours after.'

Full of concern for their sister, the brothers rallied round. The Dukes of Cambridge and Clarence came down to Weymouth to form part of the escort, and Amelia was 'much agitated' to see Adolphus again. The Prince of Wales sent her a special carriage built specially for him, which she found much more comfortable than any other she had used since her illness had worsened. It was a slow journey with several stops on the way; by the time they reached Salisbury, Amelia was very faint, and suffering from severe pain in her side, but was still 'all anxiety to get to Windsor' as soon as she could.

Several physicians were in attendance on her once she returned, and by Christmas she seemed comfortable. Yet she was still grieved by the contrast between the King and the Queen when they came to visit her; the Queen apparently told her that she was improving. 'I certainly am no better, and going on so was absurd,' she wrote pathetically to the Prince of Wales on Christmas Eve.

While hope was entertained in some quarters that the Princess's life might still be saved, one of her brothers would shortly be fortunate to escape with his. For some time, the Duke of Cumberland had been extremely unpopular. While the newspapers and public knew all about the other Princes' liaisons, there was an air of mystery attached to Prince Ernest. He was not known to have openly taken a mistress, and an extraordinary story arose that every kind of vice went on behind closed doors in his apartments at St James's.

In June 1810, news spread throughout London that the Duke of Cumberland had murdered his valet, Joseph Sellis. The valet had blackmailed his master, threatening to expose the dark secrets of his private life; or else he had discovered the Duke in bed with Mrs Sellis. Princess Augusta and the Duke had been godparents to Mrs Sellis's last child, and to a credulous few this was proof enough that she was his mistress.

Far from having murdered the man, the Duke had narrowly escaped from a murder attempt himself. On the night of 31 May, after returning at midnight from a concert in aid of the Royal Society of Musicians, he was attended by his other valet, Neale, before going to bed. At about 2.30 a.m., he was awakened by what he described as a hissing sound, and in his half-awakened state he thought a bat had flown into his room. Suddenly he received two violent blows on the head, and blood poured down his face. Putting out his hand to ward off further attacks, he almost lost a finger. With his poor eyesight, and only one screened candle for light, he could not recognize his assailant, but only see the flashing blade. He tried to grab it and received another wound; and then made for the door, wandering out dazedly into the passage, calling, 'Neale, Neale, I am murdered!'

In coming to his master's assistance, Neale tripped over a sword. Later examination revealed that it was the Duke's own regimental sabre which had been used against him, and then thrown aside. Both men were concerned for Sellis's safety, as the assailant was presumably still on the premises and might try to attack anyone nearby who approached him. Neale tied some improvised bandages round his master's bleeding head and hands and, being reluctant to leave him on his own, helped him downstairs to the office of the porter, Benjamin Smith. Though shaken by the sight of the blood-soaked victim, and by Neale's explanation, Smith had presence of mind to warn the sentries and fasten the doors to prevent anyone else from leaving.

When the other servants were up, the Duke told them to wake Sellis. As they reached his room, they heard a 'gurgling, trickling sound'. They initially thought that the would-be murderer was attacking Sellis, until Smith could make out by candlelight what had happened. Mr Sellis, he exclaimed, had cut his throat.

The inquest would later confirm what the horrified servants had been able to deduce for themselves in those dimly-lit early hours. Sellis had attacked the Duke and gravely wounded him, then run back to his apartments to wash his hands and undress. The doctors established that about half an hour had elapsed between the Duke's raising the alarm and the finding of Sellis, a basin full of bloodstained water in his room and a razor by his hand. Having heard the hue and cry, he took his own life.

The Duke had sustained several superficial wounds, and lost much blood; and the wound in his temple was so deep that the brain could be seen pulsating beneath it. In view of the wounds received as a young man in battle during the wars against France, and his poor eyesight, he was fortunate to survive, with his already impaired eyesight damaged no further. His right thumb had almost been severed from his hand when he had attempted to wrest the sword from Sellis.

The news quickly reached Brooks's Club, where the Duke of Sussex was playing whist. He was the first member of the family to be told. At once he sent a message to the Prince of Wales at Carlton House and both hurried round to their brother's bedside. As news spread, crowds gathered around the palace, ready to gape at a closed door or a lighted window. Straw was laid in Cleveland Row to deaden the grinding of carriage wheels as the doctors arrived, as the slightest sound meant more agony for the invalid. A bulletin was issued, stating that His Royal Highness's wounds were 'not immediately dangerous, and he is as well as can be expected under the circumstances of the case.' Assured that his life was not in imminent danger, the Prince of Wales left to inform his parents at Windsor, and return with them to London.

Later that day, the Duke suffered from delayed shock. In great pain, he could scarcely bear the slightest touch. An operation was performed next day to move a large fragment of splintered bone pressing on the brain, and he was taken to Carlton House, in the same carriage which had been sent to Weymouth to bring the invalid Princess Amelia to Windsor. He was slow to recover, and not until the middle of July could he go outside in the garden again.

The inquest jury brought in an unanimous verdict of suicide against Sellis. Yet pamphleteers and scandalmongers put the worst possible construction on his motives, asserting that the Duke had been committing sodomy with either Sellis or Neale and that blackmail was therefore involved. The most likely reason was that Sellis, a Corsican and not a particularly devout Roman Catholic, was of unstable and near-criminal character, and harboured republican sympathies as well. He had previously been employed by a Mr Church in America, and dismissed for stealing money from him. Three other former servants of Mr Church were in England at the time, and testified to Sellis's bad character, one professing himself astonished that such a rascal could have ever been employed by the Duke. The latter had a reputation for treating his servants kindly by the standards of the day, and a few weeks earlier Sellis had complained of the cold when attending to his master on his travels, as a result of which he had been given permission to ride inside the carriage instead of on the box behind the coachman. That, and the fact that the Duke and Princess Augusta had paid him the compliment of being godparents to his youngest child, made nonsense of the idea that the valet had been goaded by ill-treatment and harboured a grudge.

At Augusta Lodge, Princess Amelia's health had seemed to be improving slowly, but she was shattered at the news of her brother's ordeal. 'How grieved I am about poor Ernest, and how like you to be the friend and brother always in distress,'[14] she wrote to the Prince of Wales. It was always unlikely, though, that any recovery would be more than temporary. Knowing she was not long for this world, in July she drew up and sent FitzRoy a memorandum regarding her last will and testament, in which she left everything to him apart from a few mementoes which were for relatives and other close friends. Her hypersensitivity to noise had returned, and she could no longer even bear the playing of a piano in a nearby room. Princess Augusta gave her a caged bird which sang 'with a very soft note' for company.

On 16 September, Princess Mary wrote, at her request, to let the Prince of Wales know 'that the Eruption he saw the beginning of in her face had increased every day since and had run nearly all over the body.'[15] The doctors agreed that 'it had an alarming appearance.'

On 25 October, the family and certain members of the household gathered on the fiftieth anniversary of King George III's accession to the throne. Apart from the youngest and eldest daughters, all the children were present. The Queen took him by the hand as he went round the circle, each one speaking to him as he approached, so that he could recognize by their voices whom he was about to address. To Miss Cornelia Knight, the Queen's companion, he said, 'You are not uneasy, I am sure, about Amelia. You are not to be deceived, but you must know that she is in no danger.' At this he squeezed her hand so tightly that she almost shouted out loud.

It had been the practice of the physicians to report to the King every morning at 7 a.m. on Amelia, and at frequent intervals throughout the day. Sometimes he kept them for over an hour, examining them minutely about her condition. He visited her every day, but his visits were strictly limited to five minutes or less. As he could barely see her, he would peer closely down upon her, looking pathetically for some signs of improvement. But she had given up all pretence of recovery. On one of these last visits, she whispered, 'Remember me, but do not grieve for me,' and gave him a diamond ring made specially for him, with a lock of her hair enclosed under crystal. He was distressed that she had left no similar keepsake for the Queen, and to please him she relented and gave her mother a locket with her hair as well.

On 2 November, towards midday, Sir Henry Halford, with his hand on Amelia's pulse, turned to Princess Mary, suggesting, 'Your Royal Highness had better retire.' Mary replied that she was determined to stay to the last. Then the doctor took a candle, and held the flame to the patient's lips. Looking at the stillness of the flame, he said, 'It is over.'

The previous month, Herbert Taylor had given his opinion that the King was resigned to his daughter's death, 'determined to meet the melancholy event with that fortitude which confidence in the inestimable blessings of Christian faith can alone inspire.' The Tory politician George Canning thought that, once she was dead and he was over the shock, it would hasten his recovery; it was the lingering suspense that had 'irritated him into madness.'

Neither verdict would prove to be accurate. Since his illness of 1801, the family had lived in dread of the apparently dormant complaint breaking out again and threatening his reason for good. He was now aged seventy-two, and his constitution had little resistance to further attacks. During the last week of October, his behaviour had again been peculiar, and worry about Amelia may have been a contributory factor. Not until nine days after her death did the family think him well enough to be told. He took it as well as could be expected, and made arrangements for the funeral, choosing the anthems himself. Even so, he assured people at court that he knew she could be brought to life again. Later he appeared convinced that she was alive and living in Hanover where she would never grow older and always be well. One of his physicians, whose wife had recently died, was 'comforted' by the King's tender assurance that she, too, was in Hanover. Soon he told his family that Prince Octavius, the infant son on whom he had doted, was there as well. The German ancestral home, which he had never visited, had become a synonym in his confused mind for Heaven.

Soon, though, the old symptoms reappeared. Remembering the cruel treatment to which he had been subjected during earlier attacks, the King was quick-witted enough to extract a verbal promise from his physicians that he should never be left alone with any doctor 'specially engaged in the department of insanity'. For weeks the illness continued its fluctuating course, and on Christmas Eve he was seized with such violent abdominal pain that he thought he was dying. The Prince of Wales was summoned, and came to Windsor at once, but there was soon an improvement. Some days he felt calm, and found solace in playing the harpsichord. Twice in January he asked to be helped outside for a walk on the castle terrace, being anxious that members of the public should see him and know that he was not dead nor a helpless invalid.

Nevertheless, the question of a regency arose. The government decided to introduce a bill with restrictions, as in the case of Pitt's bill of 1788/89, which would lapse if the King had not recovered within twelve months. Visibly moved by the pathetic sight of his ageing father, the Prince accepted them philosophically. So did the King, who assented at an audience with Perceval on 29 January, remarking sadly that it was no more agreeable to him to be turned out of office than it was to any other man, but appearing otherwise resigned.

On 6 February, the Prince of Wales took the oaths of office as Regent and thus formally assumed charge of the government. The Whigs who had expected him to dismiss his father's Tory ministers were disappointed, and Perceval was reassured to hear him talk of his 'irresistible impulse of filial duty and affection to his beloved father' which prevented him from taking any actions which might threaten his father's recovery. There was more to the Prince's caution than this, however. He had not forgotten his horror of revolutionary France twenty years previously, and his alarm at the 'hell-begotten Jacobins', as he labelled the more radical Whigs. Moreover, at a time of war in Europe, it was not the moment for a change of government.

Few people now held much hope for the King's recovery. Though the Regency was nominally to last for only a year, the reign of King George III effectively ended when his eldest son took the oath of office.

One of the first family duties the Prince undertook as Regent was the dispersal of Princess Amelia's inheritance – or such little as she had left. An extravagant young woman, she had borrowed freely from her eldest brother, and her sisters. She had left nearly everything to Colonel FitzRoy, who was persuaded to renounce his claim on her estate as a gesture of goodwill, and the Prince presented her jewels to Princess Mary. The royal family were apprehensive at the effect the business might have on the King's disordered mind, for they had successfully concealed her passion for the General from him. However he took it placidly, and he was pleased at hearing how the Prince had dealt with matters. 'I will never call him anything but George in future,' he remarked. 'How thankful I ought to be to Providence for giving me such a son in the hour of my trial.'[16]

It was a timely reconciliation between father and son; for the first few months of the Regency were the last in which the King still had any grasp on reality. His sons paid him regular visits, he walked on the terrace with them, and even rode in the park. Sometimes he played backgammon and was read aloud to, one of the first books for which he asked being Boswell's *Life of Johnson*. Apart from occasional delusions when his mind was wandering, or when he talked long and loud, he appeared perfectly sensible. The family hoped he might recover his reason after all, and the physicians thought he would be cured within twelve months at the most.

On 21 May he rode on horseback at Windsor, accompanied by Princess Augusta and Sophia; it was his last appearance in public. Two months later, he had a relapse, and became so violent that he had to be physically restrained. Even when given laudanum he could not sleep, refused his meals, and talked incoherently. As hope was gradually given up, he was left all day with his keepers, and put into the strait-waistcoat when he threatened to become violent. He ceased to ask about his family or talk coherently, and could no longer recognize them by the sound of their voices. By the end of the year he was living in a world of his own.

7 'Noble and generous intentions'

On taking office, the Regent intended to celebrate with a grand fête at Carlton House. He would have liked to do so immediately after the swearing-in ceremony, but the physicians warned that as His Majesty might recover, it would be premature. By June he considered it safe to do so, and on 19 June 1811 the fête was held, ostensibly in honour of the royal family of France. Queen Charlotte did not attend, as she thought it unseemly for him to hold a party while his father was so ill, and she therefore forbade her daughters to attend.

Two thousand invitations were despatched, some to people recently deceased. To her annoyance, Princess Charlotte did not receive one. Mrs Fitzherbert did, but when she learnt that his current mistress Lady Hertford was to be given a place at the royal supper table, she asked whether she would too. He rejected her request, and she refused to attend the fête. They never spoke to each other again, but after persuasion he acknowledged their formal separation and agreed to the continuation of her annuity of £6,000, later increased.

The Regent enjoyed presiding over proceedings in his new, self-conferred rank as Field-Marshal with the Duke of York, whom he had reappointed Commander-in-Chief, but sometimes his zest for life got the better of him. That winter, at a party given by the Duke and Duchess of York at Oatlands, he tried to show his daughter Charlotte how to dance the Highland fling. In doing so, he landed heavily on his ankle, and had to retire to bed for a fortnight, heavily dosed with laudanum. Rather tastelessly, the Duke of Cumberland growled that the illness 'was higher than the foot and that a blister on the head would be more efficacious than a poultice on the foot.' In view of their father's condition, it was not the wisest remark.

The Duke of Clarence now saw that only three lives stood between him and the throne – his invalid, possibly dying father, the Prince Regent, his daughter Princess Charlotte, and the childless Duke of York. He had always boasted that, with his regular habits, he would outlive his elder brothers; should anything happen to his niece, he would ascend the throne, and any legitimate children would succeed him. This, and his mounting debts, made it imperative for him to choose a wife.

For twenty years he and Mrs Jordan had lived together, as husband and wife. She had borne him ten children, most of whom had inherited their father's extravagance. It was ironic that he should need to write to his eldest son, George FitzClarence, in February 1811, reproaching him for his fast friends, drinking and gambling, and that he 'must not forget you have four brothers and five sisters who have an equal claim on me. I must provide for all, I have made great sacrifices and am ready to make more for the good of you, but you must not distress me.'[1] It might almost have been his father talking. With a large and expensive family to maintain, ever-increasing debts, and a need to do his dynastic duty, the Duke reluctantly decided that he and Mrs Jordan would have to part.

Mrs Jordan was on a provincial tour in October 1811, when she was handed a letter from the Duke asking her to meet him at Maidenhead so they could discuss the terms of separation. That night on stage at Cheltenham, the script called on her at one point to laugh heartily, but she burst into tears instead. The rest of the cast managed to ad-lib, and afterwards she left for Maidenhead to keep her unhappy appointment. Distressed as she was, she could see things from the Duke's point of view; money, or the want of it, she understood, 'made *him* at this moment the most *wretched* of men.' A settlement was drawn up in January 1812 by which she was given an annual allowance of £1,500, plus £600 towards a house and coach and £800 for her daughters by her two previous liaisons. An additional £1,500 was provided for the maintenance of her youngest daughters, but in the event of her returning to the stage, she would forfeit this sum, and the daughters would return to their father's custody.

The Duke of Clarence's conduct in terminating his liaison with Mrs Jordan was difficult to excuse, but understandable in the light of conventions of the time. A royal mistress's role was never meant to be a permanent arrangement until death removed one partner, but strictly temporary; the Duke and the actress were doing no more than conforming to the expected standard, and the Duke was as generous in terminating matters as he could afford to be. He threw himself with enthusiasm into a series of doomed courtships, until gossips whispered behind his back that soon his father's doctors might have another patient on their hands.

Since his recall from Gibraltar, the Duke of Kent had been kept professionally unemployed. Bitterly jealous that the Duke of York had been reappointed Commander-in-Chief but that there was no similar reinstatement of office for him, he never forgave the Regent. However, not one to remain idle for long, he kept himself occupied with his charity work, chairing meetings for the benefit of widows, orphans, and the under-privileged. He was a close friend and admirer of the pioneer socialist Robert Owen, and chaired meetings promoting Owen's plans to establish 'experimental villages of co-operation.' Apart from the Duke of Sussex, he was the only son of King George III to embrace liberal principles with enthusiasm, and he was always keen to assist those less fortunate than himself. Unlike his father, he sympathized with the movement for Catholic emancipation, partly because of his friendship with Madame, partly as he saw no reason why followers of another religion should be so penalized. Yet in the name of family solidarity, he told the Regent that he would personally vote against emancipation in the House of Lords if required to do so, in deference to his father, but when his eldest brother (at this time, also a supporter of the Catholics) became King, he would vote in accordance with his principles.

Apart from the Regent, he was regarded as the most intelligent of the Princes. The Duke of Wellington said that he never knew any man who had 'more natural eloquence in conversation' than the Duke, who was gifted at 'choosing the best topics for each particular person,' and excelling in after-dinner speeches. While his military career had brought out the worst in him, and 'his name was never uttered without a sigh by the functionaries of every public office,' his niece Princess Charlotte was devoted to him, and Mrs Fitzherbert trusted and valued his friendship implicitly.

His abstemious way of life – rising early, eating and drinking sparingly, and frowning on gambling – was praised by some, although regarded with contempt by others. His more self-indulgent brothers called him 'Joseph Surface' behind his back.

The Duke and Madame always had a warm welcome at Castle Hill Lodge for their guests, who were always impressed by the hospitality. None more so than Mr Justice George Hardinge, who was astonished to be shown a closet with a running stream and a fountain playing, and to see that the lawn, covered in autumn leaves one morning, was cleared to the last leaf and twig by a gardener and six assistants within fifteen minutes. But his greatest amazement of all was reserved for breakfast, when he saw the Duke get up and speak in German to someone behind a glass door in the dining room. As the judge was lifting a cup of tea to his lips, an invisible thirty-strong orchestra broke into a lament written in memory of his nephew, killed in a naval battle three years earlier.

In February 1812, the Regency was made permanent. During the previous summer, the Regent had said that he wanted his sisters' allowances to be increased in the event of the King's death, and to give them their own apartments in St James's Palace. In March he notified the Chancellor of the Exchequer, Spencer Perceval, to this effect. If they were granted their financial independence, and at the same time were encouraged to appear with him more frequently on public occasions, they might perform something of the role that the Princess of Wales might otherwise have played. To Queen Charlotte, he wrote that it was necessary for his daughter to have 'the advantage of the countenance and apparent Protection of some part of my Family when she is to be seen in public.'[2] He did not add that they would serve to help protect him as well, but perhaps he felt that to have at least one Princess by his side on state occasions (as long as it was not the one to whom he was married) would ensure him some safety from a stone-throwing mob.

At the same time, he wanted to emancipate his sisters from the tyranny they endured at home in 'the Nunnery'. Sophia had written to him in great depression in December 1811, thanking him for all his 'noble and generous intentions' towards them, '*poor old wretches* as we are, a *dead weight* upon You, *old Lumber* to the *country*, like *Old Clothes*, I wonder you do not vote for putting us in a *sack* and drowning us in *The Thames.*'[3]

The Queen's health was deteriorating. She had become very fat, and suffered from attacks of erysipelas which made her face red and swollen. She became so irritable and cantankerous that her daughters were more miserable than ever. Princess Augusta, who had confided in the Regent of her love for Sir Brent Spencer, urged him to allow her to marry. She was, however, too dutiful a daughter to think of keeping such a match secret from her mother, who was so appalled at the idea that she would not let it be mentioned any further.

As everyone knew, the idea of giving the Princesses some freedom from their increasingly irascible and self-centred mother would not be well received. One morning in April 1812, four separate letters were handed to the Queen after breakfast by Madame Beckendorff, her Keeper of the Robes. One, largely drafted by Augusta, was signed by all four sisters, and the other three were written by Elizabeth, Mary and Sophia respectively.

The Queen was furious that the Princesses would have independent establishments, and liberty from her as well. In her reply to her four daughters, she attempted to take refuge behind the King's illness, 'under the present Melancholy Situation of your father the going to Public Amusements except where Duty calls you would be *the highest mark of indecency possible.*' Though the Princesses were all over thirty years of age, she still insisted that when they visited their brothers, none of them could remain indoors with a bachelor brother without a lady being present. Furthermore, she did not wish to see any of them again that day; 'I do not think I ever felt as shattered in my life as I did by reading your letter.'[4]

Having struck a blow for freedom, however, the Princesses would not give in. A joint letter, again written mainly by Augusta, was despatched to the Regent, admitting that they had 'neither Health nor Spirits to support for any length of time the life which we have led for the last two years, more Especially the Treatment which we have experienced whenever any proposal has been made for Our absenting ourselves for a few days from the Queen's Roof.'[5]

In November 1812, Princesses Elizabeth and Mary came up from Windsor to accompany Princess Charlotte to the opening of Parliament. Though they apparently had no effect on the lively young girl of sixteen, who talked and laughed a good deal at what struck her as the solemnity of the occasion, they cheered up their careworn brother, who had been given a frosty reception in the streets, 'in dead silence, and not a hat off.' After they returned to Windsor, there was what Princess Augusta described as 'a dreadfull scene', during which the Queen accused Princess Elizabeth of not caring for the King's feelings, and the latter having hysterics. It took all the diplomacy the Prince Regent could muster, assuring her how grieved he was at the feelings of dissatisfaction which she had manifested towards his sisters, 'whose conduct had been so truly proper and affectionate.' At length he persuaded her to see things from her daughters' point of view as well as her own.

All the same, the years had left their mark on her. Humiliated in early marriage by her husband's family, she was horrified at the symptoms displayed by him during his illnesses, until she feared for her life. His condition appeared abhorrent to her, and she lacked compassion; as the Duke of Kent told Halford, his mother had a 'natural want of warmth.' Her solution to her husband's pitiful

*Princess Augusta, by Peter
Edward Stroehling*

state was to try and shut herself off from it, while ready to accuse her daughters
of failing in their duty every time they showed any inclination to relax or enjoy
themselves.

The Princesses generally visited their father in pairs. The Queen spent
quarter of an hour with him one day in June 1812 but, although she lived for
another six years, it was probably the last time she ever saw him. From now on,
as far as the family was concerned, it was evidently their sons' and particularly
their long-suffering daughters' duty.

Princess Mary undertook to write the Prince Regent a daily bulletin on their
father's condition, and her regular visits to him, which she called 'going down'. 'I
went down with the Queen,' went one such report, 'and it was shocking to hear
the poor, dear King run on so, and her unfortunate manner makes things so
much worse.' What saddened her most was the knowledge that relations
between their parents were so irrevocably altered; 'I fear we can never make
them a *real comfort* to each other again, as all confidence has long gone, but I am
sure they have a *great respect* for each other, and that the Q. loves him as much as
she can love anything *in this world*, but I am clear it is in the power of their
daughters, if they are allowed to act, to keep them tolerably together.'[6]

As the King's mental state became more confused, his physical condition
improved, and he ate with a good appetite. He spoke of himself with sadness in

97

the past tense, declaring that he must have a new suit of clothes in black, in memory of King George III, who was a good man. He thought his sons were dead as well, or at least sent away to distant countries. He had nightmares that the country was being flooded, and wanted to escape to Denmark. Sometimes he wept, and then his mood would change to uncontrollable mirth, or as Princess Augusta wrote to the Regent, 'a great deal of unpleasant laughing.' 'All here goes on the same,' Princess Sophia wrote on another occasion, 'quiet days do us no good – it only shows the mind more completely gone.'

The King would never know what was happening in his own family, let alone great events abroad. In the autumn of 1813 the Duke of Cumberland was with the Hanoverian troops, although not actively engaged, at the decisive battle of Leipzig, a three-day conflict in which both sides sustained about 50,000 casualties.

The Napoleonic wars had restricted travel for high and low alike; none of the British royal family could leave England, unless on active service, between the years 1803 and 1813. While the people of Europe had watched the seemingly invincible Napoleon Bonaparte defeat their armies and subject their countries to his rule, in 1813 it was as if they had had enough. Napoleon's defeat in Russia

Ernest, Duke of Cumberland, and Adolphus, Duke of Cambridge, from plaster busts by Heinrich Hesemann

had proved that he was fallible; and after his defeat at Leipzig, English princes and British soldiers were again welcomed in Germany.

Another problem posed by the wars in Europe was the continual begging of Queen Charlotte of Württemberg. She did not refrain from exploiting the family connection with her brother by seeking financial assistance and protection for her husband, who had been one of the most devoted of Napoleon's vassals. As late as December 1813, after he had changed sides, King Frederick was suspected of treachery to the allies, and thought to be in secret negotiation with Napoleon. It was rumoured that the Württemberg ministers were planning to depose him. The little kingdom had been further impoverished by Austrian troops quartered on its territory during the war, and the rate of exchange had reduced the value of Charlotte's marriage allowance from England to a fraction of what it had been in 1796. Though the Prince Regent felt duty-bound to help his sister, the government refused to trust her and her fickle husband, and constant appeals for additional income to settle her debts and to 'enable me to live in a manner suitable to my situation in life'[7] brought nothing but expressions of fraternal sympathy.

In December 1813, the Duke of Cambridge, newly promoted to the rank of Field-Marshal, was appointed Governor-General of Hanover, representing the Regent and acting as a figurehead for the national feeling against France. His return to the ancestral home was in stark contrast to his ignominious departure ten years earlier, when the temporarily peace-loving Hanoverians had refused to put up any resistance. 'Our Adolphus is coming!' people exclaimed in the streets. It was well known that he had offered protection to Hanoverians who had gone to England while the state laboured under the Napoleonic yoke.

Riding towards the city on horseback, the Duke was asked to mount a triumphal carriage, lined with white satin and hung with garlands of flowers. Thirty brewers seized the traces and carried him through the streets to Herrenhausen Palace. As he swayed through the wildly cheering crowd, bands played 'God save the King', trumpets sounded, bells were rung, cannon thundered and handkerchiefs fluttered from every window. Deeply moved, 'our Adolphus' burst into tears.

For a Prince who had never been educated with a view to ascending a throne in future, and who had no practical experience of politics and government, it was a daunting task. It was made more so by the fact that the Germans had just rid themselves of Napoleon's tyranny, but were no more inclined to accept the scarcely less tyrannical government of their own medieval constitutions. The sovereigns of the other German states were likewise not disposed to grant new constitutions to their subjects. He was under no illusions, telling the Prince Regent that the only reason he had consented to accept the post was 'to be of use to you and the country.'

The Duke appreciated the importance of honouring Hanoverian aspirations. In opening the first Assembly of the Hanoverian Houses of Parliament, he addressed the members as 'Venerable, noble and loyal Friends and Country-men', assuring them that in time they would have a new constitution which would give them power to help in the task of reorganizing the country. At the same time he told the Prince Regent how essential it was to give the people a reformed constitution. He had reckoned without Count Münster, the reaction-ary Hanoverian Minister in London, who believed that the way forward was to build up a powerful Hanoverian kingdom as the centre of anti-Prussian feeling in Germany. He had some influence over the Regent, and regarded the Duke as a nonentity.

As Governor-General, the Duke had no political power, and would have none for several years, but this did not disturb him unduly. Hanover was more peaceful than England in the immediate post-Waterloo era. From Germany, he looked with unease at the riots in his home country, notably the disturbance at St Peter's Field, Manchester (the 'Peterloo Massacre') in August 1819. 'I trust that the Government will meet with the necessary support from Parliament in the measures which must be adopted to check this abominable revolutionary spirit,' he wrote to the Regent. 'Thank God in this part of Germany people are in general satisfied.'[8]

It was to have been expected that one of his elder brothers would be appointed, the obvious one being the Duke of Cumberland, who had had several years' experience of living as well as fighting in Germany – as well as the physical scars to prove it. However, Prince Ernest was notable for his political views and obstinacy. To have a diehard reactionary of a royal Duke might have suited the like-minded Münster; but the Duke of Cumberland would never have accepted office as a mere figurehead.

Moreover, a few disparaging remarks about the Prince Regent made by the Duke of Cumberland in Germany had been overheard. The Queen of Württemberg, who had never liked her brother Ernest, gleefully passed them on, perhaps with exaggeration. 'If it was one person that told me I would not believe it,' she wrote, 'but all say the same.'[9] Knowing what an inveterate tale-teller his sister was, the Regent probably knew better than to take it at face value; but the damage was done. Always one to avoid argument in the interests of a quiet life, and preoccupied with more pressing matters, the Regent sent an equerry to break the news to the Duke of Cumberland that their youngest brother was to be appointed instead. The Duke of Cumberland was deeply disappointed. Thwarted in one ambition, he was determined to realize another – marriage.

While in Germany he had met and fallen in love with Princess Frederica of Solms-Braunfels. Unlike several of his brothers, he had at least fixed his affections on a German Protestant Princess; but she was already married, albeit unhappily; and, to complicate matters further, she was the same Princess who had been unofficially engaged to the Duke of Cambridge, and was suspected, without good reason, of having jilted him.

Frederica's second marriage, to Prince Frederick of Solms-Braunfels, had not been a success. The Prince had become irritable and morose, a victim to early arteriosclerosis. When it became inevitable that they were growing apart, his family advised her to seek a divorce, and they separated in April 1813. A few weeks later, the Duke of Cumberland met her, they fell in love, and agreed to marry when it became convenient. Recognizing the hopelessness of their marriage, Prince Frederick agreed to release his wife.

In Württemberg, his sister Queen Charlotte strongly disapproved; 'I dread that Ernest will forget what he owes to the Prince Regent, and obstinately persist in a marriage which he knows must be a source of pain to the whole family.'[10] Divorce proved unnecessary; on 13 April 1814, the ailing Prince suffered a stroke and died within a few hours. His demise had occurred at such a convenient time that it was rumoured that he was poisoned by his estranged wife.

The year 1814 was a time of celebration by the allies. Napoleon's defeat at the hands of Russia in 1812 and the battle of Leipzig in October 1813 had marked the beginning of the end of the Napoleonic era; by April 1814, news reached England that he had abdicated after Paris was occupied by the allies. The Prince Regent had never wavered in his support for the Bourbon dynasty, and unknown to his ministers, sent for Prince Lieven, Russian Ambassador in England, to inform the Tsar that England would regard any peace as temporary which did not provide for a Bourbon King on the French throne.

When news of Napoleon's abdication was confirmed, Carlton House blazed with illuminations. The exiled King Louis XVIII, brother of Louis XVI,* had spent most of his exile at Hartwell, Buckinghamshire, and the Regent decided to give him a fitting send-off. It would be a colourful prelude to state visits from other allied sovereigns, planned for the coming months. The Regent was always at his happiest when acting as the master of ceremonies on such occasions, and he hoped that the resulting festivities would silence his critics at home and win him respect from his brother sovereigns.

On 20 April, resplendent in his Field Marshal's uniform, he drove out from Carlton House to meet his brother sovereign at Stanmore. After an emotional greeting, a procession of seven carriages, escorted by a troop of Life Guards, made a state entry into Piccadilly. King Louis stayed for three nights at Grillon's Hotel, Albemarle Street, where orders of chivalry were exchanged. Next day the King was guest of honour at a splendid dinner at Carlton House. The Regent gave him a royal send-off from Dover on board the yacht *Royal Sovereign.*

Next the Prince Regent prepared for the visit of the allied sovereigns who were due to arrive at the beginning of June. The Austrian Emperor Francis declined, sending Count Metternich to represent him, but King Frederick William III of Prussia and Tsar Alexander I of Russia came. Unhappily for their host, the people of London were far more interested in the heroes of the day. The Prussian commander, Count Blucher, and Platov, leader of the Russian Cossacks, were loudly cheered wherever they went, while only sullen looks and the most perfunctory of cheers were reserved for the Regent. None however had a better reception than the Tsar, who was popularly identified with the Russian people's heroic defiance of the French invaders in 1812. Apart from Metternich, none of them took much notice of the Prince Regent. Metternich had already met him in London twenty years previously, and delighted him by making him the first Protestant Prince to be awarded the Order of the Golden Fleece, and he was delighted to be made an honorary Colonel of a Hungarian regiment.

---

* He took the regnal number XVIII, in recognition of his late brother's son, who had been nominally King Louis XVII for two years.

Not only did crowned heads of state pay him little attention, but the Tsar, who had actually ridden into Paris a conqueror, could not but hide his contempt for his portly English host who had never seen active service himself. After a dinner at Carlton House he was introduced to Lady Hertford. He bowed but said nothing to her, and turned away with the remark, 'She is mighty old.' He further irritated the royal family by asking repeatedly to be allowed to see King George III, as though he was one of the sights of Britain, and only the most earnest entreaties of Prince Lieven, Russian Ambassador, dissuaded him from going to call on the Princess of Wales.

In his contempt, he had been influenced by his sister, the Grand Duchess Catherine, who had preceded him to London and behaved rather tactlessly. At a formal dinner at Carlton House, she complained that the sound of music gave her nausea, and asked for the band to be dimsmissed; she then lectured the Prince Regent on the value of good husband–wife relations, and on the best way of introducing Princess Charlotte into society. Under the circumstances, it was magnanimous of the Regent to commission Thomas Lawrence to portray his distinguished guests on canvas in celebration of their visit, though he stopped short of requesting a portrait of the Grand Duchess as well.

The Prince Regent had not made matters easier for himself by pointedly excluding the Princess of Wales from the festivities. In the Commons, the Whigs never ceased to ask why she was not received at court, and why she was still denied the company of her daughter. Though the Whigs had no personal admiration for Princess Caroline, they had even less for her husband, whom they regarded as a political turncoat. Moreover she still commanded consider-able sympathy among the public, who knew very little about her, and whenever she visited Covent Garden or any other theatre, they made their feelings clear. Demonstrations in her favour were made during the allied visits, and neither the Tsar nor King of Prussia could ignore them.

During the celebrations, the Duke of Clarence (who had been created Admiral of the Fleet, or Commander-in-Chief of the Navy in 1811), hoisted his flag in HMS *Impregnable*, from which the Regent, Tsar and King of Prussia were to witness a grand review of the navy. As the Duke came on board with his visitors, he saw something amiss with the top-gallant yard. Putting his hand to his mouth, he shouted out a stream of only too audible oaths to the sailors up there. Being ignorant of naval life, the Tsar and King thought this was part of the entertainment. The Regent, used to covering up for his brother at embarrassing moments, remarked solemnly, 'What a good sailor William is.'

Another highlight of the season was a fête given by the Regent in honour of the Duke of Wellington at Carlton House, attended by the Queen, and the Princesses Mary and Augusta. Starved of merriment for so long, the Queen (then aged seventy) stayed until 4.30 a.m. The three royal ladies were carried back in their sedan chairs to the Queen's House at that hour, while the orchestra was still in full swing. 'I am sure we all talk of nothing else but all your kindness,' Mary wrote to her brother afterwards, 'and all those I have *seen* are full of *gratitude* and delight with your manners and great good nature and kindness to every soul. I never saw the Queen more pleased.'[11]

The Royal Pavilion, Brighton

Brighton Pavilion, the Banqueting Room

The lonely adolescent Princess Charlotte, who lived at Warwick House, had no strong feelings for or against either of her parents. Her mother never went out of her way to visit her regularly, while her father spoke sentimentally of her at times, but apart from lavishing expensive gifts on her, he never treated her with much paternal affection. To his sisters he complained that she was always sulking. She behaved like a tomboy, which some thought was an affectation to irritate him, knowing how he admired conventional femininity. Queen Charlotte's remarks that the girl was more her mother's child than her father's was a tactless comment which did not make him look any the more fondly on her.

She disliked being encouraged to be friendly with the young men who frequented her mother's room at Kensington and Blackheath, and she was irked by her mother's incessant fault-finding. As she grew older, she preferred her father's company. He was kind enough to her, though she found her visits to him spoiled by the regular presence of her dreaded uncle Cumberland, 'Prince Wiskerandos'. The Duke of Cumberland felt himself duty-bound to warn his brother against the Whigs, against reform, against Catholic emancipation and in fact against anything remotely progressive. His bullying, rude banter and indecent jokes turned Charlotte against him. She also dreaded her visits to Windsor, where Queen Charlotte seemed to disapprove of her, and while her maiden aunts were attentive and civil, she found them dreadfully dull.

If one thing united father and daughter, it was the suggestion of an early marriage. In 1813 the Prince Regent had already authorized his Foreign Secretary, Lord Castlereagh, to make arrangements for a betrothal between his daughter and the Dutch heir, the Hereditary Prince William of Orange. Such a dynastic union would be of paramount political importance, for it would link the United Kingdom of Britain and Ireland with the projected new Kingdom of the United Netherlands, comprising Belgium, Holland and Luxembourg. Charlotte apparently accepted the fact that she was to be engaged to him, without much enthusiasm, and in the spring of 1814 a marriage contract was drawn up. She had never been attracted to 'the Young Frog', as he was popularly nicknamed, and she disliked the idea of residing abroad, thinking it inappropriate for the heir presumptive. While the Duke of Sussex thought the marriage was a good idea, he urged her to stand firm against the idea of living in Holland, and thought the matter should be discussed by Parliament.

While the foreign dignitaries were in England, her attitude hardened. She insisted that she must never be made to leave England without her consent. Knowing how obdurate she was, the Regent asked the Duke of York to persuade her, but to no avail. She disliked the Duke, suspecting that he was waiting for his elder brother to die so that he would be proclaimed Regent. At the same time she believed that he was trying to prove the validity of her father's marriage with Mrs Fitzherbert, which would have the net result of her being declared illegitimate and therefore excluded from the succession. Matters came to a head when the Prince of Orange made a drunken exhibition of himself at Ascot Races. On 16 June she informed him by letter that their engagement was at an end, but the Regent refused to hear of it.

On 12 July she slipped out of the back of her residence at Warwick House, took a hackney cab from Charing Cross and fled to her mother's house in

Connaught Place. Only the servants were there, as her mother was at Blackheath. She sent a note to her mother's legal adviser, Henry Brougham, and an hysterical, illegible scrawl to the Duke of Sussex, begging for help. The Duke had always been sympathetic to her plight, and he was the uncle she trusted most. He was dining at the time, and after glancing at it put the note in his pocket. When a second followed shortly afterwards, he realized that something serious was amiss, and hurried round to Connaught Place. Here he met Brougham and the Duke of York, who had been sent by the Prince Regent to persuade her to return to Warwick House. If she stayed where she was, a sympathetic mob might surround the house and try to prevent her from being carried away by order of her tyrannical father.

The Duke of Sussex and Henry Brougham decided that resistance on the Princess's part would be useless and might only make the situation worse. Sadly, the Duke advised his niece to return as calmly as possible to Carlton House. For his sake she agreed, and there was an emotional reconciliation between father and daughter. A few days later, however, she smuggled the Duke a note complaining that her father was keeping her virtually a prisoner. As a result the Duke raised questions in the House of Lords, demanding to know what liberties she was permitted; was she allowed bathing and sea air; and as she was eighteen years of age and heir to the throne after her father, what were the intentions of Parliament regarding an establishment for her?

Although he received nothing but evasive replies, his intervention had some positive results. The Prince Regent now accepted that the Anglo-Dutch engagement must be considered at an end. He allowed his daughter to go for a change of air to Cranborne and Weymouth, taking the bathing cure at the latter.

Yet the business had the unhappy effect of exacerbating differences between the Regent and the Duke of Sussex. Family ties, shared friendships and similar political views had bound them close after the latter's return from Europe. The change came initially when the Regent failed to give power to his Whig allies on assuming the Regency, and what they had judged to be a temporary change in affiliations was soon seen to reflect a permanent change of heart. In contrast, the Duke of Sussex held fast to his liberal principles, such as open support of full political rights for Roman Catholics and Jews, a belief that the criminal laws of England were vindictive and barbarous, and that sentences should not depend on the temper or caprices of judges; 'Christianity, common reason, and sound policy, demand that the laws which affect the liberties and the lives of men, should proportion the punishment to the offence, and not teach cruelty to the people, by examples of vindictive legislation.'[12]

This made the Regent regard his brother with suspicion; and his championship of the unfortunate Princess Charlotte drove the wedge even further between them. It was an open rupture which grieved the ageing Queen, and in January 1817, after an attempt on the Regent's life, she tactfully suggested to the Duke 'how fair an Opportunity this would be for a reconciliation between you & yr Brother, which would do Honour to both your Heart and your Understanding.'[13] Happy to accept her advice, he wrote a friendly letter to his brother expressing his horror at the attack, but it was never acknowledged.

In August, the Princess of Wales left the country. She had made up her mind to go for some time. Apart from the Dukes of Gloucester, Kent, and Sussex, most of her husband's family ignored her; her mother, who had returned to England in widowhood, had recently died; her daughter plainly did not care for her; and the visiting monarchs from Europe had also ignored her, though the Tsar would have paid a visit had it not been for his ambassador's entreaties. As for the Whigs in Parliament, it was evident that they championed her largely for party political reasons, rather than from any desire to see justice done to her personally. She would therefore go to Italy, where 'Caroline, a happy merry soul' could live and behave as she pleased, answerable to nobody.

On behalf of his sisters, Princess Mary congratulated her brother 'on the prospect of a *good riddance.* Heaven grant that she may not return again and that we may never see more of her.'[14]

Wisely, the Regent let Charlotte recover from the emotional traumas of the summer before discussing her marriage again. She spent Christmas with him at Windsor, and on Christmas Day caused a furore by remarking innocently to him and her aunt Mary that she had witnessed many things in her mother's room which she could not repeat. This was less unexpected than the horrifying news that, the previous year, her mother had encouraged her to 'be friendly' with Captain Hesse, an officer in the Light Dragoons believed to be an illegitimate son of the Duke of York, and now one of the Princess of Wales's aides on the

Princess Charlotte of Wales, by Richard Woodman, c. 1816

continent. She had first met him while riding at Windsor and her mother had arranged meetings with them in her Kensington Palace apartments, on at least one occasion leaving them together in a bedroom and locking the door. As she said ruefully, 'God knows what would have become of me if he had not behaved with so much respect to me.' Charlotte did not know whether the Captain was her mother's lover at the time, but she thought that her mother's motive 'was to draw her into this scrape' in order to bring William Austin forward as heir to the throne.

This forfeited the last remaining shred of sympathy that her husband's family may have had for the Princess of Wales. While it could have been admitted that the Regent's own conduct had given her every excuse for adultery, nothing could condone this brazen attempt to compromise her innocent daughter. It was no wonder that the Regent's hatred of his wife now hardened into contempt and disgust, and that he resolved to get rid of her as soon as conveniently possible.

By January 1815, Charlotte's determination to marry had hardened. Her father still hoped that she would accept the Prince of Orange, but she despised him, and the Regent had to accept her decision. She briefly contemplated marrying her second cousin, the Duke of Gloucester; tiresome, self-satisfied, and nearly forty he might be, and she did not particularly care for him, but he was good-natured, and might at least treat her kindly.

The Prince Regent had much else to occupy his mind during those early months of 1815; not only his daughter's future, but also the repercussions of the Cumberland betrothal, and also major renovation and extension at the Brighton Pavilion. Work had continued almost annually to the interior decoration and general fabric of the building, but while staying there in the autumn of 1814, he felt that it was too cramped for comfort. In March 1815 more rooms were added to the building. It was completed three years later, with the addition of an Oriental dome, prompting the Revd Sydney Smith to observe gravely that the Dome of St Paul's had 'come down to Brighton and pupped'.

News came from the Continent that Napoleon had escaped from Elba, where he had been permitted by the allies to reside and rule after his abdication, had landed near Cannes, and advanced on Paris, once more proclaiming himself Emperor.

The Prince Regent found few of his society friends at Ascot in June 1815. Most of the aristocratic regiments were in the Low Countries, under the Duke of Wellington's command. If Napoleon attempted to cross the boundaries of France, it was believed that his power would be swiftly broken. On the evening of 21 June the Regent was attending a ball in St James's Square. The guests, including Lords Liverpool, Castlereagh, and the Duke of York, were awaiting dinner when a messenger in major's uniform appeared at the door with the first despatches and trophies of the battle at Waterloo three days earlier, where the Duke of Wellington and the allied forces had broken the power of Napoleon once and for all. Later it was seen that tears were running down the Regent's cheeks. It was not just emotion at the news of a great British victory, and the effective end of over twenty years' intermittent war in Europe, but also the sight of familiar names on the casualty list, and the fact that the 10th or Prince Regent's Own Royal Hussars and their officers had played such a distinguished role in the combat. He knew the Hussars and their officers so well, that in later years it seemed to some that he believed himself to have been present on the battlefield on 18 June.

By this time, the Duke of Cumberland was officially engaged. Despite her private objections, Queen Charlotte wrote her son a charming letter advising him not to come to England until the year of mourning was over; and to wait until Parliament had voted them the extra allowance that he was entitled to expect on his marriage. Wishing him well, she also wrote affectionately to her prospective daughter-in-law.

Once the Prince Regent's formal permission was received, arrangements were made for the wedding. Sir George Jackson, British Ambassador in Berlin, acted as witness on behalf of the Regent, and attended the ceremony at the Palace of Neu Strelitz, on 29 May 1815. The court assembled at the palace, where the Grand Chamberlain read a declaration that the couple had been formerly affianced the previous year with the full approval of the Regent of England and the Duke of Mecklenburg. A carriage procession was then formed and bride, relatives, functionaries and guests went with an escort of Hussars to the town church where the groom was waiting in Field Marshal's uniform. After the wedding ceremony and breakfast, the couple retired for the night in the ducal palace, and left for Berlin a few days later to be cordially received by King Frederick William III of Prussia.

The Privy Council in England recorded details of the ceremony, in the form of sworn statements from the witnesses, and recommended that a second wedding should be performed in England, as any children born of the marriage might in due course be closer to the succession than the Duke of Cumberland himself.

The Duke arrived in London on 21 June, having left his wife and family behind, intending to make plans for their reception and remarriage. Shortly after his arrival, one of his English equerries handed him a letter from Queen Charlotte in which she regretted that, owing to the knowledge in England of her niece's having broken off a former engagement with the Duke of Cambridge and 'the unfavourable impression which the knowledge of those circumstances has made here,' she must refuse to receive her.

Although she added, rather incongruously, that such a step would not prevent her from showing them both 'every act of kindness and affection' in her power, the Duke was astonished that his mother should act with such coldness towards his wife. Although he did not know it yet, worse was to come. The Queen warned the rest of the family that they would incur her most severe displeasure if they received the Duchess of Cumberland. She had already announced her decision in writing to the Prince Regent the previous month, assuming that he would take on the unpleasant task of warning his brother, but he did nothing about it, thinking that she would soon have a change of heart.

The Duke was not one to give up in haste. A month later he returned to Germany, vowing to bring his wife to England for the second marriage ceremony. This took place two days after their arrival in England, on Sunday,

29 August. Though the Princesses felt unable to defy their mother, the Prince Regent and the Dukes of York, Clarence and Kent were present. The Duke and Duchess settled down quietly in his house at Kew, where he had always been popular.

The Queen was so overwrought in her determination not to receive the Duchess that she became ill, and the government advised that the Duke of Cumberland should take his wife back to Germany, as he would be blamed if her malady was to 'end fatally'. The Prince Regent was forced to ask them to return to Germany, offering them money and even considering giving him the Governorship of Hanover in place of the Duke of Cambridge, but Ernest refused. His wife's health was 'very precarious'; and 'a departure would be immediately held forth as a *proof of conscious guilt and fear of shewing*' themselves.[15] The brothers argued fiercely, but neither would give way; and the Cumberlands stayed in England for three years.

Relations between the Regent and his daughter had now improved. Charlotte had been deeply hurt by her mother's abrupt departure, and she was shocked at tales from the Continent of her scandalous conduct. The Privy Council advised the Regent that she should not be admitted if she ever attempted to return to England. Though Charlotte may have despised her father and found him heartless in the past, she could now forgive him much.

Shortly before Christmas, he told her that she was free to make her own choice of husband. Prince Leopold of Saxe-Coburg, one of the younger dignitaries who had visited London during the season of 1814, was suggested by the government, and in January 1816 he was invited to England a second time. That same month Princess Charlotte received her first invitation to the Pavilion at Brighton, and at a house party she celebrated her birthday, joined by the Queen and two of the unmarried aunts. Leopold arrived in February, his welcome somewhat overshadowed by his finding the Regent so ill with gout that he could only move down the corridors in a wheelchair.

He made an excellent impression on Charlotte; he was good-looking, considerate, and it was clear that he would make a kind husband. Others found him unnecessarily solemn, if not shifty, and the Prince Regent took an immediate dislike to him. Yet this mattered not to Charlotte, who liked him better than any of her previous suitors, and when he proposed she willingly accepted.

On their engagement Parliament voted Leopold a pension of £50,000 per year, to continue even in the event of his future wife's death. They were married on 2 May at Carlton House. At the ceremony the Princess knelt to her father for his blessing, which he gave, and then he delighted the assembled company by picking her up and giving her 'a good hearty, paternal hug'. She shook hands with the Dukes of York, Clarence and Kent, and kissed her emotionally-weeping grandmother and aunts.

The Duke and Duchess of York lent them Oatlands for their honeymoon. It was a generous gesture but not totally appreciated, as the house resembled a dog kennel, and the young couple found the air 'infected and impregnated with the

Claremont Park, Surrey

smell and breath of dogs, birds and all sorts of animals.' With relief they escaped to what would be their home, Claremont, in Surrey.

It was the first of two royal marriages that season. For several years Princess Mary had been fond of, if not in love with, her cousin William, who had succeeded his father as Duke of Gloucester in 1805. As a young woman Mary was the acknowledged beauty of the family, but too pliable in the Queen's hands. 'Mama's tool', her distrusting sisters called her, suspecting her of telling tales and pandering to their mother. She could never keep a secret, and Princess Charlotte found her 'too great a repeater'. Her sardonic wit sometimes disconcerted her brothers, and the Duke of York was offended when she drew attention to his increasing girth; 'It is so *very visible* that I could not help *making the* remark.' She had however been a devoted nurse to Amelia in her last illness. Afterwards, she was more lonely than ever, chafing against the dullness of her life, and suffering agonies from chilblains every winter. She had never been attracted to men in the same way as her sisters, and most of the family felt that she saw her cousin as the only means of escape.

The Duke of Gloucester was pompous and overbearing, with what Baron Stockmar described as 'prominent, meaningless eyes'. He was rather less than royal himself, being a product of that controversial union between the King's brother William and Maria Waldegrave, so he put on tremendous airs and graces as if to compensate. While the Regent had never liked him, and even less so since his championship of the rebellious Princess Charlotte, he readily gave his consent to the marriage of his favourite sister. To everyone's surprise, Queen Charlotte raised no objection, apparently mollified by the Duke's assurance that he would never place any obstacles between his wife and her relations in time of trouble.

'I don't know what other people feel when going to be married,' Mary wrote to Lady Harcourt, 'but as yet I have done nothing but cry.'[16] After her engagement, she was 'half killed by the kindness of the Queen and all my brothers,' though upset at being unable to receive the 'Blessing and Approbation' of her unhappy deranged father. She indulgently overlooked the fact that he would almost certainly never have given his consent to the betrothal, least of all to the son born of his brother's marriage which had so compromised family dignity early in his reign.

The wedding took place on 2 July at the Queen's House. Mary's gown and train were 'a mass of silver, very elegant yet light,' and her dressing struck everyone as being 'of a sentimental kind – that she should wear on this awful day the present of each of her Brothers and Sisters and the Queen.' Among the jewellery she wore was a ring set with a lock of the King's hair, saying, 'This I would not for the world omit. I have a superstitious dread of misfortune if I did.'[17] At the ceremony the Duke of Gloucester 'looked very serious, and pronounced his vows with right good will – the Queen, tho' much agitated, restrained her tears, but Pss Elizabeth and Sophia of Gloucester cried (almost) aloud.' The bride looked close to fainting, while the ever-emotional Prince Regent 'was exceedingly affected, and had several times recourse to his Pocket Handkerchief.'[18] The room was very hot and overcrowded, and the seating so badly arranged that only a few guests could see what was happening. The congregation were so restless and talkative that the Lord Chief Justice announced sternly that if they persisted in making such a noise, they would be married themselves.

The Duke and Duchess made their home at Bagshot Park. On 26 July the Duchess wrote to the Regent that their house was 'comfort itself, and to crown all, the Duke all affec [sic] and kindness, and has no object but my happiness.' She evidently recognized the doubts entertained by her family as to the success of their marriage, and explained that she had purposely held back before writing; 'The assurances of a day or two after marriage, I felt would not satisfy your *anxious mind*, and that alone made me delay writing.'[19] When the Regent and Queen Charlotte visited Bagshot three days later, they were glad to see that they were 'most rationally Happy and Comfortable.'

Three days after the marriage of Princess Mary, the almost forgotten Dorothy Jordan breathed her last in France. For her there had been no happy ending. Her children, the FitzClarences and those born of her previous liaisons, either ignored her or involved her in financial problems. Despite returning to the stage to make ends meet, losing custody of her younger daughters as agreed in the separation settlement, she fell deeply into debt. Applying to the Duke's 'man of business', John Barton, for assistance, he promised her vaguely that if she went to live in France, he would discreetly sort out her affairs in her absence, with the minimum of fuss and publicity. In so doing, he never revealed to his master the true extent of her debts. Her health ebbing away, installed in a squalid apartment at St Cloud near Paris, waiting for letters from England that never came, she died on 5 July 1816, aged about fifty-five.

Though the Duke could be charged with thoughtlessness, it was most unlikely that he would have condemned her to spend her last days thus if he had been aware of her circumstances. He was deeply upset when he heard of her death, and bitterly angry that he had not been given a chance to make amends.

Since leaving Mrs Jordan, he had gone seeking a wife with more enthusiasm than dignity. Six times he proposed to the heiress Miss Tilney Long, adding the final time rather untruthfully that the Queen sent her best wishes and regards, but six times she refused him. After several more almost farcical and equally fruitless proposals to attractive and wealthy young heiresses from the British nobility, he turned to the continent. Princess Anne of Denmark was suggested, but she would have nothing of him, and by the time he was thinking about the twenty-five-year-old widowed sister of Tsar Alexander I, Grand Duchess Catherine of Oldenburg, he was almost desperate.

One day he was at the Brighton Pavilion with the Regent when the Russian Ambassador's wife, Princess Lieven, a fellow guest, was leaving. As she was about to drive off, the Duke, who was saying goodbye, knocked the footman aside and jumped into the carriage, ordering the coachman to drive on. Hatless and slightly drunk, he asked her if she was cold. 'No, Monseigneur,' she replied. 'Are you hot, Madame?' 'No, Monseigneur.' 'Permit me to take your hand.' 'It is needless.' He insisted on doing so, and she was terrified that he was about to assault her. Racking her brains for something to distract his attention, she quickly changed the subject. Apparently he had intended to ask her what were his chances of marriage with the Grand Duchess, but this strange encounter was not calculated to make Princess Lieven recommend him as a prospective husband to anyone.

Thwarted in his marital aspirations, and considering the quest for a wife less urgent than it had once seemed, he turned his attention once more to naval and ceremonial duties.

On 30 October 1816, the King of Württemberg died, and in England, Queen Charlotte decreed that she and her daughters should wear mourning for a month. The Queen of Württemberg had been totally isolated from her family, destined never to see her parents again once she was married. Without any children of her own, she declared that religion alone would give her the courage to look forward to 'a life which must now ever be clouded with sorrow.'

Though they had often wondered if she was happy with a man commonly regarded as a tyrant in public and private life, she always insisted that she was content with her lot. Not for one moment would she have changed places with her unmarried sisters.

That autumn the Duchess of Cumberland, who had already given birth to a daughter and three sons (one already deceased) in her two previous marriages, was expecting another child. The pregnancy was a difficult one, due partly to her age (thirty-eight) and distress at her father's death. On 27 January 1817 she produced a stillborn daughter. It was ironic that the fifteen children of King

George and Queen Charlotte should so far have only produced three grand-children born from officially-recognized marriages. All three had been princesses, and two had been stillborn. The hopes of all devolved on Princess Leopold of Saxe-Coburg, now living in domestic bliss at Claremont.

By the spring of 1817, after two miscarriages, she was pregnant again. Much depended on the infant who would be third in succession to the throne, and on 5 November the Prince Regent was alarmed when told that his daughter had been delivered of a stillborn son, although she was 'doing extremely well'. He retired to bed, only to be roused at 4.30 next morning by the Duke of York with the news that she was dead.

In his grief, he struck his forehead violently with both hands and collapsed into his brother's arms. On regaining his composure, he asked to be driven out to Claremont before her body was laid out in the coffin. After scenes of terrible emotion, he was escorted back to Carlton House, the blinds of his carriage drawn to shelter him from inquisitive eyes.

The Duke of Cumberland hurried to Claremont to convey his sympathy to the disconsolate widower. Meanwhile her favourite uncle the Duke of Sussex made a special journey to Carlton House to condole with the bereaved father, but the latter refused to see him.

During the funeral on the evening of 19 November, the Queen and her daughters sat in their apartments at Windsor listening to what Princess Augusta called 'the dreary, heavy sound which is sad and melancholy to the Ear and most painfull to the Heart', the sound of the mourning coaches in the procession and the Dead March. The Dukes of York, Clarence, Cumberland and Sussex kept solemn pace with the chief mourner, the widowed Prince Leopold, beneath the banners of the Garter Knights in the wavering torchlight.

The Prince Regent remained in shattered seclusion until after the funeral. Later he went to Brighton, where he spent three months in deepest mourning. For a time he seemed beyond the reach of sympathy. When the Duchess of Gloucester came to visit him, she was so distressed by his condition that she had to go into an anteroom to compose herself before leaving the house.

To the family and the country, Princess Charlotte's death was an unexpected and harrowing tragedy. Henry Brougham called it a 'most melancholy event' which produced 'feelings of the deepest sorrow and most bitter disappointment' throughout the country. Extraordinary though it seemed, the royal line was heading for extinction. Of the twelve legitimate living descendants of King George III, the youngest of the seven princes was aged forty-three and the youngest princess forty. Between them, none had a legitimate child to inherit the throne.

8 'John Bull is a very odd animal'

The year 1818 was destined to see a procession of royal marriages. Already three of the Dukes had given earnest consideration to matrimony. The prospects of increased parliamentary grants, settlement of debts, and of providing an heir to the throne, were temptations they could not ignore.

Parliament was reluctant to provide expensive establishments for the Dukes who now seemed hell-bent on racing each other to the altar, especially as they feared anger from the people who had groaned under the weight of heavy taxation required to finance twenty years of war in Europe. The prospect provoked one of the Duke of Wellington's most oft-quoted remarks, as recorded by his fellow-parliamentarian Thomas Creevey. The Dukes were 'the damnedest millstone around the necks of any government that can be imagined. They have insulted – *personally* insulted – two thirds of the gentlemen of England, and how can it be wondered at that they take their revenge upon them when they get them in the House of Commons? It is their only opportunity, and I think, by God, they are quite right to use it.'[1]

Before the Dukes' turn, however, one of their sisters was to make good her escape from the Nunnery. In January 1818, Princess Elizabeth was informed that the Hereditary Prince of Hesse-Homburg was about to arrive in Britain, in order to ask for her hand in marriage. Though she was unaware at the time, he had come to England in 1814, during the allied heads of state visits. 'I am no longer young,' she wrote to the Prince Regent, 'and fairly feel that having my own home will be a comfort in time, tho' it causes me a degree of pang which I feel *deeply* – more than I have words to express – but God knows our lives have been times of *trial* and ever will be so.'[2]

She dreaded the effect that her marriage would have on the Queen, who was visibly declining. She found such effort in getting her breath that Elizabeth was frightened to be alone with her. On 29 January she plucked up courage and told her mother she was going to be married. At first the Queen seemed resigned, but that evening she realized what it would mean to be deprived of her daughter's company, and grumpily refused to join them at dinner or play cards afterwards. 'Do as you please,' she snapped at her daughter, 'you are of age.'

Elizabeth complained bitterly to the Regent that she was 'hardly used', and that the Queen was so incensed by her conduct that she could not bear to see her. Princess Augusta, angered by her dutiful sister's plight, tried to reassure her by telling her what a 'spoilt child' their mother was, and that she was vexed as she could not manage things her own way for once. After two conciliatory visits from the Regent, a truce was arranged, and the Queen was reassured that she would not be deprived of her daughter's companionship immediately on marriage.

The wedding took place at the Queen's House on 7 April 1818. The Prince Regent, laid up with a severe attack of gout, was unable to attend, though the Queen was present, behaving to guests with a graciousness that pleasantly surprised her daughters. The bride was clad in rich silver tissue with flounces of Brussels lace, her head plumed with ostrich feathers.

Though happy to be free at last, she could not help looking anxiously at her mother, whose mainstay she had been. Always ready to make allowances for the sick, ageing woman in her twilight years, she had at the same time helped to bring a touch of humour to the sad atmosphere at home, poking fun at herself by saying that she was 'nobody', and in the next breath declaring that with 'my fat figure' anyone might be excused for doubting her.

Her husband-to-be was not handsome; 'an uglier hound, with a snout buried in hair, I never saw,' declared one observer. However he was kind-hearted, and a war hero, having been wounded at the battle of Leipzig. He was so unaccustomed to riding in a closed carriage that as they set off for the honeymoon at Windsor, he was so violently sick that he had to get out and ride on the box. The honeymoon was spent at the Royal Lodge, where he passed much of his time in the Gothic conservatory, smoking vigorously, clad in dressing gown and slippers.

The Princess celebrated her forty-eighth birthday six weeks after her wedding, and thus had no expectations of motherhood. This mattered less to her than her freedom. But parenthood and dynastic needs were to dictate the purposes of the next three royal marriages.

Of the bachelors, the Duke of Cambridge was regarded as the most eligible. Unlike the Dukes of Clarence and Kent, he had neither mistress nor illegitimate family; unlike the Duke of Sussex, he was not already married to (albeit separated from) a wife not recognized by the Royal Marriages Act. He was musical, enjoyed singing and playing the violin, wore a blond wig and talked endlessly. With his income in Hanover he was the least debt-ridden of his brothers, and always ready to lend generously to them. Still comparatively young – at the time of Charlotte's death he was only forty-three – and untouched by any taint of scandal, well respected in Hanover where he had lived as Governor-General for some years, he would surely make some princess an excellent if somewhat eccentric husband.

By Christmas 1817, he was unofficially engaged to the twenty-year-old Princess Augusta of Hesse-Cassel. It was said that the Duke of Clarence had asked him to 'keep an eye open for a likely bride for him in the course of his travels.' Bearing in mind his previous, farcical quests for a Duchess of Clarence, the Admiral of the Fleet evidently saw the wisdom of delegating such a delicate mission to somebody else for a change. Adolphus's glowing description of Princess Augusta, whom he said 'would make an ideal Queen of England,' made the naval Duke roar with laughter, exclaiming that Adolphus was in love with her himself; 'I'll write and tell him to take her himself, bless him!' It was a generous gesture which the Duke of Cambridge was pleased to accept.

The marriage took place on 7 May at Cassel, and they arrived at Dover three weeks later. Though they were married in Germany, it was a match which caught the imagination of people in England, for the Duke of Cambridge was respected, if not nearly as well-known, far more than his elder brothers. As the royal yacht anchored and the Duke led his bride to board the barge, thousands cheered. Louder still rang the cheers as they stepped ashore, the seasick and thoroughly nervous Duchess just able to nod that she appreciated the welcome. She had recovered by the next morning, when they were seen strolling arm in arm along the pier. That evening they arrived in London, and a further marriage ceremony was held at the Queen's House in the presence of Queen Charlotte.

Shortly after the Duke of Cambridge brought his bride to England, he wrote to the Duchess of Cumberland – the woman said to have jilted him some twenty years before – to express his regret at Queen Charlotte's prohibition on bringing his wife to visit her in England, but he hoped they could meet on the continent as soon as possible. When the Duke of Cambridge met both the Cumberlands soon afterwards, his pleasant manner made it clear that he bore no grudge for past events. The Duchess of Cumberland, still *persona non grata* at the English court, suggested that they should all meet at Kew, and with some trepidation the Duke of Cambridge took his wife with him. As she could barely speak a word of English, when she met the Duchess of Cumberland, she was so relieved to meet a fellow-German that she spontaneously embraced her, and they struck up an immediate rapport. The Duchess of Cumberland never forgot which was the first member of her husband's family to risk displeasure by giving her such a warm welcome. When the Queen heard, she was so angry that the doctors feared her rage could bring on a fatal heart attack.

The Duke of Kent and Madame de St Laurent were now installed at the Hotel de Maldeghan, Brussels, where the cost of living was much less than in England. Although Madame did not know it, the Duke of Kent had also been looking for a bride. It had been suggested to him that Victoire, widow of Prince Emich Charles of Leiningen and elder sister of Princess Charlotte's widower Prince Leopold, might be suitable for him. A discreet visit to the Princess and her two small children, Charles and Feodora, in the autumn of 1816, confirmed his favourable impression, but soon after his return to Brussels, he wondered if he might not have been too precipitate. Not until the news of Charlotte's death, when the horrified Julie de St Laurent read in their newspaper over breakfast one morning an editorial recommending that the Duke and his brothers should marry forthwith, did the matter become imperative. For twenty-seven years they had lived together, but like Mrs Jordan, she recognized that as a son of the King of England, he had to do his duty. Unlike the actress, she had no brood of bastards to be provided for. With unobtrusive dignity she took her leave, and settled in a Paris convent.

Once the Prince Regent had given his approval, the Duke of Kent wrote to

Edward, Duke of Kent, engraving after a portrait by Charles Dawe, c. 1816

Princess Victoire proposing. Flattered and delighted, she accepted him. Tenderly he replied that he was 'nothing more than a soldier, 50 years old and after 32 years of service not very fitted to captivate the heart of a young and charming Princess, who is 19 years younger.'[3] He would, however, make her 'the first object' in his life.

On 29 May 1818, the Duke and the Dowager Princess of Leiningen were married according to the rites of the Lutheran church at Schloss Ehrenburg, Coburg. The Duke was attired in his Field Marshal's uniform, while his bride wore a pale silk lace dress with orange blossoms and white roses.

Dutifully, the Duke of Clarence had also resumed his deferred quest for a bride. An heiress in Oxfordshire, Miss Wickham, was briefly the object of his affections, until the Prince Regent was advised by the Cabinet that she would not be acceptable. Close examination of the German courts revealed a suitable candidate in Princess Amelia Adelaide of Saxe-Meiningen. The marriage negotiations were conducted in a curiously cold-hearted fashion. Twenty-seven years his junior, the princess was said to be personable, home-loving, and so fond of children that she would be pleased to welcome the FitzClarences as part of the family. As the Saxe-Meiningen line was said to be 'good breeding stock' in the phrase of the day, there would undoubtedly be young Clarences as well in due course.

The Duke's reaction on hearing that this dutiful young woman was prepared to accept him failed to lift his melancholy spirits. 'She is doomed, poor innocent young creature,' he wrote to George FitzClarence on 21 March. 'I cannot, I will not, I must not ill use her.'[4]

Lord Liverpool, the Prime Minister, had rashly promised the Duke a greatly increased income on marriage. Aware that Parliament was in no mood to countenance large expenditure, he reduced a proposed increase to £10,000 a year, but the House cut it further to £6,000. Grossly insulted, he informed the House that such an increase was so irrelevant to his needs that he would refuse it altogether, and probably forget the marriage as well. Hearing however that the diffident Princess Adelaide (perhaps less than confident of attracting a more dashing suitor herself) was loath to give up her chance of marriage, and being told that her character was really as good as he had been advised, he was persuaded not to abandon the project. A wife who would tolerate the Fitz-Clarences was not to be lightly dismissed, and in any case Bushey had become much less homely since the departure and death of Dorothy Jordan.

He still approached the marriage in a sombre frame of mind. He stayed in England, while Adelaide and her widowed mother made the journey on their own, arriving on 4 July, and installed themselves at Grillon's Hotel, Albemarle Street, London until the Prince Regent and then the bridegroom himself came to call.

The marriage ceremony, a double, was to be celebrated at Kew Palace on 11 July 1818, but postponed for two days as the Queen was ill. An altar covered with crimson velvet was placed in front of the fireplace in the drawing-room, and at a service printed in English and German, shortened for the benefit of the Queen, the Prince Regent gave Princess Adelaide away, and Prince Leopold his sister. The brides knelt to receive the blessing of their mother-in-law, who answered in a cracked, unemotional voice. She retired to her boudoir as soon as she could, leaving the rest of the family party to a large dinner presided over by the Regent.

The nuptials over, both couples left for Germany. The Duke of Clarence had indignantly refused the meagre increase in his allowance; while the Duke of Kent had not been too proud to accept his £6,000, he still appreciated the virtues of thrift and inexpensive living on the continent. The Clarences settled in Hanover, where they were welcomed by the newly-married Cambridges, while the Kents went to Amorbach.

The Duke and Duchess of Cumberland also returned to Germany. The Duke felt that his wife's spirits had been undermined by the strain of being treated as an outcast, and it was clear that the Queen would never give way. In addition, though their style of life was quite spartan, they were unable to live in England on their modest income.

Shortly before their departure, the Duke wrote to the Regent of his 'most heartfelt gratitude for all your brotherly kindness to me during my stay in England which believe me will never be effaced from my recollection, in short you ALONE among eleven *brothers & sisters* have proved to me that you are really a *brother & friend*.'[5] As the butt of pamphleteers and caricaturists, the brothers had a common bond in their unpopularity. The Duke was hated even more than his brother, as at least the Regent could display tact and charm when occasion demanded. Though the Duke never attempted to court easy popularity, he was not as insensitive as he seemed, especially where his wife's happiness was concerned. The Duchess likewise recognized with gratitude and affection how much the Regent had stood by them.

By autumn, the Queen was clearly dying. Bluntly she asked her doctors whether they believed her constitution was giving way, and she was irritated by their evasive replies. Aged seventy-four, she had suffered from dropsy for some time, and she was gradually losing the will to live.

To Princess Augusta, on whom fell much of the brunt of providing her with companionship, she appeared to express some regret for her selfishness. In October, the Queen remarked to her sadly, 'I had hoped to see you all happy, and now I fear I shall not arrive at that wish of my Heart.' When Augusta gracefully told her that they were 'all sensible of your Affection and most gratefull for it,' she replied apologetically, 'I have caused a very dull summer *to you all,* for the Prince would have given his Brothers balls and parties on account of their marriages, and poor I have been a bane to everything . . . I wish to God I could see *your Brothers* – tell them I love them – but I am too ill. I can only see you and Mary.'[6] She regretted not being near the King at Windsor, but by now she was too ill to be moved from Kew.

On 17 November, Queen Charlotte breathed her last, sitting up in her favourite horsehair-covered armchair, her hand in that of her eldest son. The previous day she had completed her will, bequeathing the house and farm at Frogmore to Augusta, and Lower Lodge, Windsor, to Sophia. 'We had the consolation of seeing her expire without a pang,' wrote the Duchess of Gloucester, '& a sweet smile on her face. My two elder Brothers, Augusta & myself *nearly* received her last breath.'[7]

Her death brought no reconciliation between the Regent and the Duke of Sussex. The latter wrote saying that although he had 'drawn your own line with regard to me . . . I never can forget that we are both the offspring of that revered mother whose death we as sons, and brothers, have now to lament.'[8] As an olive branch, it failed. He came to hear the reading of their mother's will, and the Regent kept him waiting four hours, then asked him to come again next day. He was enraged to discover that it had been read while he was waiting.

The Regent was overcome with grief at his mother's death. Though she had treated him severely in his youth, a close relationship had grown between them since he turned to her for consolation when it was evident that his marriage would prove to be a disaster. For her part, she was lonely when the King became incurably ill, and as there was little love lost between her and her daughters, once they proved they had minds of their own, it was to her eldest son that she turned for companionship and affection. He always treated her with the utmost consideration, the soul of tact when championing the rights of his sisters. When she was invited to Brighton and Carlton House, he waited on her himself at table, taking pains to see she had everything she wanted.

After her death he suffered another nervous breakdown and spent a month in seclusion at Carlton House, finding diversion in the novels of Walter Scott. At fifty-six, racked by years of indulgence, gout and the frustration at living for so long in the shadow of his father, he seemed like an old man himself.

'A Scene in the New Farce called The Rivals, or a Visit to the Heir Presumtive' [sic], *cartoon, April 1819, ridiculing the Dukes' race to produce an heir to the throne in the next generation.* From left: *the Clarences, the Cambridges, the Kents, and the Cumberlands*

The year 1818 had seen three marriages, and the following year brought several royal births in the next generation.

On 24 March, the Duchess of Cambridge had a son. Couriers were sent to England to announce that at last a grandson, to be christened George, had been born to His Majesty the King.

Later that week the Duchess of Clarence went into labour. Unhappily she had caught a cold while walking in the garden, and developed pleurisy. The doctors prescribed a course of bleeding, which hastened a premature delivery. On the morning of 29 March she gave birth to a puny daughter, Princess Charlotte Augusta, who was baptized at once and died that same evening. She was laid quietly to rest beside the body of her ancestor, King George I, in the palace crypt. For several days, the mother's life was also in danger.

The Duke of Kent had been determined that his child would be born in England. The Regent and the Prime Minister saw no need for the Kents to move from Germany, but once the Duke had resolved to borrow money to meet his expenses, the Regent sent the royal yacht to await them at Calais, and arranged for apartments in Kensington Palace to be prepared for them. Alone of the family in England, the Duke of Sussex supported his brother's intention to return home. While the Princesses sided with the Regent, Augusta in particular being '*outrageous with Edward* for he is acting like a fool and *a Madman,*' Sussex added words of encouragement. 'John Bull is a very odd animal, and he must be cajoled,' he wrote. 'You will find it *very difficult* to drive into his Head that *his Sovereign if born in a foreign Country* is *not a foreigner,* and this *at any price* you must prevent.'[9]

In March the Duke and Duchess set out from Amorbach, in a huge shabby coach driven by the Duke himself to save the expense of hiring a driver. A midwife and qualified doctor, Fraulein Siebold, travelled with them in case the Duchess should give birth prematurely. They reached Dover in April and proceeded to Kensington, where the Duchess was delivered early in the morning of 24 May, of a daughter, the future Queen Victoria.*

Three days later the Duchess of Cumberland produced a son, named George. At her age, she was unlikely to bear further children. Until February, the blind, deaf and deranged King had no legitimate surviving grandchildren; by the end of May, although he would never know, he had three, and there would doubtless be more. The Hanoverian line had been saved.

Of these new infants, the Princess of Kent would be the first in succession. At her birth she was fourth in line, after the Prince Regent, her uncle Clarence (and any children he and the Duchess might have), and her father. That the Duchess of Kent had produced a daughter, not a son, did not matter to the Duke. 'Take care of her, she will be Queen of England,' he remarked proudly as he showed the infant off to friends. To the Duke of Orleans, he wrote proudly that she was 'rather a pocket Hercules, than a pocket Venus.'

On 24 June, family and guests gathered in the Cupola Room at Kensington Palace for her christening. Her godparents were to be the Prince Regent, Tsar Alexander I of Russia, the Dowager Queen of Württemberg and her maternal grandmother, Augusta, Dowager Duchess of Saxe-Coburg. Of these, only the Regent was present; the Tsar was represented by the Duke of York, the Duke and Duchess, Prince Leopold, Princesses Augusta and Sophia, and the Duke and Duchess of Gloucester also being present. The list of names – Georgina Charlotte Augusta Alexandrina Victoria – had been submitted by the father to the Regent, who would not allow Georgina as his name could not come before that of the Tsar, but he would not let it come after. As the Archbishop of Canterbury stood with the child in his arms, waiting for the Regent to pronounce the first name, there was a pause before he muttered 'Alexandrina'. He stopped and the Archbishop waited. The Duke of Kent prompted him with 'Charlotte', but the Regent shook his head fiercely. Discomfited, the Duke proposed 'Augusta'. Again the Regent objected. 'Let her be called after her mother,' he muttered, glaring at the now sobbing Duchess. Thus christened amid family discord, the infant was known for the first nine years of her life as 'Drina'.

The coldness with which the parents had been treated at the christening was indicative of the feeling with which the rest of the family were to treat them. The Duchess of Gloucester and her sisters might have harboured some feelings of affection towards the little girl, but loyalty to their eldest brother took precedence over all other considerations. The Prince Regent snubbed the Kents; they therefore followed suit. From Claremont the widower Prince Leopold observed that they all seemed to be 'looking to the Clarence family', and the baby princess was 'a real thorn in their side'. When the Duke of Kent took her at the age of three months to a military review, the Regent was furious.

---

* Fraulein Siebold returned to Coburg, and the next child she delivered, born three months later, was Albert, the future Prince Consort.

George, Prince of Wales, by Sir Thomas Lawrence, c. 1819

'What business has that infant here?' he bellowed. This young niece was an unpleasant reminder of the daughter he had so tragically lost.

Meanwhile the Clarences were travelling home from Hanover. The Duchess had rallied after the death of their daughter, and by August they knew that another child was on the way. It should be born in England, the Duke had decided, and en route they paid visits to the Duke's sisters in Hesse-Homburg and Württemberg, and to the Duchess's mother in Ghent. Unhappily, this protracted, uncomfortable journey was too much for her delicate health. She miscarried at Calais in September, and had to spend six weeks convalescing at Walmer Castle in Dover.

Only the generosity of Prince Leopold – who could well afford to be bountiful with his grant of £50,000 – enabled the Kents to live in comfort. He entertained them unstintingly at Claremont, but recommended that they move back to Germany. Maliciously, twenty years later he told the Princess (by then Queen) that, as Regent and King, George IV's greatest wish had been to get her and her mother out of the country, as he had always hated the Duke of Kent and was jealous of his family's popularity.

In July, on the advice of his trustees, the Duke attempted to sell Castle Hill Lodge through a lottery, since a normal sale was unlikely to bring in its valuation price of about £50,000. He was prevented by Parliament, which felt that such a move would be rather demeaning for someone of his exalted birth.*

Believing their rightful place to be in England, but recognizing that London was far too expensive for them, the Duke took the advice of his old tutor Dr Fisher, Bishop of Salisbury, and decided to retire for a while to the west country. In October 1819 he and his equerry Captain John Conroy visited Devon to look for suitable accommodation. Rejecting houses at Dawlish, Torquay and Teignmouth, they found a small two-storey cottage at Sidmouth: Woolbrook Glen, about a hundred yards away from the sea.

To his brothers, the Duke insisted that the move was for reasons of health rather than economy, 'in order that the Duchess may have the benefit of tepid sea bathing and our infant that of sea air.'

On the afternoon of Christmas Day, the family and their entourage arrived at Sidmouth in a snowstorm. The winter of 1819/20 was severe, and all the family had caught colds while breaking their journey at Salisbury. In spite of snow, gales and pouring rain, the Duchess and Drina quickly recovered, but the Duke had a gastric attack. All of them were well, he wrote optimistically, 'except that the water had already begun to play the very deuce with my bowels.' He made light of it, declaring that with his regular ways of living and strong constitution, he would outlive the rest of his family.

One afternoon the Duchess and Drina were playing in the nursery, when a shower of pellets shattered the window, flew over the baby's head, and tore the sleeve of her nightgown. The Duchess was terrified, but the Duke was less alarmed. It was no underhand attempt at assassination, merely an accident due

---

* The Duke's goods and chattels were sold by auction in 1820 after his death, but two attempts to sell the house and land were unsuccessful. They were purchased by his lifelong friend General Wetherall in 1829, in order to help pay off his creditors.

Woolbrook Glen, Sidmouth, Devon, from a drawing by George Rowe

to the carelessness of a trigger-happy youth out shooting birds. The Duke lectured the lad, pardoning him 'on a promise of desisting from such culpable pursuits'. To others, he joked that the girl 'had stood fire as became a soldier's daughter'.

As the new year of 1820 dawned, the fierce weather continued, with heavy snow and bitterly cold nights. Despite his cold and gastric attack, the Duke was determined to enjoy the Devon scenery, with brisk walks along the cliffs admiring the view of Torbay. One afternoon he and his equerry arrived back with soaking feet. Conroy changed his boots immediately, but the Duke did not bother. He was more interested in the sight of his daughter, who 'now between seven and eight months old looks like a child of a year.'

The Duke had long been susceptible to colds in winter, and a martyr to attacks of rheumatism. That night he retired to bed complaining of hoarseness. By the end of the week his lungs were inflamed and he had become feverish. One doctor after another came from London to Sidmouth, and despite blistering and blood-letting, the symptoms continued. The slightest sound sent him into delirium, and Prince Leopold hurried to be with his distraught sister. On 22 January the Duke realized that he was dying, a will was hastily prepared, and with some effort he added his signature. Next morning, with his hand in that of his wife, he died.

The rest of the family were dumbfounded at his sudden death. Though they had rarely been on good terms, the Prince Regent burst into floods of tears when he was brought the news, while from Berlin the Duke of Cumberland said he thought Edward 'would have outlived us all from his regular habits of life which he has pursued ever since I can recollect any thing. . . . His heart was good, but he was an unfortunate man from his onset in life, and from having seen very little of the world in his youth he got imposed upon by men who certainly did him much mischief.'[10] Augusta was shocked to think that, only five weeks earlier, he had been on his way to Sidmouth; 'so happy, with His excellent, good little Wife, and his lovely child; and within so short a time was perfectly *well – ill -* and *no more!* It's an awfull [*sic*] lesson, even to those who did not know Him; but it's a severe blow to those who loved Him *as I did.*'[11]

Even in death, the Duke's misfortunes were not over. It was ironic that he predeceased his father and sovereign by six days, so that his demise went virtually unnoticed. Posterity, however, brought its own reward, for his belated marriage had proved the salvation of the dynasty. Within a century, his descendants would occupy the thrones of almost every kingdom in Europe.

The slow journey which Leopold and his twice-widowed sister made from Sidmouth to Kensington with the baby of eight months created unfounded rumours that the Duchess was expecting another child.

On the death of Queen Charlotte, the Duke of York had been appointed his father's official guardian, and was consequently voted an additional £10,000 a

King George III and Edward, Duke of Kent, from an 'In Memoriam' pearlware spill vase, 1820

year. Unlike his late mother, he was more conscientious in visiting the tragic white-haired figure in his solitary room at Windsor Castle, overlooking the North Terrace. Until deafness added to his other afflictions, the King would sometimes hear the tramp of soldiers' feet when the guard was relieved, and go to the window. As the guard passed, the ensign in command would give 'Eyes right', and the King would raise his hand in acknowledgement. When awake, according to the Duke of York in summer 1819, he would amuse himself 'playing on the harpsichord and singing with as strong and firm a voice as ever I heard him and seemed as happy and cheerful as possible.'[12] But by the autumn of 1819 the King began to lose weight, and in November the physicians thought he was 'declining fast'. At Christmas he suffered the last violent onset of the malady, talking restlessly for a period of fifty-eight hours without sleep. He lost his previously hearty appetite, and became little more than a skeleton.

On 27 January he was unable to rise from his bed, and ceased to speak. Two days later, at 8.35 in the evening, the end came. The Duke of York was the only member of the family present; also at the deathbed were the King's secretary Herbert Taylor, his physicians and several attendants, all of whom had been warned that their sorely-tried master's physical sufferings would soon be over.

The Duke sent a message to his elder brother, now King George IV, at Carlton House, informing him that 'it has pleased Providence to take to himself our beloved King and Father; the only immediate consolation under such a calamity is the almost conviction that his last moments were free from bodily suffering and mental disorder.'[13]

9 'Like some gorgeous bird of paradise'

Sunday 30 January was the anniversary of the execution of King Charles I, and it was decided to postpone the proclamation of the new King until the following day. At midday on 31 January 1820, therefore, His Majesty King George IV, supported by his brothers and his son-in-law, stood in the forecourt of Carlton House as the Garter King at Arms read the proclamation, to an outburst of acclamation and cheering.

King George III had reigned for fifty-nine years and three months, and attained the age of eighty-one, a reign and life easily surpassing those of any previous monarch. At first it looked as if the longest reign would be followed by the shortest. The Prince Regent had been seriously ill at Brighton during his father's last days. Excitement at his accession and exposure to the bitter January weather after being cosseted in overheated rooms at Brighton brought on an inflammation of the lungs. On 1 February he was critically ill, and by the evening the doctors feared for his life. For four days, bulletins were issued twice daily, as the nation contemplated the tragic prospect of two Kings, father and son, being buried together. As Princess Lieven remarked to Metternich, 'Shakespeare's tragedies pale before such a catastrophe.' Brougham was not alone in praying for his recovery, dreading the accession of King Frederick I, who would probably turn out to be a 'shady Tory-professional King'. However, King George rallied, and when he was well enough to travel, he went to Brighton for two months' convalescence. He was advised not to attend the funerals of his brother and father, as the emotional stress of such a 'dangerous effort of respect and piety' might lead to a relapse.

The embalmed body of the Duke of Kent lay in a coffin over seven feet five inches long, and weighing more than a ton. A cavalry escort brought him on his last journey from Sidmouth to Windsor, and he was laid to rest on the evening of 12 February in the Chapel of St George. The coffin was followed by the chief mourner, the Duke of York, and his younger brothers, all in long black cloaks. Throughout the service the Duke of Sussex, who had been closest to Edward, sobbed uncontrollably as he mourned 'one of the best of men, my most steady friend and the best of brothers.' They had been members of the Masonic fraternity, keen Whigs, and involved in several of the same charities and causes. No closer bond had existed between any of King George III's sons than that between the Dukes of Sussex and Kent.

Four days later, a similar ceremony was held as King George III was buried at Windsor, the Duke of York acting again as chief mourner.

The two deaths brought about a temporary reconciliation between King George IV and the Duke of Sussex. Although the Duke of Cumberland's politics were very different from those of his younger brother Augustus, he respected the cause of family unity and wrote approvingly to the King of his joy at the chance of their being able to 'live happily together, of which you have given us such a handsome example by shaking hands with Augustus, the news of which gratified me beyond everything.'[1]

As King George IV recovered his health and spirits, he realized that a new problem had to be confronted. His hated wife was now Queen Consort. Divorce had never been far from his mind, and after the death of Princess Charlotte it had become more urgent than ever; but the marriages of his bachelor brothers and his mother's death had distracted him. To such vexing questions as to how prayers for the royal family should be worded in the Anglican liturgy, what role if any Queen Caroline should play in the Coronation festivities, and what advice should be given to foreign courts discreetly enquiring about the honours they should accord her in her odyssey around Europe, the King was adamant. A speedy divorce must take place, and meanwhile Church and State should simply ignore her existence.

However, the cabinet insisted that no bill of divorce could be brought without being heard by judges in an ecclesiastical court, and if the Queen decided to fight for her rights, recriminations would no doubt be made. Nobody needed to remind His Majesty that unedifying revelations regarding his relationships with Maria Fitzherbert, Lady Jersey, Lady Hertford, and others, would be made – and made extremely public. The King briefly considered dismissing his Ministers in the hope of finding some that would be more compliant, but at length he realized that this would be impossible. The Tories were firmly in power, and the opposition would be far less sympathetic to his case. A threat to retire to Hanover was seen as nothing more than empty bluster.

Reluctantly, he agreed that the Queen should be granted an annuity payable only on condition that she remained abroad; but he insisted that she should not expect to take her place as Queen at the forthcoming Coronation; and that her name should be omitted from the prayer book. This last move brought protests from the Duke of Sussex and many of his friends, on the grounds that as in common law a person was innocent until proved guilty, prayers for her should not be omitted until she was convicted of immorality.

The new Queen Consort did not intend to give up without a fight. She was well on her way to England by the end of May when the Prime Minister received her letter asking for the royal yacht to be available to receive her at Calais on 3 June. Undeterred by his refusal, she crossed the Channel on 5 June and was welcomed with loud cheers. She made a triumphal entry into London, being cordially welcomed by the Lord Mayor, Alderman Wood, who offered her hospitality at his home in South Audley Street. As her landau passed Carlton House, the sentries presented arms. 'Long live the King!' she cried as the carriage swept down Pall Mall.

The King himself was at Windsor, doubtless considering himself fortunate to be there at the time. He had slipped away quietly to the Royal Lodge with his latest female companion, the Marchioness of Conyngham, where he stayed until

Queen Caroline, by Samuel Lane

September, only appearing in public at the Ascot races. If he had appeared in London, the authorities could not have guaranteed his safety, as the public was so fervently pro-Caroline. The King may have been a coward, but he was a wise one; he knew better than to brave the mob's discontent.

In June 1820, the government prepared a Bill of Pains and Penalties. The King was determined to find a legal solution to depriving his wife of the title of Queen, and dissolving the marriage which had only briefly been more than a marriage in name only.

The proceedings, lasting nearly three months, were limited to the alleged adultery between Caroline and her Italian chamberlain and companion Bartolomeo Pergami. If the case was proved, she would technically be guilty of treason, and there would be no need for the government to bring up the matter of the King's own extra-marital liaisons. The Queen was permitted to attend, but not to give evidence. Sometimes she went to the hearing, on other days she stayed in an adjoining room playing backgammon with Alderman Wood.

By the beginning of September the Prime Minister wanted to drop the last four lines of the bill, enacting the divorce. The whole business produced mixed feelings in the House of Lords. Attendance at the proceedings was compulsory for all peers except for Roman Catholics, minors, those who were absent from the country, and those recently bereaved. Despite his wife's death in August, the Duke of York insisted that he would be 'ashamed' if not present to do his duty. The Duke of Sussex begged to be excused on the grounds of consanguinity to both parties. Yet a brief visit to the Queen at Brandenburg House, Hammersmith, in October, shortly before proceedings were completed, angered the King.

Most of the peers and bishops knew too much about the Queen to consider her totally innocent of gross foolishness if not actual adultery, but they found the whole idea thoroughly undignified, and the alleged revelations distasteful and demeaning. The evidence was heard by October, and was subject to a debate in the Lords afterwards. On the final reading of the bill in November, the government had a slender majority of nine votes. Liverpool recognized that this was tantamount to defeat; to introduce such a contentious bill in the House of Commons would almost certainly result in its rejection and the fall of the government, and he therefore withdrew it. Brougham had obtained a copy of the King's will in which Mrs Fitzherbert was named as his 'dear wife', and threatened to produce it as proof that he had forfeited his throne by marrying a Catholic. In view of his dislike of the Duke of York, his threat was probably not that serious, but it was sufficient to halt the bill in its tracks.

There was widespread rejoicing throughout London and other cities. Queen Caroline may not have been worthy of much respect, but she was certainly the object of sympathy, and there was even less respect for her husband. The King once again considered using his royal prerogative of seeking an alternative government and inviting the Whigs to take office, but thought better of it. From his sulky seclusion at Royal Lodge, he accepted defeat as gracefully as he could. Nobody took seriously his protestations that he would retire to Hanover, leaving the kingdom of England to his brother. He could at least take comfort from the government's successful motion that the Queen's name should still be excluded from the liturgy, and that she was not to be crowned, nor permitted to reside in any of the royal palaces.

As the King's health was none too good, the Duke of York watched him carefully. He was said to be 'all activity and business, and goes about a great deal, and is very popular and becoming more so.' The Duchess, who had suffered from consumption for some time, died on 7 August in his presence, after begging him to let her be buried in Weybridge Church, not at Windsor. As she had meekly borne all his infidelities, it was a request he could hardly refuse.

Yet it made little difference to his way of life, for they had long since ceased to be much more than companions. Looking askance at the Duchess of Kent and her daughter, the King urged him to marry again in order to provide an heir. The Duke did not intend to, for he was in love with another ineligible lady – the Duchess of Rutland. One day they were both seen walking up and down Kensington Gardens, the Duke at such a brisk pace that he did not notice the Duchess was close to fainting with exhaustion. When he realized, he rushed off and returned a few minutes later, puffing and panting, leading a pony which he insisted she should ride.

Though he was next in succession to the throne, the Duke of York was as debt-ridden as ever. Most of his annual allowance was absorbed in the interest on his debts, and he was obliged to sell Oatlands, but debts likewise took care of the proceeds. Yet lack of money did not discourage him from a decision to build a new house in Stable Yard, St James's Palace. Initially it was to be a small dwelling, but after work had begun on it, he realized that it might not be finished

Royal Lodge, Windsor

before he became King. So he thought it would be more economical to turn it into a palace, and then there would be no need for him to move to Carlton House or Buckingham Palace when King George should die and be succeeded by King Frederick. Benjamin Wyatt was commissioned to design a suitable dwelling, and all the plans were submitted to the Duchess of Rutland for approval. By the time she had laid the foundation stone, the building was heavily mortgaged, and the government was obliged to advance money to rescue the scheme.

There would be no Princes or Princesses of York, but the prospect of a Clarence heir remained. During the summer of 1820, the Duchess was expecting another child. On the doctors' advice, the Duke had moved his wife from the draughty quarters of St James's, to the more spacious, country air of Bushey. Although it might be indelibly associated with his life with Dorothy Jordan, the Duke and Duchess soon transformed it into its old homely self again. As she had promised, she made an admirable stepmother to the FitzClarences; she shared in his pleasure when he became a grandfather for the first time, and was happy to attend the wedding of his third daughter Elizabeth to the Earl of Erroll at St George's Church, Hanover Square, on 4 December, though she was over seven months pregnant at the time.

Although he had taken the greatest possible care of his wife, she gave birth six weeks prematurely to a daughter, weighing nearly eleven pounds, at St James's Palace on 10 December 1820. Sir Henry Halford remarked rather coldly that the mother was a 'poor wishy-washy thing' but the baby would live provided she survived the dangerous first month or so. The Duchess of Clarence was left in a delicate state of health following the birth, and her life was once again thought to be in danger. Once she recovered, though, the newspapers were able to give the customary news that mother and infant were 'doing very well'.

The Duke and Duchess wanted to name their child Georgina, but they deferred to the King's requests that she should be called Elizabeth. That Christmas was a happy one, and the baby princess appeared to thrive. However, she fell ill in the new year, and on the morning of 4 March 1821, she died in a convulsive fit, the cause of death being given as 'an entanglement of the bowels'.

These tragedies darkened the lives of the Duke and Duchess of Clarence, but shared unhappiness brought them closer. In view of the fact that Prince William had only grudgingly agreed to marry on condition of a considerably increased allowance, and in furtherance of producing an heir to the throne, and that the marriage had succeeded in neither, he was all solicitude to his wife. As his twenty years with Dorothy Jordan had shown, he was more home-loving than most of his brothers, and having a wife to make home and hearth comfortable appealed strongly to his sense of domestic virtues, in which he took greatly after his father.

Though Adelaide was plain, prudish, and gave people the impression of being dull and lacking character, her gentle but firm influence on him had been all to the good. After meeting him at dinner at Portsmouth on one occasion, Lord Lyttelton hardly recognized him, and wrote afterwards that the Duke behaved perfectly well, was civil to everyone, and did not say a single indecent or improper thing. The Duke, in his mid-fifties, found it difficult to change the habits of a lifetime. Though still inclined to say the first thing that came into his head, under his wife's influence he cleaned up his language considerably, and appeared to appreciate the importance of not offending other people's susceptibilities so much. From time to time his outbursts would still embarrass other people, but less often than before.

There was less domestic happiness for Mary, Duchess of Gloucester. She and the Duke were now established at Gloucester House, Piccadilly. Creevey noted that her husband 'Slice' (a nickname derived from Gloucester cheese), who professed to be a Radical in politics, was in his domestic life a tyrant. When her sisters and friends called upon her, they were surprised to be marched up to the top of the house. The Duchess apologized to them as they sat down exhausted and out of breath, explaining that it was 'owing to the cruel manner in which she was treated by the Duke.'[2] Deciding that the rooms on the drawing room floor were not kept in good order, he had them locked up and pocketed the keys himself. The King was indignant at this treatment of his sister, and behaved so coldly to his brother-in-law when he came to court that the latter declared he would never go there again. The Duchess was afraid to show her private letters to the Duke, but meekly submitted to his will, even to the extent of not travelling to visit anybody on a Sunday, because of his strict Sabbatarian scruples, or allowing the King's invitations to determine the date and duration of her absences from Gloucester House and Bagshot.

Yet she enjoyed herself whenever she could escape to visit her brother at the Brighton Pavilion, where she was treated like a normal human being rather than a prisoner. She took pains to try and maintain friendly relations between the King and her husband, and interceded for the latter that he might be allowed to keep all the game that fell to his gun in the Great Park. But when the governorship of Guernsey fell vacant and he tried to solicit the post himself, she refused to do anything to help, as if he was simply not worth the effort.

By early 1821 the pro-Queen Caroline hysteria had died down. When the King attended the theatre at Drury Lane and Covent Garden in February he was loudly cheered and applauded. At last, he could turn his attention to the Coronation, to take place at Westminster Abbey on 19 July.

As one who loved pageantry, dressing up and being the centre of attention, the King was determined that his Coronation would be a splendid occasion which none of its spectators would ever forget. In a surprisingly generous mood, Parliament granted nearly quarter of a million pounds for the service and festivities.

At 10.25 in the morning, a procession set out from Westminster Hall for the service, moving along a covered walk raised three feet high, so that spectators could see everything. It was headed by the Royal Herbwoman and six attendant maids, scattering nosegays along the route. They were followed by a Household

George IV Coronation jug, 1821

Band, the Corporation of the City of London, Peers in full robes, Privy Councillors in special Elizabethan costume, dignitaries of state carrying the crown, orb, sceptre and sword, church dignitaries bearing a Bible, patten and chalice. Last came the King himself, walking slowly beneath a canopy of cloth-of-gold, a train of crimson velvet twenty-seven feet long relieved with a pattern of golden stars. His vast plumed hat was decorated with ostrich feathers, and a long curly wig hung down over his shoulders. The painter Benjamin Haydon, carried away by the picturesque scene, described his sovereign as 'like some gorgeous bird of paradise'. 'By God! I'll have everything the same at mine!' exclaimed the Duke of York, lost in admiration.

The ceremony in the Abbey lasted for five hours. It was extremely hot inside, and early on the King seemed about to faint. Very pale, and weighed down heavily by his robes, he was only saved from sudden collapse by sal volatile. The Archbishop of York preached a sermon on the need for the ruler to preserve his subjects' morals 'from the contagion of vice and irreligion', at which the King's attention wandered, and he was seen nodding and winking at Lady Conyngham. At the banquet at Westminster Hall afterwards, over three hundred guests sat down to a vast meal, watched by the peeresses in the gallery who had to go without.

Exhausted but exhilarated by the day's proceedings, he returned to Carlton House in his carriage, amid wild scenes of enthusiasm. Although he had rarely been popular, at least he could be guaranteed to put on a splendid display of Majesty as befitted his station.

As the King had feared, the festivities did not go ahead without the Queen attempting some show of strength. She had driven to the Abbey and tried to gain admittance at each door in turn, but was turned away as she had no ticket. For once the crowd's sympathies were with the King rather than her, and she was booed away.

Unlike his father who had barely travelled at all during his long life, the new King had decided that his Coronation would be a prelude to a tour of his dominions at home and abroad.

Twelve days later, he embarked at Portsmouth in the *Royal George*, sailing down the Channel around Land's End and up towards the Welsh coast. By 6 August the yacht had reached Anglesey and anchored off Holyhead, about to cross the Irish Sea, when news came that the Queen was gravely ill. The previous week, she had been seized by abdominal pains while attending the theatre at Drury Lane. Her physician, Henry Holland, thought that her spirit had given way after the humiliation of not being admitted to the Coronation. Diagnosing acute inflammation of the bowel, he ordered that she should be blooded and heavily dosed with calomel, topped up with 'a quantity of castor oil that would have turned the stomach of a horse.'

It was all to no avail. Although he felt little regret, the King knew that it would ill become him to be seen enjoying public celebrations at such a time, and he decided to wait at Anglesey for further news.

Queen Caroline died on the evening of 7 August. She had expressed a wish to be buried in Germany, with 'Caroline of Brunswick, the injured Queen of England' engraved on the coffin. The King was happy to grant her wish to be returned to the land of her birth, if not her choice of inscription. He received a copy of her will, by which William Austin was to receive the whole of her inheritance on reaching his majority. There were, however, many demands on her estate, and she had in fact died insolvent.

After a suitable interval of mourning, the King made a ceremonial entry into Dublin, dressed in a uniform he had designed for himself as a Field-Marshal, with a thick black armband and a spray of shamrock in his hat. The Irish, who had until then entertained no particularly warm feelings towards the King of England, were flattered by his attention and impressed with the pomp and pageantry, and the visit, the first by a reigning sovereign since that of King Richard II, was a great success. One spectator, who was proud to have been 'a rebel to old King George in '98', declared that he would die a hundred deaths for his son, 'because he's a real King, and asks us how we are.' He returned to Carlton House in mid-September, 'a most determined Irishman', declaring that his hosts had offered to build him a palace in Dublin and christen him 'Paddy the First'.

After a week's rest, he crossed from Ramsgate to Calais in his yacht, and toured the continent for seven weeks. While staying at Brussels, he was escorted round the field of Waterloo by the Duke of Wellington. At Hanover, he was welcomed with a hundred-and-one gun salute and a university address of welcome. Although he found the solemn and conventional way of life of his

Hanoverian subjects tedious, his sojourn was enlivened by a visit from Metternich, at which the King was indiscreet enough to criticize most of his ministers. But by now he was feeling the effects of his travelling exertions, and by the time he was on his way back to England he was suffering from his old enemy, gout. He spent most of the winter and much of the spring convalescing at Brighton.

In the spring of 1822, the Clarences' last hopes of parenthood were dashed. On 8 April the Duchess miscarried of twins, and the Duke was brokenhearted 'at these repeated misfortunes to this beloved and superior woman.'

The marriage had failed to provide an heir, but far from his bearing her any ill-will, which a more selfish prince might easily have done, he found himself drawn ever closer to his young wife. Whereas King George IV had given the impression, both before and after he became King, of resenting the presence of his niece Princess Victoria of Kent, as a reminder of the daughter he had lost, the Clarences were genuinely fond of the girl. 'My children are dead,' the Duchess wrote to her sister-in-law, the Duchess of Kent, 'but your child lives, and she is mine too.'[3] To some, it might have seemed a little possessive, but such a trait had no place in the former Princess Adelaide's kind-hearted nature. Nobody expected any more heirs to the Duke and Duchess of Cumberland, although the Cambridge line was evidently secure, with the birth of a second child, a daughter Augusta, later that year.

After the King's European sojourn, he planned to visit Vienna in 1822 and renew his acquaintance with the continent's political arbiters, especially his friend Metternich. However the government did not look kindly on him identifying himself and them with Metternich's policies, and Sir Walter Scott, whose works had been so much enjoyed by the King as Regent that he had bestowed a baronetcy upon him, was urged to encourage the King to visit Scotland instead.

Although the house of Hanover aroused nothing but hatred among those who remembered the defeat at Culloden in 1746 and its aftermath, the King and Scott stirred their enthusiasm with a series of royal progresses and pageantry that were little less splendid than the Coronation. He stayed at Dalkeith Palace outside Edinburgh, and used Holyrood House for state ceremonies, including a levee where he appeared in full Highland uniform, sporting the Stuart tartan. When he accepted an invitation to attend the Caledonian Hunt Ball, he diplomatically requested no foreign dances, as he disliked 'seeing anything in Scotland that is not purely national and characteristic'.

By the time he returned on board his yacht to Greenwich at the beginning of September, carrying a knife, fork and spoon used by the Young Pretender in 1745, the reconciliation between the godson of 'Butcher Cumberland' and his Scottish subjects was complete.

The following January, the King presented to the nation the library of nearly 70,000 volumes which his father had collected over half a century. The British

Museum had been founded in 1759, its exhibits housed in Montague House, Bloomsbury, and it was decided to replace the building with a series of galleries and libraries worthy of a great national collection. Work on the King's Library began later that year.

At the same time, he encouraged the foundation of the National Gallery, by persuading the Liverpool government to purchase the paintings collected by Sir John Julius Angerstein, which formed the nucleus of the gallery's display. Work did not begin on the building until after his death, but it was a fitting memorial and testimony to his patronage of the fine arts.

Ill health gradually restricted the King's movements. The Brighton Pavilion was completed in 1822, but ironically he started to lose his affection for it almost at once. It was as if one of the great dreams of his life was now finished, and could hold no more for him. He continued to pay short visits there until 1827, but the growth of the town gradually destroyed its privacy, and he seemed fearful that its exposed position might encourage would-be assassins.

Carlton House, too, fell from favour. Although he had loved it while he was heir to the throne, he found it too small for royal grandeur as monarch, and after fire damage in 1825 he lost all enthusiasm for it. In 1827 it was demolished, the pillars which stood outside it being transferred to the site of the National Gallery when building began on it in the next decade.

Windsor and Buckingham House henceforth became the chief royal residences. The King commissioned John Nash to convert the latter into a palace,

Frederick, Duke of York, by William Yellowlees after Sir William Beechey

although again he did not live to see the culmination of the work; and Sir Jeffry Wyatville was charged with modernizing Windsor Castle as a home fit for a Sovereign. Royal Lodge was improved and enlarged, and between 1824 and 1828, a series of state apartments replaced the small castle drawing-rooms, while the Waterloo Chamber was built as a monument to Britain's victory, providing a suitable place for Lawrence's portraits of the allied heads of state.

King George III, who had given the impression of being content with, if not actually revelling in, physical discomfort, had had no sense of creating a physical background worthy of the Crown. His partial rebuilding of Windsor Castle had done little to redress the balance, and it fell to his eldest son to complete the process.

As observed recently, this most self-indulgent yet sensitive monarch, who had often felt so useless to his country, who had experienced such an unhappy family life as husband and father, who had been ruthlessly exploited by his mistresses, was compelled to withdraw into his own world, his own dreams, to create a deeply personal setting for his private life.[4] Having failed in so much, he could at least leave behind some living testimony to his love of the fine arts and architecture. He was responsible for making Windsor Castle and Buckingham Palace the two official residences of the monarch, and although the Brighton Pavilion was ridiculed much in its day and by the Victorians, it survives as a splendid personification of the Regency and a monument to the dreams and aspirations of the Regent himself.

As heir to the throne, the Duke of York had considerable influence with the King. The brothers had long enjoyed a love–hate relationship. They made fun of each other, and the Duke delighted in telling stories about the King to his friends. However the banter was never meant unkindly, and beneath it all there was, as the King had written in his letter of condolence after the Duchess of York's death, 'the most unvarying, the steadiest affection between them.' Despite the occasional arguments, their past differences were long forgotten.

Early in 1825, a bill was introduced giving relief to the Roman Catholics, and passed the House of Commons by twenty-one votes. When the House of Lords met in April, the Duke produced a petition from the Dean and Chapter of the Collegiate Church of Windsor, begging that no concessions should be made to the Roman Catholics. His solemn and emotional speech in the House that day, piously invoking his father's memory, and affirming his Protestant convictions, left the radicals and Catholics in no doubt that as heir to the throne, and probably King before very long, there was no hope of the Emancipation Bill becoming law. As Lord Melbourne would later tell the Duke's niece, by then Queen Victoria, 'Your uncle the Duke of York declared many times that he would have gone to the scaffold sooner than give way about the Roman Catholics.'

The Duke had his champions among the public, the Protestants being fervently grateful to him for defending their cause. The King, they knew, did not have the heart to stand up to his ministers, and would grant them anything within reason in return for a quiet life; but the veteran of the war against France was made of sterner stuff.

Frederick, Duke of York, from a Worcester bust in unglazed china

In private, the Duke was very different. Princess Victoria of Kent remembered him as 'tall, rather large, very kind but extremely shy', and giving her 'beautiful presents', such as a donkey to ride, and planning little amusements for her, including a Punch and Judy show in the garden.

Reminiscing in 1872, long after she had become Queen, Victoria recalled arriving at the Royal Lodge as a girl of seven, and the King taking her by the hand affectionately, saying, 'Give me your little paw.' 'He was large and gouty but with a wonderful sense of dignity and charm of manner. He wore the wig which was so much worn in those days. Then he said he would give me something for me to wear, and that was his picture set in diamonds, which was worn by the Princesses as an order to a blue ribbon on the left shoulder. I was very proud of this – and Lady Conyngham pinned it on my shoulder.'[5] Next day, she was invited for a drive to Virginia Water in the King's phaeton, sitting between him and 'Aunt Gloucester'. In her old age, she told her granddaughter Princess Marie Louise of Schleswig-Holstein how the coachman had given her a ride, but left the Duchess of Kent to continue on foot – 'most rude!' She also recalled how the King paid great attention to her half-sister Princess Feodora, 'and some people fancied he might marry her!' Even in his last years, thoughts of remarriage and providing the kingdom with an heir crossed the King's mind, but perhaps even he appreciated how undignified and unpopular it would be for him to seek the hand of a princess almost forty-five years younger than him.

One last shadow was to fall across the Duke of York's declining years. Early in 1826 the Duchess of Rutland died. On his return to London from the funeral at Belvoir Castle, it was noticed that his zest for life seemed to have gone. He was suffering from heart trouble, aggravated by dropsy, and by the summer he was seriously ill. According to his physician, Dr Parr, the Duke's 'fatal habit of sitting up at night – he would play cards so long as anyone would play with him – had led to a fatal dropsy and corrupt state of the blood; for the extremities not getting rest by a recumbent position the blood was determined to them. He found at last that, when he did attempt to lie down, he could not do so, as a feeling of suffocation came on.'[6]

At Brighton during the summer, where he had gone for a change, it first struck him 'that he did not gain ground'. Returning to London, he could not bear the loneliness of his lodging at South Audley Street, and he stayed with the Duke of Rutland in a room overlooking Green Park. Recovering a little, he went to Ascot races in June, but on returning to London, he appeared weaker, and was urged to send for Sir Henry Halford. From the doctor's concern, he knew that his condition must be serious. Warned thus by Sir Herbert Taylor, a close confidant of the family since being attached to the Duke of York's staff during the campaign of 1794–5, and subsequently as King George III's private secretary, he remarked, 'I was not mistaken in my suspicions, and my case is not wholly free from danger; but I depend upon your honour, and you tell me there is more to hope than fear.'[7]

By autumn he was resigned to his death. Princess Sophia, who had always been his favourite sister, came to see him at the Duke of Rutland's house nearly every afternoon. She found him propped up in a crimson chair, wearing a grey dressing gown. As he grew worse, those around him noticed that her presence seemed to give him new strength, while she 'supported herself wonderfully'. When Sophia visited him, 'the manner in which he roused himself when she was announced was very striking.'

At Christmas he made his last will and testament, and two days later the Bishop of London came to administer the sacrament, which Halford, Taylor and Princess Sophia received with him. The Bishop was the most affected of all, while the Princess 'supported herself wonderfully throughout this trying scene, and the Duke was quite free from agitation.'[8]

On new year's day, 1827, the Dukes of Clarence and Sussex visited him, and he received them affectionately, but could no longer speak. After rallying and sinking again over the next few days, he died in the evening of 5 January, after what the doctors called 'a long and painful struggle, borne with exemplary resolution and resignation.'[9]

The King had been too ill to visit his brother, and Sophia wrote to him on 16 January how his letter of condolence 'made me shed tears for the first time since the blow *was struck*, and thus relieved my poor head, for I am still a piece of marble, and can catch myself for ever inclined to call out, "And is it all true?"'[10]

It came as no surprise that the Duke had died deeply in debt. His will had entrusted Taylor and Colonel Stephenson with the task of settling his affairs, and expressing the hope that his property would supply a fund more than sufficient to meet his debts, the residue if any to go to Princess Sophia. 'Of course there is *nothing* to inherit,' she wrote to a friend, 'but the naming me in such a manner has made me feel I am Heir of his *affection*, which is the most precious gift I could receive.'[11]

As Sophia and the Duke of York had always been so close, their sisters were anxious at the effect his death would have on her. Noting that she had been 'the constant soother and comforter to him in his hours of pain', the Landgravine of Hesse-Homburg noted, 'I tremble for the consequences now, for all she most valued and loved is gone.'[12]

The King had always thought that Frederick would make a more suitable King than William, more politically and temperamentally suited to the high office. According to Princess Lieven, what most distressed him about the Duke of York's fatal illness was the prospect of William becoming heir, referring to him bitterly as 'that idiot', and saying sarcastically what a fine King he would be. Yet for all the King's doubts about the bluff quarterdeck manner of the Admiral of the Fleet, it was unlikely that he would have expressed himself in such scathing terms about his brother, particularly to such a notorious gossip as Princess Lieven. William too believed that Frederick would have worn the

Memorial to Frederick, Duke of York, statue by Richard Westmacott on a 124-foot pillar by Richard Wyatt, on the site where Carlton House had stood, unveiled 1834. The cost of £25,000 was reportedly met by a 'voluntary' contribution of a day's pay from every man in the British army. Contemporaries joked that the statue was placed high enough to keep him out of reach of his creditors

crown admirably. On new year's eve, he had written to his son George, saying how he had looked forward to 'poor dear Frederick . . . filling the throne to the advantage of all of us his future subjects. . . . But alas that fond hope is now over and I have therefore if possible stronger reasons to pray to the all-mighty to prolong the *life* and *health* of his present majesty.'[13]

The Duke of York's funeral was held at Windsor Castle on the bitterly cold night of 20 January. Due to an error in the arrangements, the coffin was two hours late arriving at the Chapel. With damp paving stones, and no matting, the occasion took its toll of several of the elderly gentlemen in attendance. Within a few weeks two bishops, five footmen and several soldiers had died, as well as two cabinet ministers who caught severe chills which hastened if not ultimately caused their deaths.[14]

10 'In short a medley of opposite qualities'

Although saddened by his brother Frederick's death, William could hardly pretend that he was not excited at the thought of being King before long. He did not make a very decorous Chief Mourner at the funeral, speaking to everyone very much as usual, and enquiring from a guest how many head of game he had killed on a recent shooting expedition. Creevey noticed that several peers paid more attention to the Duke than they had in the past, and that whenever there was a gap in the proceedings, he turned to the Duke of Sussex, remarking gleefully, 'We shall be treated now, brother Augustus, very differently from what we have been.'

As heir to the throne, the allowance of the Duke and Duchess of Clarence was raised by Parliament. Although the increase granted was less than the figure Lord Liverpool had suggested, the Duke was content. Marriage had thoroughly domesticated him, and husband and wife lived quite frugally. They ate sparingly, much as King George III and Queen Charlotte had done, the Duke usually dining off roast or boiled mutton. Though he enjoyed a glass of sherry, and occasionally wine, the only drink he took in quantity was lemon-flavoured barley water. Their regular travelling companion when they visited Saxe-Meiningen, Dr Beattie, noticed how he looked over all the accounts himself, scrutinizing and balancing everything carefully. Like his father, perhaps it indicated a parsimonious streak, but the Duchess had taught him the value of money; and such attention to detail was warmly approved by the government of a nation impoverished by war and continually having to cope with the extravagance of their sovereign.

The Duke of Clarence was up and dressed every morning by seven o'clock, and after breakfast walked for about an hour. The next two or three hours were devoted to correspondence, and he always answered letters in his own hand. When Beattie suggested that he might do a little less, he answered with a twinkle in his eye that he needed to keep up the practice of letter-writing, as one day he might still have more occasion for it. Then he would walk until dinner, never venturing out in the rain without his galoshes. Companions might innocently suggest a short walk with the Duke, and find themselves taken on an exhausting two-hour stride. On his own, the Duke would think nothing of walking for four hours, generally in the hottest part of the day. If the weather was bad, he would pace up and down the drawing room with the windows wide open. Apart from annual attacks of asthma each June, and regular pains in the legs which were probably gout, his health was good.

In February 1827, the Prime Minister, Lord Liverpool, had a stroke, and the King requested George Canning to form a government. Several other politicians distrusted him and were reluctant to serve under him. Canning felt that his grip on the highest office would be strengthened if he had the support of the heir to the throne, and accordingly decided to revive the office of Lord High Admiral for his benefit.

The post had fallen into abeyance since the death of the last holder, Prince George of Denmark, Queen Anne's husband, in 1708. The Lord High Admiral was not only supreme commander of the Navy, but at the head of naval administration at Whitehall with a seat in cabinet. In the nineteenth century, however, the government thought such powers were too much even for their next sovereign; and it was decided that the Duke should not sit in cabinet, and that the majority of his powers should only be exercised through a council, drawn from officers at the Admiralty.

The Duke was undaunted at the terms set out in his letters of appointment. Like the government, he knew that he would surely succeed to the throne before long, and this was a desirable way of giving him some experience of public affairs. Any mistakes which he might make as Lord High Admiral, and the lessons he would thus learn, were best made now rather than as King, when the results might be disastrous for the country.

At first, all went well. The Duke genially requested that all members of the existing Admiralty Council should stay in their posts to assist him with his new responsibilities. He busied himself sailing around southern ports, while the Duchess, who was a bad sailor, travelled overland to attend the receptions he hosted in the evenings. But he was not content to be a mere figurehead, confining himself to hospitality and making speeches. During the daytime he poked his head round the corners of the dockyards at Portsmouth and Plymouth. The dockers were startled, but flattered, to see this elderly gentleman nosing round the docks quite unattended, chattering away to all and sundry without a trace of pomposity. It was difficult to realize that this man was the heir to and brother of the ailing recluse at Windsor. When not inspecting dockyards, he would hurry round to the Admiralty with a volley of questions on matters which had not been bothered with since the battle of Trafalgar. In the evenings he delighted in giving balls on board his yacht.

When Wellington, who had become Prime Minister in August 1827, tactfully suggested that the Duke's exhausting devotion to duty might undermine his health, the Duke cheerfully replied that 'The eye of the Lord High Admiral does infinite good.' He took matters into his own hands when Admiral Codrington, stationed in the Eastern Mediterranean to assist the French and Russians in defending the Greeks and preventing any massacres by the Turks, destroyed the Turkish fleet at Navarino in October 1827 without explicit Admiralty orders. A belief that the Duke had encouraged Codrington by adding a codicil to his written orders, encouraging him to go in 'and smash those Turks', was probably the result of one of Princess Lieven's exaggerations, but news of the battle certainly delighted him. He promoted a bevy of Codrington's senior oficers, and recommended to the King that the Admiral himself should be awarded the Grand Cross of the Order of the Bath. But the Admiralty were embarrassed and

William Henry, Duke of Clarence, as
Lord High Admiral, 1827

received the Lord High Admiral coldly. The King's speech at the next session of Parliament in January 1828 referred to Navarino as 'this untoward event', and Codrington was recalled and dismissed his post.

Although the Duke displayed a predictable sense of the farcical during his appointment, he was responsible for several long-overdue reforms. He initiated a system of half-yearly reports for each ship in the Navy on their state of readiness for battle, introduced milder punishments and abolished the use of the cat-o'-nine-tails except in the case of mutiny, criticized and resolved to overhaul the lamentable state of naval gunnery, and modified the anachronistic system of promotion. The senior member of the Admiralty Council, Sir George Cockburn, an obstinate, arrogant-minded conservative, resented such encroachment on his powers. He and the Duke had disliked each other for many years, and friction was inevitable.

That the Duke's reforms were popular in the Navy only increased Cockburn's resentment. The Duke established a committee on gunnery and summoned its members to discuss the issues with him at Portsmouth. Cockburn was furious with what he regarded as this interference, and an angry exchange of letters resulted in the Duke calling for his dismissal. The Duke of Wellington was not prepared for this, especially as he knew that should Cockburn resign the entire Council would follow suit. The Prime Minister appealed to the King, who wrote to his brother saying that he regretted the embarrassing position in which he found himself, but he must give way. After threatening to resign, the Duke met Cockburn and Wellington together, and a grudging reconciliation was reached.

However, it was clear that the two men could not work together, and that a further clash was merely a matter of time. While on another inspection of outlying ports, the Duke came across a squadron of ships waiting for the arrival of Admiral Blackwood. Without more ado he hoisted his flag in *Royal Sovereign*, and gleefully ordered his ships out to sea. He remained at sea for several days, while wild rumours circulated about his whereabouts and those of the fleet. Nobody else had any idea where he was. Exasperated, the Duke of Wellington complained to the King. The latter sadly affirmed that, if the Lord High Admiral could not agree to fill his station according to the laws of the country, it would be impossible to retain his services in the present situation.

On 14 August, more in sorrow than in anger, the Duke attended his final council meeting and announced his immediate resignation. His eldest son, George FitzClarence, had been convinced that his frustrated father was close to a nervous breakdown, at irritation with the resistance his reforming zeal met from the Admiralty diehards. Ever one to exaggerate, Princess Lieven said that he was about to end up in a straitjacket. Yet he shook hands magnanimously with Cockburn afterwards, and invited him and several of the other council members who had regularly opposed him, to his birthday party a week later at Bushey. As King George III had remarked, 'William was ever violent when controlled,' but though he might have a sudden temper, he was just as quick to forgive and never bore a grudge.

Moved by his brother's climbdown, the King afterwards studied the terms of the patent of Lord High Admiral and concluded that they were unnecessarily restrictive. He suggested to Wellington that they might be modified, but the Duke was reluctant to open the matter again and said he could not recommend any change. It would have been purely academic, for the office was henceforth abolished.

In March 1827, the Duke of Cumberland was advised by his doctor that the time was right for an operation for cataract. As one eye was very clouded, it was a risk which threatened virtual blindness if anything went wrong. He was prepared to take the risk of 'couching', an operation which involved piercing the cataract to let light through. It was performed in April, and after a few days of waiting with bandanged eyes to know whether it had been successful, the Duke was delighted to find that he could see distant objects far more clearly than he had done for a long time. The effect had been to make him long-sighted instead of short-sighted, and he now had to use glasses for reading and writing, but he was overjoyed to find he could attend military parades and see every line of the corps with the naked eye as well as any other officer.

Unhappily, his son also had problems with poor eyesight. During boyhood he became blind in his right eye, but whether from illness or an accident is not known. The parents lived in fear that the left eye might suffer, and he was indeed completely blind by the age of about twenty.

The Dowager Queen of Württemberg had been cut off for so long from her family in England, that she was always pleased when any of her brothers and sisters came to Germany and visited her. Though she had little desire to see Ernest, the Dukes of Kent and Cambridge had visited her at Louisbourg; Elizabeth of Hesse-Homburg visited her in 1819 and 1820, and in 1821 she saw Princess Augusta at Bessigheim, for 'a very crying meeting'. Augusta was rather startled at the change in her elder sister. 'Had I not had the picture previous to seeing Her, I should not have guessed it was Her,' she wrote to Lady Harcourt. 'She is very large & bulky. Her face is very broad and fat, which makes Her features appear quite small and distended. But what strikes the most is, that from not wearing the least bit of Corset, Her Stomach and Her Hips are something quite extraordinary.'[1] Elizabeth had helped to prepare her for the change, as in November 1819 she had written of her as being 'certainly very large,' and though neat and clean, did not dress to advantage, her hair being very thin, combed flat upon her face, 'which is three or four times larger than it was.'[2]

She had kept up her correspondence with the family, the Harcourts, and others in England, and took an interest in the young nephews and niece. Politics she normally avoided, though once she wrote to King George IV encouraging him to 'put an End to the democratical Meetings which must make every British Heart blush.' Early in 1827 she wished to come to England again, apologizing in advance for being 'troublesome from not being able to go in a shut carriage or walk, my breath being so short that I must be carried downstairs as well as up stairs. However I hope my dear Brother will have patience with my infirmities.'[3] In particular, she looked forward to seeing her goddaughter 'Vicky', now aged eight, 'and hope she will take a little bit of a fancy for me.' Forty-five years later the Princess, now Queen, recalled seeing her aunt driving through the Park in the King's carriage with red liveries and four horses, in a Cap and evening dress, her sister Augusta sitting opposite her, in evening attire, both having just dined with the Duke of Sussex at Kensington. 'She had adopted all the German fashions and spoke broken English – and had not been in England for many many years. She was very kind and good-humoured but very large and unwieldy.'[4]

Her expedition to England was partly for medical reasons. Like several of the family, she suffered from dropsy, and none of the German doctors could treat her satisfactorily, so Sir Astley Cooper and others were called in to attend to her while she was in England. She underwent the operation of tapping while staying at St James's Palace. For a while she stayed at Frogmore, where she fell ill and was unable to venture out for several days. Once she was strong enough to drive to Royal Lodge, she stayed with the King. For her amusement he arranged a dinner-party in a large tent on the banks of Virginia Water, and afterwards they rowed out to the island. After coffee they took a picturesque row by moonlight, and, added Princess Augusta, her brother and sister 'were as happy as it is possible to be.' In earlier years, relations between brother and eldest sister had been distant, probably because of her inveterate tale-telling. She had been hurt at only learning of the date of the forthcoming wedding of Princess Charlotte to Prince Leopold from the papers. But in the evening of their days, much was forgiven and forgotten.

The Dowager Queen may have had a premonition that it was the last time she would see her family in England. Soon after her return to Germany she fell ill again. Visits from her brother Adolphus, her sister Elizabeth, and old friends revived her spirits, although she was evidently dying. Early in October 1828 she entertained Lord and Lady Shrewsbury to dinner, and 'kept up for nearly two hours a most interesting conversation upon a variety of topics.' Two days later, a Sunday, as was her usual custom, she asked her English maid to read her a sermon. After listening attentively, she remarked, 'There, my dear, you have done, and I thank you – you will never read me another.'[5] Next day she asked the King of Württemberg to bring his family to her bedside. As she put out one hand to him in farewell, she had an apoplectic seizure and died. She was sixty-one years of age.

Though he had not seen her since her departure from England as a bride, the Duke of Cumberland – who had less reason than any to remember her with affection – observed that 'one cannot help feeling deeply when one branch of the old tree drops off.'[6]

By this time, King George IV was reluctant to show himself in public. Grotesquely fat and swollen-legged, he could only walk with difficulty, and he disguised his facial ravages with much greasepaint. Ever sensitive to ridicule, he would not even allow his servants to stare at him, and when he drove out into the park at Windsor, a groom had to ride out first, ordering everyone to retire, so that His Majesty should not be seen. In December 1826 he made a rare appearance at the Drury Lane Theatre, and was rapturously received, with

Windsor Castle, showing the heightened Round Tower and other modifications carried out during the reign of George IV

deafening applause and repeated singing of 'God save the King', but he looked bored and displeased by the attention. Mrs Harriett Arbuthnot, one of the more sympathetic diarists of his reign, echoed the thoughts of many when she said sadly that he would be much more popular if he appeared more often in public.

Those who knew him well could testify that he was not the selfish ogre of popular legend. One of the first acts of his reign had been to abolish the legal use of torture in Hanover. At home, he warmly encouraged various parliamentary measures taken to lessen the severity of legal punishment, such as the abolition of the flogging of female prisoners. He was also interested in the protection of animals from cruelty, and as a close friend of the Irish parliamentarian Richard Martin, he encouraged legislation making wanton ill-treatment of animals a criminal offence. Not only the family benefited from his financial generosity. Dr Knighton, his secretary and formerly his physician, would say that he only had to hear of anybody in distress, and he genuinely wished to help. Exceptionally kind to artists and actors, he gave liberally to countless others who aroused his admiration or pity.

By 1828, the issue of Catholic emancipation in England could no longer be ignored. As a dynasty, the Hanoverians were traditionally opposed to it; they had been called to the throne because they were Protestants, and considered themselves bound by their Coronation oath to uphold the Protestant faith. Any concession to Catholicism would be a violation of their oath and undermine the British constitution. It was a matter which the government hoped to avoid by maintaining a neutral stance. However, it was forced into the open by the election of Daniel O'Connell, leader of the movement for Catholic relief, but as a staunch Roman Catholic himself he was barred from sitting in the House of Commons. Buoyant at his victory, the Catholics announced that at the next election they would contest every seat in Ireland. All but the most passionate supporters of the established church now saw that there was little constitutional reason for keeping Catholics out of Parliament. The possibility of a Stuart restoration to the British throne had long since passed, and the Protestants' most fervent supporter in England, the Duke of York, was dead. Although the Duke of Cumberland – who spent most of his time in Hanover – was traditionally almost as fervently pro-Protestant as his late brother, he was reassured by a talk with the Duke of Wellington, who expressed himself as against the principle of making concessions to the Catholics, and maintained that any negotiation with the Pope was contrary to the principles of English law. Yet Cumberland did not altogether trust the Prime Minister, fearing that he would be unable or unwilling to resist the demands of his ministers.

He was right. During the summer of 1828 the government decided to bring in an Emancipation Bill, partly as they hoped to cling to office by stealing a plank from the Whig platform, partly as they thought that emancipation might solve the Irish problem and avert the threat of civil war over there.

By the time the King attended the Council to approve the speech for the opening of Parliament in February 1829, ill health and ministerial pressure had worn down his opposition to emancipation. The Duke of Cumberland returned to England, maintaining that Wellington had reneged on his word, and thinking it would be an ineffective sop to Ireland and do nothing to avert civil strife in the country. Hurrying to Windsor, he persuaded the King to withdraw his support. The Duke of Wellington had heard rumours that Cumberland was planning to assemble a mob of 20,000 Protestants to march on Windsor to petition the King and frighten him into refusing to grant any concessions. If this was true, Wellington declared, he would happily send him to the Tower 'as soon as look at him'.

When the King told the officers of his household to vote against the Bill, Wellington announced that the government would resign unless assured of his complete support, and asked him to order Cumberland out of the country. The King prevaricated, and a few days later Wellington and two of his senior ministers went to Windsor. Fortified with repeated sips of brandy, the King talked, raged, wept for five hours, and accepted their resignations. The Duke of Cumberland and his fervent ally Lord Eldon threatened to form a government, but although they were supported by Protestant champions in the Lords, they had few in the Commons. A messenger therefore went from Windsor to Wellington to say that the government's resignation was not accepted.

A lively debate ensued in the House of Lords. The Duke of Cumberland vigorously denounced the Bill, which he described as 'one of the most outrageous measures ever proposed to Parliament.' The Catholics, however, found an unexpected ally in the Duke of Clarence. The heir to the throne had been rather ambivalent in his attitude. His pro-Protestant fervour had been more a matter of family loyalty rather than personal conviction, but now that the Duke of York was dead, he had evidently had a change of heart and realized that the time for change had come. On the night before the debate, he had dined with Lord Ellenborough, and told a long story about Lord St Vincent and a host of many other Admirals, 'and supposed them all to put up their heads, and express delight at seeing the Irish sailors who had fought the lower deck guns emancipated.' Carried away by his powers of oratory in the Lords, he attacked his brother, saying that he had been abroad for so long that he had almost forgotten 'what is due to the freedom of debate in this country.' When the Duke of Cumberland rose to reply to the speech, he said that he objected strongly to having his conduct described as 'facetious' and he had forgotten the other epithet. 'Infamous,' added William helpfully. At one stage, the King threatened that if made to give way he would retire to Hanover, and leave his subjects a 'Catholic' King in the shape of the newly pro-Catholic Duke of Clarence, but nobody took this seriously.

True to his principles, the Duke of Sussex was a faithful ally of the Catholics. With enthusiasm if dubious relevance, he traced in his speeches the history of the doctrinal disputes which had shaken the Church of Rome in the Middle Ages. During one spell of oratory, a Tory peer whispered to his neighbour that His Royal Highness was 'deep in the Councils of Trent.' 'I could wish it was the river,' the other replied wearily.

The Bill was passed in the Lords, and Cumberland was observed to leave the House looking 'like a disappointed fiend'. The government did not trust him and his influence on the King, and feared that he would continue to make

Ernest, Duke of Cumberland, by George Dawe, 1828

mischief. The cabinet suggested that he should be made Viceroy of Hanover, and the Duke of Cambridge recalled and appointed Commander-in-Chief. Wellington vetoed the suggestion; though he privately thought Cambridge 'mad as Bedlam', he was popular and efficient in his present post, and unless he offered to resign it was out of the question.

Ernest decided to settle in England again, sending for the Duchess and their son to join him. *The Times* acidly commented that the Duke and his family were coming to live at Windsor, and would 'occupy that portion of the building called the Devil's Tower.' In fact he reopened his house at Kew, and sent Prince George to the Eldon School, Vauxhall. This enabled him to draw the £6,000 per year which Parliament had voted him on condition the boy was educated in England.

The Duke of Cumberland was irritated by the pressure on the King to send him back to Hanover. Moreover, the King had told him in an emotional moment that he could not bear the thought of his leaving, perhaps for fraternal reasons, and perhaps as he had felt that after giving way to the pressures of the more liberal Tories, he needed his influential (if highly disliked) brother at home in the Lords to give some heart to the status quo. Once it was known that the Cumberlands were staying in England, an extraordinary series of slanders against the Duke began. There was no doubt that they were intended, and timed, to drive him out of the country for political ends.

The first was a rumour that Captain Thomas Garth, son of Princess Sophia, had been fathered on her by Ernest, and that General Garth had been begged by King George III to acknowledge the boy's paternity. Shortly before the Emancipation Bill, General Garth had become seriously ill, and did not think he would live for long. He had apparently possessed what were described as 'very incriminating' papers concerning Thomas's parentage, and passed them to his son. The latter attempted to blackmail the royal family, suggesting to Herbert Taylor that the documents should be deposited in Snow's bank in return for a lump sum and a pension of £3,000 per annum. General Garth unexpectedly recovered, and demanded the return of the papers. Thomas refused to do so, as he had realized how easy it would be to make money out of blackmail. He then attempted to obtain an injunction against Taylor on the grounds that the papers were not deposited in the bank as promised; Taylor countered with the accusation that Thomas had disclosed their contents to certain newspapers which relieved him of his obligation.

The story was leaked to less reputable elements in the press. Who started the rumours that Ernest was Garth's father was never known, though the finger of suspicion pointed at Princess Lieven.[7] It was too far-fetched to be possible, but society gossip-mongers and lampoonists rubbed their hands at the idea. Cumberland's opponents whispered that only fear of exposure of this terrible secret had made the King pay heed to his advice to withhold consent to the Emancipation Bill. It seems not to have occurred to those who took this view that it would have been an act of madness for the Duke to have threatened the King with a weapon which he could not use without destroying himself.[8] Even the Duke's worst enemies could never have accused him of such gross stupidity.

Though his more respectable opponents publicly denounced the lie, fresh scandals soon followed. In July 1829, the press reported that the Duke had been thrown out of the house of the Lord Chancellor, Lord Lyndhurst, after assaulting his wife. So many different versions of the story were circulated that it is impossible to know which to believe, but the most likely (if the least lurid) was that he met Lady Lyndhurst at a reception, or called at her home socially, and allowed his tongue to run away with him, haranguing her over her husband's political cowardice. His language may have been blunt, even insulting; but to suggest that he physically attacked her, or indeed attempted rape, was gross exaggeration.

In April 1829 the Landgrave of Hesse-Homburg died of influenza, complicated by an infection to the wound in his leg. Though grieved by his death, his widow was grateful that she had been granted the pleasure of a married life denied to many; 'No woman was ever more happy than I was for eleven years, and they will often be lived over again in the memory of the heart.'[9] From his sickbed at Windsor, the King sent a generous donation to ensure that his sister should suffer no financial hardship.

After her husband's accession as Landgrave in 1820, Elizabeth had been allowed a free hand in decorating the old castle at Homburg. Now, in widowhood, she threw herself into her art with renewed enthusiasm. In the evenings, she wrote to a friend, she would read and work until 11 p.m., 'now I have taken up my drawing and am painting fruit with success.' Her drawing master gave her renewed inspiration; 'he proves there is nothing so fascinating as one's pencil.' Many of the hangings and much of the upholstery in her apartments at Bad Homburg were worked or painted by her, and with the assistance of her architect she designed and helped build a number of small buildings in the castle grounds.

At Kensington Palace, her sister Princess Sophia was playing an interesting role. She had become friendly with Sir John Conroy, the Duchess of Kent's Comptroller, and had appointed him her Comptroller as well. Conroy was a tactless and impatient man, and although married with a family, he behaved indiscreetly. Though it was unlikely that either of the royal ladies was ever his mistress, Princess Victoria was nauseated by his flirtatious and over-familiar behaviour with them. Sophia was regarded as Conroy's spy, and in 1829 the Duchess of Kent dismissed her lady-in-waiting, Baroness Späth, ostensibly as she wanted to surround herself and her daughter with English ladies, but really because she was jealous of her daughter's affection for the faithful Späth. She let it be known that she intended to dismiss the equally faithful Baroness Lehzen for similar reasons. In a memorandum of 14 October to Conroy, Sophia, 'the spy', reported a conversation with the Duchess of Clarence, who was grieved that Späth should have been dismissed after so many years of service. The question of Lehzen's departure arose, and the Duchess said it would be impossible to find a second Lehzen. Princess Sophia remarked coldly that a second Lehzen was not required. In the event Lehzen kept her place, as King George IV and the Duke of Clarence recognized how devoted Princess Victoria was to her, and acted as her protectors.

During the winter of 1829–30, caricatures, scurrilous articles and crude broadsheets hinted at an affair between the Duke of Cumberland and Lady Graves, wife of a former member of the King's Household, and Comptroller to the Duke of Sussex.

For several weeks all three shrugged off the rumours, and Lord Graves made a point of being seen in public with his wife in order to show the world that nothing was wrong with their marriage. Yet it was all to no avail, and by January 1830 Lord Graves was so worried that he confronted the Duke of Cumberland, who had long been a close friend. The latter, long since hardened to scurrilous

Frederica, Duchess of Cumberland, engraving by Thomson after a drawing by Carbonnier, c. 1830

attacks, advised him to ride out the storm. On 5 February Lord Graves called on Cumberland and seemed in better spirits than he had been for some time, but the following morning he received another set of insulting cuttings, with an anonymous letter saying that he had only rejoined his wife because Cumberland had bribed him. In despair he cut his throat.

Although the coroner at the inquest attributed his suicide to a fit of depression (to which he had long been prone), gossips asserted that the Duke had driven a cuckolded husband to take his own life. *The Times* published an article the day after the inquest, headed 'Melancholy Suicide in High Life', drawing readers' attention to the other 'mysterious and inexplicable suicide – with which a name that has been so often mentioned of late was also connected.' This was an underhand attempt to remind the public of Sellis's death in 1810, and led some to believe – or affect to believe – that both men had been murdered by the Duke. Lord Ellenborough, a political adversary of the Duke, wrote gleefully that Graves's suicide would surely drive him 'out of the field' (the country). Although the Duchess was distressed and ill with worry, and the Duke himself grew haggard and thinner than ever, he would not be shifted, and wrote to Lord Eldon: 'That Party thought to *frighten* me and make me leave the country but by God *nothing shall.*' To Lord Wynford, he said, 'If you can think me such a damned coward as to run away, by God I am *not* and will face that and every other false and infamous libell and cabal.'[10]

By this time the King was dying. He slept badly, and seemed in permanent need of company and reassurance during the night, ringing his bell several times each hour to ask the time, or to ask his valet to pour him a glass of water from the jug by his bed. Greville reported that his servants came and opened the window curtains at 6 or 7 a.m. He breakfasted and did as much business as he could in bed, reading the newspapers through, getting up at 6 p.m. in the evening, and going to bed between 10 and 11 p.m. His sight was failing, and sometimes he alarmed his doctors by going almost black in the face as he struggled for breath. Afraid that he was about to have a heart attack, they would hand him a large glass of brandy, which made him feel so much better he would suddenly decide to go for a long ride in his carriage. Despite lack of exercise, his appetite was still prodigious. On 9 April 1830, Wellington noted, his breakfast consisted of a pidgeon and beef steak pie, three parts of a bottle of Mozelle, a glass of champagne, two glasses of port, followed by a glass of brandy.

The Duke of Cumberland, with his wife and son, spent much time at Windsor during March and April. The King, he wrote sadly, was 'as blind as a beetle', in pain, his legs alarmingly swollen with the dropsy. Yet still the King remained cheerful, delighting in mimickry and chaff with Ernest. The Duke of Clarence, another regular visitor, was deeply concerned, always returning to Bushey 'greatly affected and crying like a child'. The Duchess, who with her lack of ambition for high office dreaded becoming Queen Consort, felt that they were 'passing through a very dark time'. Yet the Duke was so excited at his imminent accession that he wrote to the Duke of Wellington reassuring him that he meant to keep him in office upon accession, an unconstitutional action which the Duke wisely ignored.

The King's babblings made little sense. After cheerfully telling his brothers or friends that he would be dead by the next Saturday, a few minutes later he would be discussing the horses he wanted to buy for the races at Ascot. Another time he reminisced about being told as a young man that he should stick to his father; 'as long as you adhere to your father you will be a great and happy man. But if you separate yourself from him you will be nothing and an unhappy one.' 'And by God I never forgot that advice, and acted upon it all my life,' he went on. Those who heard this declaration in astonishment felt that it was some kind of belated atonement for the frustrations George III had felt with his eldest son.

By June his heart, enfeebled by a series of minor attacks and strokes, could no longer withstand the strain. Early in the morning of 26 June, he was clutching the hand of Sir Wathen Waller, the physician sitting up with him, and suddenly exclaimed, 'My dear boy! This is death!' A few minutes later, as the clock struck quarter past three, he breathed his last.

The nation, as a whole, greeted his passing with indifference. His profligacy, indulgence, and reactionary political views were all that most people remembered, and the crown was held in low esteem. Expecting some kind of emotional demonstration in the city of London, John Cam Hobhouse noted that he saw 'nothing like grief or joy – only a bustle in the streets.'

The Times remarked bluntly that 'there never was an individual less regretted by his fellow creatures. . . . If he ever had a friend – a devoted friend in any rank of life – we protest that the name of him has never reached us.' With more

King George IV, equestrian statue by Francis Chantrey, Trafalgar Square, with the National Gallery and the pillars from the front of Carlton House in the background

loyalty than accuracy, the *Morning Post* mourned 'the loss of a monarch so conspicuously endowed with all the qualities calculated to endear him to the hearts of his subjects.' Among the few to appreciate his contradictory character was the Duke of Wellington, who spoke of 'the most extraordinary compound of talent, wit, buffoonery, obstinacy and good feeling – in short a medley of opposite qualities with a great preponderance of good – that I ever saw in any character in my life.'

Perhaps the most understanding tribute was paid by his sister Elizabeth, widowed Landgravine of Hesse-Homburg, who wrote that her eldest brother 'was *all heart,* and had he been left to his own judgment would ever have been kind and just. But people got hold of him, and Flattery did more harm in that quarter than anything.' The contrast with their father was acute; 'My father ever acted on the finest of feelings, and as an honest man, and with his ideas of justice would never have done what a man of the world would do; but different characters must always act differently. My Father was a man after God's own heart, the finest, purest, and most perfect of all characters; the other God made perfect but the world spoilt him.'[11]

11 'An immense improvement on the last unforgiving animal'

As dawn broke during the early hours of 26 June, Sir Henry Halford rode along the chestnut avenue of Bushey Park. At 6 a.m. the third son of King George III, who had been known for over forty years as the Duke of Clarence, was woken by his servants and told that the doctor wished to see him. Without being told, he knew what the news was.

Within hours, he was on his way to Windsor, with a long piece of black crepe flowing from the crown of his white hat, grinning and bowing to everybody as he passed. As yet very few people knew that King George IV was dead, and still fewer knew what the new King looked like. A small crowd had gathered outside St James's Palace, and as he drove into the palace a faint, dutiful cheer was heard.

The Privy Councillors were all assembled to be sworn in by their new sovereign. He had lived in such retirement that few knew anything about him, beyond his reputation for being somewhat eccentric and given to salty language, yet more affable, less remote or pompous than his predecessor. They were standing in groups, talking solemnly together, when the doors were suddenly flung open and a short, red-faced figure bustled in. Without acknowledging anyone, he walked up to the table, seized a pen, and signed boldly, 'William R.'. Then he remarked, 'This is a damned bad pen you have given me.' One by one the Councillors knelt to kiss his hand.

The late King's funeral took place at night on 15 July, with much solemnity but little grief. King William, as chief mourner, walked behind the two-ton coffin. Dressed in a long purple cloak, relieved only by the brilliance of the Star of the Order of the Garter, his train was carried by his nephew Prince George of Cumberland. The congregation were astonished to see the King suddenly dart up to Lord Strathavon, greeting him with a hearty handshake. They were further embarrassed to notice him nodding to left and right as he recognized friends in the congregation. After two hours, as the anthem was being sung, he rose from his seat, thanked the Earl Marshal genially for making all the arrangements, and walked out.

These touches of affability were not isolated. A few days later, the King made his first official public appearance reviewing the Guards, wearing military uniform for the first time. After it was over, he changed back into ordinary clothes, and decided to take a stroll down St James's Street. Meeting a friend, Mr Watson Taylor, both men strolled along arm in arm. Members of White's Club were astonished to hear a noisily enthusiastic crowd coming past their windows, looked out and saw the King being kissed on the cheek by a street-walker. Thinking he might be in danger, they rushed out to form an improvised bodyguard, and escorted the King (still holding on to Mr Taylor) safely to his palace. The King was a little startled but unconcerned, and in thanking them for their assistance, said, 'Oh, never mind all this; when I have walked about a few times they will get used to it, and will take no notice.'

Thus did His Majesty's loyal subjects observe the contrast between him and his late brother. 'Though our adored sovereign is either mad or very foolish,' commented the diarist Emily Eden, 'he is an immense improvement on the last unforgiving animal, who died growling sulkily in his den at Windsor. This man at least *wishes* to make everybody happy, and everything he has done has been benevolent.'[1] He never appreciated that there were times when his natural bonhomie was slightly misplaced, and how thin the line was between affability and lack of dignity. Yet he brought a reassuringly human touch to the monarchy, at a time when it stood in low esteem. 'This is not a new reign,' commented the Duke of Wellington, 'it is a new dynasty.'

King William was quick to show himself conscientious in discharging his duties as a sovereign. In his last months, King George IV had become so indolent that he refused to sign state papers altogether, and his brother had a backlog of several thousand to see to. Queen Adelaide sat beside him as he worked laboriously through the piles of documents, helping him at intervals to bathe his cramped fingers in a bowl of warm water. Wellington claimed that he had done more business with him in ten minutes than with his predecessor in as many days. The King was quick to grasp problems concerning matters of state, giving his own views 'with perfect candour and fairness', and relishing contradiction, 'in order that he might come to a full understanding with his ministers.'

The new reign brought the Duke of Sussex back into favour at court. Greville noted approvingly that the King 'is very well with all his family, particularly the Duke of Sussex.' He attended King William's first levee in July, and was appointed Ranger of the Royal Parks, the first honour he had received from the Crown since being made a peer.

At the end of July, the King dissolved Parliament, as a new House of Commons had to be elected after the sovereign's death. The election campaign coincided with the abdication of King Louis XVIII of France, and the accession of his more democratic Bourbon rival as King Louis Philippe – a striking reminder of the democratic forces of reform afoot in Europe. Fifty seats were gained by the Whigs; Wellington was left in office with a small Tory majority. The Tories were split, as their right wing had not forgiven Wellington and Peel for introducing Catholic emancipation. After defeat in the Commons in November, the government resigned, and with some trepidation the King asked Lord Grey to form a Whig administration.

One of Grey's first objectives was to pass a Reform Bill for England and Wales. Introduced in March 1831, it proposed to transfer 168 seats from small

Queen Adelaide, by Sir William Beechey

boroughs to large towns and counties, increasing the franchise by nearly 50 per cent. The Tories, who had most to lose from the abolition of rotten boroughs, agreed to let it pass unchallenged on the first reading, but they were determined to defeat it on the second. It passed its second reading by one vote, thanks to the votes of more moderate Tories. In April the government was defeated in Committee stage, and the King agreed to dissolve Parliament. The subsequent election compaign resulted in a comfortable majority for the Whigs and for reform, and in July the Bill passed its second reading with a majority of 136.

On 8 September 1831 the King and Queen were crowned at Westminster Abbey. The King had not wanted a Coronation at all, calling it a 'useless and ill-timed expense', and consulted legal opinion on the possibility of dispensing with it altogether. He was told, though, that some such ceremony was required for swearing the oath before Lords and Commons, and the Duke of Cumberland demanded the Coronation in its entirety as some compensation for the King's support for the Reform Bill. Still, the King was determined that there should be a considerably curtailed ceremony, shorn of many of the outrageous trappings of his brother's in 1821. Its final cost was about one-seventh of the previous one. When Tory peers, smarting from what they regarded as his Whig partisanship, threatened to boycott the 'Half-Crownation', he retorted that from this he would expect 'greater convenience of room and less heat'.

After the ceremony he gave a large private banquet at St James's, asking his guests to join him in a toast to 'the land we live in'. With one eye on the Duke of Cumberland, he said, 'I think the Coronation has been unnecessary but I am quite as anxious as before the ceremony to watch over the liberties of my people.'

This declaration was to be put to the test in the ever-rising temperature surrounding the Reform Bill and the Whig government. There was disorder in the industrial towns, which had most to gain from the increase in franchise proposed, and even the royal family themselves were not immune. Mobs surrounded and attacked the carriages of the King and Queen, travelling separately, as they returned to St James's Palace.

Conflict between the Commons and the Lords was inevitable. Twice in the last quarter of 1831, the Whigs introduced modified Bills which passed the Commons but were defeated by the Tory Lords. With riots in Bristol, after which order was restored only by the cavalry, the threat of major unrest if not revolution grew apace. In January 1832, Lord Grey asked the King to create a small number of Whig peers to ensure the Bill's passage. The King was reluctant, seeing this as unconstitutional, but later assented so to do 'if the dreaded necessity arose.' In April the Bill was narrowly passed by the Lords, who were anxious at the threat of being 'swamped' with new creations, but a month later the government was defeated in the Lords at the committee stage. Grey informed the King that unless a sufficient number of peers was created to pass the Bill, his government would resign. With regret, the King accepted their resignations, and asked the Duke of Wellington to form an administration to carry through a Bill more acceptable to the Lords than that of Grey.

Though Wellington had been a bitter opponent of reform, he realized the expediency of such a measure. The Tories, however, were still deeply divided, and he was unable to form a government. Grey and the Whig ministry were

'A Cheap Coronation for the Good of a Trading Community', cartoon by Robert Seymour, September 1831, mocking the frugality of King William IV's Coronation. The outer figures represent Lord Brougham (Lord Chancellor) and Earl Grey (Prime Minister)

therefore recalled, with a promise wrung from the reluctant King to create as many peers as necessary to force the measure through the Lords. Rather than see the peerage thus cheapened, the Tory Lords and bishops followed Wellington's advice, most absented themselves from the division, and nearly two years of bitter struggle culminated in the Bill being given the royal assent on 7 June 1832.

In retrospect, the monarchy was fortunate that William was King at the time. As Roger Fulford remarked a century later, the skill with which he met the reform struggle can be appreciated by imagining what would have happened if either of his next surviving brothers had occupied the throne instead. The Duke of Cumberland, as King Ernest, might possibly have allowed Grey to form an administration, but he would never have granted a dissolution in April 1831, and would have relied on an extreme Tory government to stamp out the enthusiasm for reform – and been driven off the throne within months. On the other hand the Duke of Sussex, as King Augustus, would have sided so completely with the Whigs that he would have put the Royal Prerogative at the disposal of Grey's administration, and risked transforming many of the moderate Whigs into bitter opponents of reform, thus making it only possible for the Bill to be passed by a display of arbitrary sovereignty not seen since the Stuart era.[3] In fact the latter temporarily disgraced himself, by attempting to present his brother with a sharply-worded petition from the political union at Birmingham. The King did not take it seriously, but he temporarily forbade his brother to come to court.

For several years, the Duke of Sussex had been on friendly terms with Lady Cecilia Buggin, whose husband Sir George Buggin, a City merchant, had died in 1825. Lady Augusta Murray had died at Ramsgate on 5 March 1830 after several years' illness. The Duke was saddened; 'When one looks back to events of *thirty seven years ago* one cannot do it without a sigh.'[2] Their daughter Mademoiselle d'Este had kept in close touch with her father, and spent much time at Court in attendance on Queen Adelaide.

On 2 May 1831 the Duke married Lady Cecilia, who had taken her maiden name of Underwood after her first husband's death. He knew better than to fight against the Royal Marriages Act, though had his brother not been so preoccupied with other political matters during his reign, it was possible that he might have enlisted support in having it repealed. For the time being, however, he made no effort to attempt to gain a peeress's title for her.

King William IV and Queen Adelaide divided their time between London, Windsor and Brighton. Though they retained Clarence House, their main home in the capital was St James's Palace. The King disliked Buckingham Palace, in spite of his brother's alterations which were nearing completion, calling it 'a most ill contrived house', and when the Houses of Parliament were burnt to the ground in 1834, he offered it to the government as a replacement.

At Windsor he opened the East Terrace to the public, though he objected when they scribbled their names on the statues. Recognizing the need for economy after his brother's extravagances, he cut the castle staff, replaced the

King William IV, from a biscuit porcelain bust

162

German band with a smaller English one, and dismissed the French cooks, provoking a grumble from the gourmet Lord Dudley, a regular guest at court, about 'cold pâtés and hot champagne'. The more exotic animals and birds in the royal menagerie were sent to London Zoo, and a large collection of paintings and other treasures – 'damned expensive taste', in the King's words – was given to the nation. The royal yachts were reduced from five to two, and part of the Royal Lodge at Windsor was demolished, as were the Royal Mews in Central London, clearing an area for the public which would later be developed as Trafalgar Square. Only at Brighton, however, did he feel free to 'cast off the trammels of royalty' and indulge his penchant for entertaining.

His reign brought a new respectability to court, although some found it dull after the splendours of King George IV. After dinner the Queen did little but her needlework and knitting, while the King nodded off in his chair, occasionally waking to mutter, 'Exactly so, Ma'am,' to guests, and then going back to sleep. At the Queen's request, gamblers, drunkards and their like were barred from court. She declined to receive the very rich, fashionable Duchess of St Albans, widow of Coutts the banker, as she had previously been 'an actress of doubtful reputation' – a stricture which the King must have found embarrassing.

Though the King had come through the storms of Reform unscathed, no such fortune heralded his role in a change of government two years later. When Lord Grey resigned the premiership in July 1834 and was succeeded by Lord Melbourne, the King was concerned at some of his cabinet appointments, notably that of Lord John Russell, whom he regarded as a 'dangerous radical'. Matters came to a head in November when Russell was chosen as Leader of the House of Commons. Fearing that such an appointment would lead to further resignations in the government, the King vetoed Melbourne's decision, asked him to resign, and sent for the Leader of the Opposition, Sir Robert Peel, to form a Tory administration.

In an attempt to strengthen his position, Peel went to the country in January 1835, but the results failed to give him a majority government. After heading a minority administration for several precarious weeks, he resigned in April, and the King was forced to recall Melbourne. His relations with the ministry were far from amicable, however, and when asked whether he would be entertaining on the customary scale during Ascot week, he remarked irritably that he could not give dinners without inviting the ministers, 'and I would rather see the devil than any one of them in my house.'

There was no escape for the King from political arguments at home. The ardently pro-Tory Queen had feared eventual revolution if the Reform Bill was passed, and prayed that she would behave as bravely as Queen Antoinette if the same fate should befall her, while the FitzClarences and the King's surviving sisters in Britain were equally extreme Tories. Though they knew better than to attempt to influence their brother unduly, at heart he was a family man, and he was distressed that he should seem so out of step with them. To the Duchess of Gloucester, he admitted tearfully that 'I feel my crown tottering on my head.'

Like his predecessor, King William particularly liked to have Mary close to

*Royal William Victualling Yard,
Stonehouse, Plymouth,
surmounted by a statue of King
William IV by John Rennie*

him at times of stress. The Duchess of Gloucester had spent much time with the dying King George IV, and William also found her company sympathetic. She seemed more fond of her two eldest surviving brothers than of her own kindly but uninspiring husband.

When the Duke's health was failing, Earl Grey noted that 'if he dies all I can say is he won't leave a greater fool behind than himself.' The Duchess nursed him devotedly in his last days, his cause of death in November 1834 being 'the bursting of a scrofulous swelling in the head.' The ever-jaundiced Princess Lieven suggested that his widow would now make a great improvement in health from her constant minor complaints; 'There is nothing so bad for the health as small daily worries, and nothing so trying as continual *ennui*.' When the widowed Landgravine of Hesse-Homburg came to visit her the following spring, she was pleasantly surprised to find her in such cheerful spirits.

On her return to England, the Landgravine was unimpressed by the changes in London, which had altered so much in the seventeen years since she had left; 'all is gone of what formerly was familiar to me, so that I came home not knowing where I have been, or what I have seen.'[4] At Windsor it took her courage to enter 'the Cathedral', as the family called St George's Chapel, for both parents and so many members of the family had been laid to rest since she was last there.

Queen Adelaide was still in her late thirties when her husband ascended the throne, and from time to time the press announced that she was with child again. 'Damned stuff,' was the King's bitter comment. Yet he harboured no jealousy of his niece Princess Victoria of Kent. He and the Queen were fond of the girl who was now heir to the throne, and were saddened at seeing so little of her. The King detested her mother, the widowed Duchess of Kent, who made her contempt for the King and the FitzClarences evident. She had caused offence at the start of his reign by demanding that, as mother of the heir to the throne, she should be treated as the Dowager Princess of Wales, and granted an income commensurate with such rank. A series of unofficial royal progresses around England, with the Duchess and her secretary, John Conroy, showing off the Princess to her future subjects, angered the King still more. The breach was widened by the behaviour of Princess Sophia, who maliciously repeated all the King's impatient criticisms of the Duchess to her. Every evening after dinner she would visit the Duchess's apartments at Kensington Palace and regale her with the latest tittle-tattle.

This feud came to a head in the summer of 1836, when the King invited the Duchess and her daughter to Windsor for the Queen's birthday on 13 August, requesting them to stay for his birthday (his seventy-first) on 21 August and a celebration dinner the next day. The Duchess ignored the Queen's birthday and

Victoire, Duchess of Kent

announced that she would arrive on 20 August. Indignant at this insult to his wife, the King was angered even more when told that his sister-in-law had appropriated a suite of rooms at Kensington Palace in defiance of his previous orders.

The dinner was attended by over a hundred guests, with Princess Victoria opposite him and the Duchess on his right. After his health had been drunk, he rose to his feet and delivered an angry speech in which he announced: 'I trust in God that my life may be spared for nine months longer, after which period, in the event of my death, no regency would take place. I should then have the satisfaction of leaving the royal authority to the personal exercise of that young

King William IV, by Sir David Wilkie, 1837

lady [pointing to the Princess], the heiress presumptive of the crown, and not in the hands of a person now near me, who is surrounded by evil advisers, and who is herself incompetent to act with propriety in the station in which she would be placed.'[5]

Having declared that the same person had continually insulted him and that he was determined his authority would be respected in future, he ended on a more affectionate note, alluding to the Princess and her future reign 'in a tone of paternal interest and affection', but the damage was done. The Queen was thoroughly embarrassed, Princess Victoria burst into tears and the stony-faced Duchess remained silent. After dinner she announced the immediate departure of her daughter and herself. Only with difficulty was she persuaded to stay. She and the King were both dismayed that the quarrel should have been made so public, yet it had cleared the air. Although no reconciliation took place between them, for the rest of the King's life they were on civil if cold terms.

His wish to be spared for another nine months was granted. On 24 May 1837, Princess Victoria celebrated her eighteenth birthday, and her mother's hopes of a Regency vanished. By now the King was ageing fast. Since April he had been particularly affected by the death of his favourite daughter Sophia, Lady de L'Isle, in childbirth. Only the Queen's death, thought Sir Herbert Taylor, could have upset him more. Returning from a levee in May, he was unable to climb the stairs, and collapsed, breathless and exhausted, on a sofa. A few days later he fainted at lunch and again at dinner, and never left his private apartments again. At the end of the month he attended his last council meeting, arriving in a wheelchair.

By the beginning of June, Taylor was privately warning politicians and officials that the King was dying. On the morning of 18 June, recalling the anniversary of Waterloo, he addressed his doctor, 'Let me but live over this memorable day – I shall never live to see another sunset.'[6]

Propped up in a heavy leather chair to ease his breathing, he gradually lost his iron grip on life. By the afternoon of 19 June he was unconscious, and at 2.20 the following morning he died, his hand in that of Queen Adelaide.

Often regarded merely as a figure of fun, King William IV was undoubtedly the right King for the British throne at the time. Excitable, undignified and short-tempered, he was kind-hearted and had the common sense to accept advice from those with whom he disagreed. In a way, he was the first modern monarch of Britain. He came to the throne at a time when the institution of monarchy was held in low regard; within seven years, it was respected again, and the crown which his niece Victoria inherited was secure within their subjects' affection and respect.

12   *Hanoverian Sunset*

Dressed plainly in black, without jewellery, the young Queen Victoria held her Accession Council at 11.00 on the morning of 20 June 1837, in the Red Saloon at Kensington Palace. After she had read her speech and taken the oath, the Privy Councillors were sworn in, her uncles the Dukes of Sussex and Cumberland going first to swear allegiance and kiss her hand.

In the words of Sidney Lee, the previous three occupants of the throne had been an imbecile, a profligate, and little better than a buffoon.[1] While such a verdict did scant justice to the Queen's predecessors, it suggested that those who were well acquainted with the court, if not the nation at large, expected a very different kind of monarchy.

Now His Majesty King of Hanover, Ernest was faced with a dilemma. Did he have the right, as sovereign of a foreign territory, to take the Oath of Allegiance to the Queen as a British peer of the realm? Lord Cottenham, Lord Chancellor, was reported to have said that he would refuse to administer the Oath to the King of Hanover. The government hoped that he would prove to be such an unpopular King over there that he would soon be sent back to England, and if he was prevented from taking the Oath, as an exiled monarch he would not be permitted to sit in the House of Lords. If the situation arose, it would be almost as embarrassing for the crown – and all individuals concerned – as the episode of Queen Caroline returning to England after her husband's accession in 1820. If anything happened to Queen Victoria, Ernest would succeed her as King of Great Britain as well. Whether more than a handful of the Whigs were serious about trying to deny the Queen's uncle his legitimate rights purely on grounds of political enmity is open to question, but on consultation with Tory peers and lawyers, King Ernest was assured that his rights as a peer were not affected by his change of status. When he presented himself at the Lords, the Chief Clerk administered and recorded his Oath without any objection.

Returning to Kensington, he took his leave of the Queen, who was very friendly. 'I embraced her tenderly,' he wrote to his wife, now Queen Frederica, 'and said, "My dear you may depend upon me on *all* occasions in support of your rights . . . "'.[2]

After paying his farewell respects to his sisters Mary and Augusta and the Duchess of Kent, he sailed from Woolwich to his new responsibilities as King of Hanover. On 28 June he arrived at the city for the first time as sovereign, under a triumphal arch erected at the Calenbergstrasse. At a ceremony heralded by the booming of cannon, pealing of bells and cheering of citizens, he was presented with the keys of the city. He delivered a short speech of thanks in German, promising to be 'a just and gracious King'. During the next three weeks, he

Queen Victoria at her first council meeting, at Kensington Palace, 20 June 1837, engraving after a portrait by David Wilkie. Other figures include the Dukes of Cumberland (with hand raised, seated behind table), Wellington (standing on his left), Sussex (seated in front), and the Prime Minister, Lord Melbourne (at end of table, holding papers and pen). The Queen should have been portrayed wearing black in mourning for King William IV, but Wilkie showed her in a white dress for artistic and symbolic reasons. Though she commented at the time that the likenesses were excellent, ten years later she called it one of the worst pictures she had ever seen

dined frequently with the Duke and Prince George of Cambridge, as Queen Frederica and Crown Prince George were still in Berlin, closing up the home which would now be theirs no longer.

King Ernest began his reign, it is said, by revoking the Constitution of Hanover in order to impose his own arbitrary rule. What actually happened was that a Constitution for Hanover had been signed by the Prince Regent in 1819, but did little more than confirm that the territory had been raised from the status of an Electorate to that of a Kingdom five years previously. Radical Hanoverian elements, encouraged by moves towards reform in England and the July revolution in France, resulted in the drafting of a new constitution, of which the main aim was to transfer the Hanoverian Domains (the equivalent of the English crown lands) from the sovereign to the state, thereby reducing the monarch to a virtual cypher.

There was some half-hearted rioting, and as Governor-General the Duke of Cambridge was presented with anti-government petitions protesting loyalty and devotion to His Majesty King William of Great Britain and Hanover, but blaming Count Münster, the Hanoverian Ambassador, for all their woes. The Duke of Cambridge reported to King William that a complete reorganization of the Hanoverian Government and Constitution was essential in order to avoid disaster, and a new Constitution was signed in 1833. King William was distracted and disturbed by civil unrest at home, and though the Duke of Cumberland was perturbed by the proposals, his protests went unheeded. That the Radicals were thus assuming a degree of control over the Domains was undeniable, but they had been alarmed by the extravagance of King George IV, who had raised a considerable loan from the Rothschilds on the security of his Hanoverian revenues without consulting the Estates. They wished to ensure that it would never occur again.

King Ernest now exercised his prerogative of disputing the legality of the new Constitution. A Hanoverian lawyer, von Falcke, had pointed out that his consent as Heir Apparent was legally necessary in 1833; but this had never been obtained. After consulting with his lawyers, and a commission of jurists to report on the legal position, he issued a patent in November 1837 declaring the Constitution void because of legal defects. Such action was not nearly as despotic as might have been supposed, as he guaranteed that all laws passed under the Constitution in 1833 would remain inviolate unless repealed or amended in the normal course of events. The Radicals were disappointed if not angry, but as the net result on the public was to reduce their taxation, the move made the King popular among his subjects.

At Göttingen University, seven university professors were dismissed from their posts for defying a Cabinet rescript requiring all civil servants, military officers and government officials to renew the oaths of allegiance to the sovereign. Protesting that the suspension of the 1833 Constitution was invalid, they called upon colleagues and sympathizers throughout Hanover to refuse the oath and to hamper government elections in any way possible. Three, who had been most active in circulating a manifesto at home and abroad, in order to try and gain continental sympathy for their cause, were ordered to leave Hanover. History has condemned King Ernest's behaviour as tyrannical; but such history was largely written by the academics who thus felt their liberty infringed. In fact, only one of the seven professors was a native of Hanover, and the King must have felt that foreign-born academic agitators would do better to foment discord in their own countries instead. That the King's action was popular was proved when the citizens of Göttingen sent a deputation to thank him. The lawlessness and hooliganism of the university students had become a menace, and such agitation by their tutors could only fan the flames.

With King Ernest's succession to the Hanoverian throne, there were only two surviving sons of King George III in England. As the senior of these, the Duke of Sussex hoped that his long experience of protocol and precedent would be of value to the young Queen. When she was about to make her first visit to the City of London, he sent her, through her Prime Minister, Lord Melbourne, a long letter of information about similar visits made by Kings George II and George IV. Perhaps such eagerness to proffer unsolicited help was received less than warmly, as from time to time the Queen's journals referred to visits from the Duke 'talking away the whole time'.

It was unfortunate for the Duke that the Queen's mind had been poisoned against her uncles. Her main male mentor, Lord Melbourne, was always ready to disparage the elder royal family. 'Blundering man, the Duke of Sussex; always has been and always will be,'[3] was a typical judgment. Ever critical and sarcastic about others, it was unkind of him to pour scorn on someone who was genuinely fond of the Queen, the daughter of the brother to whom he had always been closest.

However, his liaison with and secret marriage a few years previously to Lady Cecilia Underwood had done nothing to redeem him in the Queen's eyes, especially as the Duchess of Kent had made plain her disapproval. As the Queen and her mother were on far from friendly terms at the time, this in itself would not have been sufficient to prejudice the young sovereign against her 'Uncle Sussex', had it not been for Lord Melbourne's scathing comments about 'that woman', Lady Underwood.

Yet the Queen gave her uncle the respect and deference she knew were due to him. She appointed him Grand Master of the Order of the Bath in December 1837, and in place of the late King she gave him the rank of Captain General of the Honourable Artillery Company, of which he had been Colonel since 1817. She also offered him the Governorship of Windsor Castle, but he asked that it should be left with King William's eldest son, the Earl of Munster. The honour which pleased him most, however, was being granted permission to move the Address to the Throne in the House of Lords at the opening of Parliament in September 1837. As it was the first session of a new parliament in a new reign,

Adolphus, Duke of Cambridge

171

the occasion was of special importance, and the Queen was pleased that her uncle 'made a very able and judicious speech.'

As there was now no role for the Duke of Cambridge in Hanover, he brought his family back to England within a few weeks of the new reign. They took up residence at Cambridge House, Piccadilly, and at their country retreat of Cambridge Cottage, Kew.

The Duke regularly attended Sunday morning service at St Paul's, Knightsbridge, where the rest of the congregation must have found his presence quite an entertainment. He had a disconcerting habit of thinking aloud, and also his father's mannerism of 'triptology', or saying certain phrases three times. An exhortation from the officiating clergyman to pray evinced a good-natured bellow from the Duke's pew of, 'Aye, to be sure; why not? Let us pray, let us pray, let us pray.' Another day, while the commandments were being read he was heard to comment just as loudly, 'Steal! no, of course not; mustn't steal, mustn't steal, mustn't steal.'

At the Queen's Coronation in June 1838, the senior generation were given a rousing reception. The diarist Mary Frampton noted that the Duchess of Kent and the Duke and Duchess of Cambridge had been 'excessively cheered . . . but not so much as "Old Sussex", as the mob called him',[4] who received an ovation on his way to the Abbey and on returning afterwards.

Of her surviving aunts, the Queen was most fond of Princess Augusta, who called her niece 'a dear, good little creature, and so affectionate and kind to us all.' Princess Augusta watched her niece with great interest and compassion. During the first political crisis of the reign, the 'Bedchamber affair' in May 1839, when Queen Victoria refused to allow Sir Robert Peel to replace her Whig Ladies of the Bedchamber, and thus retained Lord Melbourne as her Prime Minister, the Princess was saddened 'to see my poor *innocent child* made a tool of . . . but I hope people will be gentle to her, and *pity* more than blame her, poor thing.'[5]

In Homburg, the Dowager Landgravine lived with her memories, her art and her charities. In Hanover she founded a nursery school, a facility which was then little known. Every year she fondly remembered the date of 14 February, the anniversary of her first meeting with her husband; 'I can go on hour after hour, thanks to the blessing and pleasure of memory, to look back at the sun beginning to shine upon me, as it did when he arrived, and I am sure it never set afterwards.'[6]

Failing health led her to travel around the spas in search of a cure. For the last two years of her life she was rarely free from pain, and by Christmas 1839 her strength and eyesight were failing. 'Now I am useless,' she confessed sadly in a letter to Princess Augusta from Frankfurt, where she spent the festive season. She died on 10 January 1840, and was buried in the family vault at Homburg, where the Anglican burial service was read. Five English parsons followed her on her last journey.

The death of 'dearest dear Eliza' was a heavy blow to Augusta, who was far from well herself. They had written to each other every day for many years, and Augusta found the writing her 'daily pleasure, comfort, and occupation'.

The year had begun with a royal death; exactly one month later there was a royal wedding. In October 1839 Queen Victoria had announced her engagement to His Serene Highness Prince Albert of Saxe-Coburg Gotha. They were cousins, Albert being the second son of Ernest, Duke of Saxe-Coburg, elder brother of the Duchess of Kent, and of King Leopold of the Belgians. The bridegroom's rank had precipitated some argument in the family, for Queen Victoria created him Royal Highness by Royal Letters Patent soon after his arrival in England for the wedding. An Act of Parliament was necessary to confirm this, and that Prince Albert would have precedence at court next to his future wife, over the 'old royal family'.

For this, the consent of the Queen's uncles had to be obtained. The Dukes of Sussex and Cambridge agreed, after some hesitation, but the King of Hanover refused to give way to one whom he described contemptuously as 'a paper Royal Highness'. A stickler for etiquette, he maintained that as the standing of the various Kingdoms, Grand Dukedoms, Dukedoms, Principalities and lesser states, and the order of precedence of their ruling families, had been settled by the Congress of Vienna, no alterations could be made without the consent of the Diet. Such matters of precedence counted for less in England than in Europe, but Ernest refused to give way and persuaded his younger brothers to rescind their consent. The Queen was furious with him, and a bill for her bridegroom's naturalization as well as his new rank had to go through with the question of his precedence unresolved.

Yet she bore her uncles in England no lasting ill-will. On new year's eve, 1839, the Duke of Sussex wrote her a charming letter; 'God grant that you may feel yourself blessed with the selection which you have made, and that your Bride Groom will prove himself worthy of participating in your glory as well as in your good fortune.'[7]

At the Queen's wish, Lord Melbourne wrote to the Duke of Sussex, asking if he would give Her Majesty away at her marriage 'as her nearest relation at present in this country and one who stands in place of a Father.'[8] The Duke was delighted to accept. On Monday, 10 February, the Queen and Prince Albert were married at the Chapel Royal, where her grandparents had been married nearly eighty years before. The Duke of Sussex, conspicuous as ever in his familiar black skull-cap to keep his head warm, sobbed emotionally throughout the service, while the Duke of Cambridge made his customary loud but good-natured comments. As a mark of her gratitude, the Queen created Lady Cecilia Duchess of Inverness, Duke of Inverness being the second of her uncle's titles. Lady Cecilia's lack of rank equal to her husband had created many an unfortunate situation with regard to precedence at court, such as whether she should be placed at the Queen's table with other Duchesses or not. Now the question no longer arose.

The Cambridges had been less well-disposed to the marriage. Prince George was at one time considered as a possible candidate for his cousin's hand, although he himself had showed little enthusiasm for the idea, and she referred to him privately as that 'odious boy'. Once the engagement between Victoria and Albert had been announced, she found George 'quite different towards me, much less reserved, and evidently happy to be clear of me.'[9]

Princess Augusta, who was now installed in Clarence House, St James's, turned with tenderness towards Princess Sophia, whose eyesight had given her problems for some time. A few years earlier, the latter had lost the sight of her right eye, and in 1838 she underwent an operation for a cataract. The Duke of Sussex had already been through the ordeal with success in June 1836, but in Sophia's case it was followed by three months of pain and inflammation, shortly after which she went totally blind.

In April 1840, Augusta noted that her sister was 'wonderfully well, and so sweet-tempered and resigned to her affliction of blindness, which is the greatest of all trials. She bears it with such calmness and piety, and even cheerfulness, now that her mind is made up never to be any better, but it is painful to witness the poor dear, who used to be so often and so well employed, reduced now only to open books and tear up paper for couch-pillows.'[10] She had been told that pillows filled with torn-up paper were comfortable for the sick, and she set to work tearing up books for the purpose.

Augusta's last months were cheered by the solicitude of Queen Victoria and Prince Albert. In April 1840, Augusta and Queen Adelaide attended the opera, and 'the young couple', as she referred to them, came into their box between the acts, to have 'a delightful chat'.

The sisters-in-law were ready to make the Queen and her husband feel welcome. But the Duke of Cambridge, still evidently smarting at the Queen's scathing comments on his son, continued to be somewhat touchy about Prince Albert. A few days after the wedding, he declared that he would refuse to walk behind any 'young foreign upstart'. As he had it on good authority that there was yet 'nothing in writing' about the order of precedence at court, he consulted the Duke of Wellington, regarded by all as the fount of wisdom. Much to his anger, the Iron Duke, who had said only a few months earlier that Prince Albert would take precedence over his wife's uncles 'over my dead body', now defended the right of Her Majesty to give her husband whatever precedence she pleased, and that the Duke of Cambridge would be wise not to make difficulties. Against this judgment there was no appeal, but the Duke and Duchess still felt slighted. Determined to defend the rights of 'the *old* royal family', the Duchess ostentatiously remained seated while the Prince's health was drunk at a dinner given by Queen Adelaide at Marlborough House. The Queen retaliated by not inviting any of the Cambridges to her next ball at Buckingham Palace.

Late that summer Prince Albert received the Freedom of the City of London, but regretted that owing to bad reports on the health of Princess Augusta, he could not dine with the Lord Mayor and Aldermen after the presentation, having promised the Queen he would return. She was expecting the birth of their first child within a few weeks, and he was anxious that she should not receive news of their aunt's death without him by her side. The Duke of Cambridge was accompanying the Prince. He said that the reports of his sister's health were more favourable than before, and that if he could attend the banquet, there was no reason why Prince Albert should not. Albert would not be dissuaded, and it was left to the Duke to reply to the Prince's health at the banquet. Afterwards he said that the guests were so disappointed that they might have turned down their glasses. Lightheartedly, he remarked in his address that he could account for the Prince's absence, as he 'had lately married a very fine girl, and they were somehow or other very fond of each other's society.'

The guests roared with laughter, but when the Queen read the speech in her papers the following day, she was horrified. She wrote to the Duchess of Gloucester, complaining bitterly of his behaviour and asking her to rebuke him.

On 22 September, Princess Augusta died at Clarence House. Queen Adelaide held her hand during the last moments, and both her surviving sisters, as well as the Dukes of Cambridge and Sussex, were also at the deathbed.

On 10 June 1840, a half-witted youth, Edward Oxford, fired at the Queen as she and Prince Albert were driving along Constitution Hill. This attempt on the pregnant sovereign's life persuaded Parliament of the wisdom of Albert's attempts, and those of their adviser Baron Stockmar, to pass a bill making Albert Regent in the event of anything happening to the Queen.

The Commons and Lords agreed to his appointment as full Regent, without a Council, but there was one dissentient voice, that of the Duke of Sussex. He told Lord Melbourne that he felt compelled to protest, 'since if the measure proposed be adopted I conceive it will be derogatory to the credit of those Branches of the Royal Family who are resident in England being totally excluded from any participation in the Government of the Country.'[11] Ill health, financial worries and old age made him irritable and easily insulted, clutching at what remaining privileges were still left to him. Moreover, he saw that if Prince Albert was to become a widower and make a second marriage, to a foreign princess, the monarchy, and any heir to the throne, would be out of British hands. Unfortunately he could do no more than bluster and make himself look foolish. At the second reading of the bill, he made what the Queen called 'a most injudicious speech'.

Albert told his brother that he 'declared it to be an affront against the rightful family. He intended to bring a protest into the House, but, when his friends abandoned him, seeing the superior power of the Ministers, Whigs and the whole Tory party, he let the matter pass without intervention.'[12] The Queen declared that she could not readily forgive her uncle, but the fuss soon died down. When the Queen gave birth to her first child, Victoria, Princess Royal, she asked him to be one of the godparents, another honour he was pleased to accept.

The Queen of Hanover had been unwell for some time. Poor health and a retiring disposition had kept her out of the public eye in Hanover since her husband's accession. In the summer of 1841 she became ill, and on 27 June, after hurrying to escape a thunderstorm while out walking, she caught a chill which proved fatal.

It had been a happy marriage, and the bereaved King was shattered. To Lord Strangford he wrote of this 'unbearably heartbreaking business, one which has completely annihilated me and destroyed all my worldly happiness. . . . The loss is to me irreparable, and I can say that life is now become to me a burden.'[13] Before her death, he had given orders for improvements and alterations to the

The christening of Victoria, Princess Royal, at Buckingham Palace, 10 February 1841, engraving after a portrait by Charles Robert Leslie. Figures include, from left: Mary, Duchess of Gloucester; Victoire, Duchess of Kent; Leopold, King of the Belgians; Augustus, Duke of Sussex (with skull cap); Queen Adelaide, facing Archbishop of Canterbury; Queen Victoria and Prince Albert in group on right

city of Hanover, including proper sanitation, gas lighting in the streets, and a new residential quarter of terraces and squares. The plans included demolition of the small Altes Palais where the King and Queen had lived; but after her death, he requested the architect to leave the Palais intact, as a memorial to his wife. He kept it as his town house for the remaining ten years of his life, and every night before going to bed he spent some time in prayer or meditation in what had been her bedroom. He remained in seclusion for several months after her death, finding solace in long rides and in his work.

Though a septuagenarian born and raised in the pre-industrial age, he took a keen interest in such innovations as railways, or what he called 'Loco-Motive Machines'. As King, he considered it his duty to acquaint himself with detailed plans for the first Hanoverian railway. Hanover's geographical position and sea ports made her ripe for development as a transit centre, and with the development of rail, the little kingdom became a staging post on the journey to Berlin and the East. Crowned heads, ambassadors, diplomats, business men and tourists came to Hanover, which benefited greatly from the resulting trade.[14]

Several English visitors came to make their number with the man once regarded as the most unpopular person in England. Among them was his former opponent Brougham, who had at length accorded him grudging respect. The King invited him to tea one day, and they reduced themselves to helpless laughter at each others' caustic comments and outrageous jokes. Though he had mellowed with the passing years, the King was never one to mince words. To another English visitor who complained that she had lost her way in Hanover, he retorted good-naturedly that it was impossible; 'the whole country is no bigger than a fourpenny piece.'

When the Prince of Wales, born on 9 November 1841, was to be christened, the Queen asked the Duke of Cambridge to be one of his sponsors, as the Duke of Sussex had for the Princess Royal. The Queen's younger surviving aunt, Sophia, received a similar invitation; she was represented by Princess Augusta of Cambridge. The olive branch, however, soon withered.

Late in 1842, it was rumoured that the Queen's cousin, Prince George of Cambridge, had made his mother's lady-in-waiting, Lady Augusta Somerset, daughter of the Duke of Beaufort, pregnant. A formal denial was printed in *The Times,* and there the matter should have ended. But a few months later, in order to make a firm demonstration of her innocence, the Duchess of Cambridge presented Lady Augusta at a drawing-room. The furious Queen ordered that her ladies should not speak to Augusta. After the Duchess had left, the Queen sent for the Duchess of Gloucester, said that she knew the rumours were true, and asked her to tell the Cambridges how angry she was. It was very wrong, she said, for the Duchess of Cambridge to have brought her. Astonished, the Duchess of Gloucester remarked that this was a very serious charge against the girl and the Duchess; if Her Majesty wished her to make such a complaint, would she please put it in writing.

The Cambridges were just as angry, and reiterated the innocence of both parties involved. At length Prince Albert was forced to reply rather ungraciously that as Prince George had given his word of honour that the story was untrue, 'I suppose that we *must* believe *it is so.'* Greville commented that the storm in a teacup had arisen through a combination of Albert's prudery and the Queen's own love of gossip.

In view of the disgrace Queen Victoria had brought on herself in 1839 by believing that her mother's lady-in-waiting Lady Flora Hastings was pregnant when she was suffering from terminal cancer, and in view of the notorious lack of morals of Albert's own father and brother, it was surprising that such a matter should have arisen. Yet Albert still distrusted his wife's surviving uncles and their families. Some strange sense of persecution mania inspired in him the idea that the King of Hanover had been behind, or in some way implicated in, the attempts on her life by Oxford in 1840, and two further attacks in the summer of 1842. While the Queen would later rightly dismiss any talk of threats to her on the part of her uncle Ernest as an 'invention' of the detested Sir John Conroy, Albert was less certain.

Early in 1843 the Duke of Sussex became ill with erysipelas. The Duchess of Inverness and the Duke of Cambridge were with him on the morning of 21 April. At around midday, realizing that he had not long to live, he sent for his servants to come and take their leave of him. As they came into the room, he made an effort to speak and fell back, dead.

'No death in the royal family short of the actual demise of a monarch could have occasioned a stronger feeling of deprivation than in the case of the Duke of Sussex,' *The Times* lamented in its black-bordered obituary the next day, as it paid tribute to his wide-ranging knowledge of many subjects, his appreciation of literature and the sciences, and his active support of diverse charities. Few of his brothers and sisters had achieved as much popularity and respect in their last years as 'good old Sussex'.

Knowing that burial at Windsor might cause difficulties for his widow, he left a wish that they might be buried in the public cemetery at Kensal Green. A simple mausoleum marks the site where he was laid to rest, and where she joined him thirty years later.

On his accession, the King of Hanover had decided to maintain a *pied-à-terre* in London for what he imagined would be annual visits home. He had been asked by the Queen if he would surrender his apartments at St James's for the use of the Duchess of Kent. Queen Victoria had not wanted her mother under the same roof, but as a matter of form it was essential for her to have her nearby, and Kensington Palace was inconveniently far from Buckingham Palace. The King, however, retorted that he was damned if he would. Apart from wanting to keep his apartments, he had no intention of giving them up for the benefit of a sister-in-law who had shown so little respect to the late King William. Queen Victoria therefore had to rent a house for the Duchess in Belgrave Square. To her it was an unnecessary expense, as she was attempting to pay off her late father's debts, and she never forgave her uncle.

The King paid what would be his last visit to England in the summer of 1843. As Greville commented, he must have been rather astonished to find himself so well received in a country where he had been so disliked years before; 'Everybody seems to think it necessary to treat him with dinners and balls, and he is become the lion of the season with this foolish inconsistent world.'[15] Though he issued all his invitations in the name of Duke of Cumberland, he was treated as a reigning monarch. Every day *The Times* printed a list of those who had come to pay their respects to His Majesty. He had been invited to stand as godfather to Queen Victoria's third child Princess Alice, but state business had prevented his departure from Hanover in time for the christening on 6 June.

Despite Prince Albert's letter to his brother Ernest that the King 'looks very miserable and old, but he is in good humour and full of tenderness for us,'[16] it was soon apparent that he was less than welcome in the palace of his niece than in the houses of friends or even former foes. Nevertheless he was twice the Queen's guest. On 14 June he was invited to dinner at Buckingham Palace, and she noted that he had 'grown very old and excessively thin, and bends a good deal.'[17] After all she had heard said about him in the previous six years, she was agreeably surprised to find that he was not the Lucifer incarnate of her youth. Though she was a little nervous as she asked him to do the honour of proposing her health afterwards, his speech was graciousness itself; he emphasized that he did so 'as one of Her Majesty's subjects, and as I have frequently said in the House of Lords that she has not a more faithful subject than the individual who addresses you now.'[18]

Yet he had been warned by the Cambridges how the 'old' royal family was now at a discount. For example, only Coburg relatives had been invited to state dinners immediately after the Queen's wedding. King Leopold of the Belgians, who had evidently forgotten the former Duke of Cumberland's condolences on the death of Princess Charlotte, had sneeringly written to Queen Victoria of 'your immediate successor with the moustachios', and similar disdainful remarks. For the second family occasion during his visit, he was determined to make a stand for 'Brunswick dignity against Coburg pretension'.

The Duke of Cambridge had invited his brother to give his elder daughter Princess Augusta away at her wedding to Prince Frederick of Mecklenburg-Strelitz. As Prince Albert wrote to his brother, 'It almost came to a fight with the King. He insisted on having the place at the altar, where we stood. He wanted to drive me away and, against all custom, he wanted to accompany Victoria and lead her. I was to go behind him. I was forced to give him a strong push and drive him down a few steps, where the First Master of Ceremonies took him and led him out of the chapel.'[19]

After the ceremony, all assembled in the round salon at Buckingham Palace to sign the register and certificates. The Queen signed first, and as she laid down the pen, the King stepped forward to take it and add his name below hers. Albert edged in smartly, grabbed the pen and took care to put his signature so close to that of the Queen that there was no room for the King to insert his between them.

It says much for how deeply both men felt about precedence for one, a youngster of twenty-three, to be prepared to push the other, a half-blind septuagenarian, down a set of steps in the chapel. However the King took it in his stride, and afterwards he proposed that they should both go for a stroll in St James's Park. Albert declined, saying that they might be inconvenienced by crowds, to which the King replied wryly that this did not matter; 'When I lived here I was quite as unpopular as you are, and they never bothered me.'

For the rest of his stay, there were no invitations to the palace, and he sent members of his suite to represent him at the Drawing Rooms. This was not done out of pique, but simply because he had injured himself in another fall soon after the wedding. 'Happily, he fell over some stones in Kew and damaged some ribs,' Albert remarked maliciously to his brother.

Of more pleasure were his visits to the House of Lords. He found the proceedings a welcome change from the conduct of business in the Estates at Hanover, and wrote to his son how gratifying it was to hear *good* speaking, 'and seeing how much better, clearer and more concisely all carry on a debate here. I lost not a word, and my old parliamentary passion revived in me and I could have spoken myself.'[20] Before his first attendance, the Duchess of Gloucester said she hoped that he would take no part in the debate, to which he replied characteristically that he would not unless the Devil prompted him.

In the House of Commons, the King's old adversary Joseph Hume asked if it was proper for him to draw his income as a Prince of Great Britain now that he had left the country. To this Sir Robert Peel, Prime Minister, replied that Civil List incomes were voted for life, and parliament could not go back on an undertaking. He omitted to point out that none of the King's income left the country. Much was spent on salaries and pensions in connection with his establishments, and the remainder was dispersed in charity.

Although, in his own words, he had been 'certainly very miserably treated by the Court', soon after his return to Hanover he made tentative plans to come back to England the following year, but home affairs absorbed his attention. In any case, with increasing age and infirmity, he was reluctant to travel far.

A further cause of contention between both sovereigns was the matter of Queen Charlotte's jewels. On her marriage in 1761, the Queen had been given some very fine jewellery, but no specific provision had been made in her will for its disposal. King Ernest regarded it as belonging to the crown of Hanover, and claimed it in his capacity as male heir; Queen Victoria and her advisers maintained that it was Crown, not family, property, as such to be kept in England and used at the discretion of the English sovereign.

The King proposed that the issue should be settled by arbitration, and the Attorney-General appointed a commission of three judges. In 1846 they were about to publish their findings, in favour of the King of Hanover, when the senior judge died, and legal protocol demanded that the commission's findings should be laid aside. As a compromise, the King offered to let the English Crown retain all but a few of the pieces which his mother had particularly favoured, but the English authorities refused, evidently believing that possession was nine-tenths of the law. Rather ill-advisedly, Queen Victoria made the best use she could of the jewels, and on more than one occasion the King wrote bitterly to English friends, remarking that 'The little Queen looked very fine, I hear, loaded down with *my* diamonds.'*

King Ernest's way of life was spartan. Every morning he breakfasted in bed with weak tea and toast. He then opened his letters, though as his eyesight grew weaker he had to rely more on his secretaries, heard reports and dictated replies, usually staying in bed. Soon after midday he was dressed and ready to receive ministers and other officials. Next, he would have the police reports and newspapers read to him, then attention would be given to official and private correspondence. Weather permitting, he would drive before dinner, at which he ate little. If there was no further business after dinner, he would relax with an hour or more of gossip and banter with Countess von Grote, the widow of an old friend, who acted as his hostess and companion. It was unlikely that she was his mistress, but she eased his loneliness after the death of Queen Frederica.

So did the marriage of his son and heir, who married Princess Mary of Saxe-Altenburg in February 1843, having sought permission as a matter of form from Queen Victoria. His son was still technically an English prince, and therefore subject to the Royal Marriages Act. The first grandchild, named after him, was born in September 1845, and the King was so delighted at the news

---

* The matter lapsed, despite the King's protests. After his death in 1851, his son King George revived the Hanoverian claims. Another Commission was appointed in 1857, and its findings were published later that year. Much to the chagrin of the Queen and Prince Albert, the question was settled in favour of Hanover, and the jewels were delivered to the Ambassador, Count Kielmansegge, in January 1858.

that he would not wait for his carriage but set off on foot to congratulate and thank his son and daughter-in-law.

He was often ill during the last four or five years of his life, with regular colds and influenza. The medicines his doctors prescribed were usually handed to his valet with instructions to put them in the cupboard. When unwell, he believed in a starvation diet, and so probably suffered from malnutrition. Unlike his brothers, he had always been slender. While they had all become excessively fat in their last years, with his 'regular habits' he grew thin to the point of emaciation in old age. Later in the evening, he would often give or attend a reception or party. His love of such social life increased with age, and he was seldom in bed before the small hours.

His dictation often surprised his secretaries. One had to ask the English Chaplain what His Majesty meant by his denunciation of a 'bomb-rusher' in the House of Lords. The Chaplain explained that the King was merely inveighing against the elevation of a former schoolmaster (or in Ernest's vernacular, a 'bum-brusher') to a bishopric.

Though he set great store by etiquette, some of his mannerisms were strangely informal. He would inspect his assembled guests at evening receptions almost as though they were troops on parade, but while resplendent himself in Hussar uniform, his erect carriage bolstered by yards of muslin wound tightly around his slender frame and a cravat around his neck to keep his head from falling forward, he invariably walked down the line with his hands in his pockets, as he peered carefully at each guest.

When revolution swept across Europe in 1848, Hanover was little affected; the kingdom was contented and well-governed, and her King too well respected. Ultra-radicals in Hanover made a token display of revolt, and a few sporadic riots in the towns were put down by the cavalry without bloodshed.

By the time of her seventieth birthday, 3 November 1847, Princess Sophia was very frail. Blind and partly deaf, she 'could not move from her seat without being carried; yet still she was as patient and uncomplaining as ever.'[21] Living quietly at Kensington, she was cheered by regular visits from the Duke and Duchess of Cambridge and their children. After Augusta's marriage, Princess Mary Adelaide became her aunt's particular favourite. Her most faithful visitor of all was 'dearest Minny', the Duchess of Gloucester, who sometimes took her sister out for a ride in her carriage around Hyde and St James's Parks. Sometimes the Queen came to call.

The Duchess enjoyed better health than her youngest sister, though she was becoming increasingly absent-minded. In May 1848 she attended the christening of her great-niece Princess Louise but, related Queen Victoria, was 'in one of her nervous states, and gave us a dreadful fright at the christening by quite forgetting where she was, and coming and kneeling at my feet in the midst of the service. Imagine our horror!'[22]

By now, Sophia was sinking, and on the morning of 27 May 1848 the rest of the family were warned that she was not far off. The Duchesses of Gloucester, Kent, and Inverness came to her bedside, as did the Duchess of Cambridge and

*The grave of Princess
Sophia, at Kensal Green
Cemetery*

her younger daughter Mary, and were with her as she breathed her last at
6.30 p.m. 'Thank God my poor dear Aunt Sophia did not suffer much in her last
moments, and died without a sigh, with Mama's hand in her own,' wrote
Princess Mary. 'She had been insensible for two hours before death released her
from a life of suffering.'[23]

At her request, she was buried at Kensal Rise, close to the Duke of Sussex's
last resting place.

After her death, the Duke of Cambridge and the Duchess of Gloucester
appointed a solicitor to examine her affairs. All were astonished to find that,
notwithstanding her large income and trifling expenses, she had left only
£1607. 19s. 7d. in her bank and a few shares of negligible value. On the death of
Queen Charlotte, she had been granted an income of £15,000, increased to
£17,000 after the death of Princess Augusta. Sir John Conroy, who had been
responsible for handling her finances (and had bought himself property and
houses in Wales and Berkshire which he could not have afforded out of his own
salary), 'declined to give any account of her money'. Whether she had willingly
made him gifts or whether he had taken advantage of a gullible, blind and elderly
lady was left for her surviving relations to judge.

In his last years, the Duke of Cambridge and his niece became reconciled.
Increasingly deaf, when he attended the church at Kew, he sat in a pew near the

pulpit. Close by were local schoolboys. Every Sunday he counted them, and if any were missing he would lean over his pew and tell Simpson, the schoolmaster. 'They are ill, Your Royal Highness,' Simpson would reply on behalf of the absentees. 'Send to my house for soup for them,' were the Duke's instructions. One very dry summer, the rector read a prayer for rain, the Duke heartily joining in at the end with a loud 'Amen, but we shan't get it until the wind changes.' Another Sunday, during the reading of the offertory sentences, when the words, 'Behold, the half of my goods I give to the poor,' were read, he exclaimed, 'No, no, I can't do that; a half is too much for any man, but I have no objection to a tenth.'

The Duke was endearingly eccentric, but lacking in pomposity, having as little patience as King Ernest did with pomp and officialdom for its own sake. When taken to see a cricket match at Eton, he broke away from the Provost who had been rather stiffly showing him round, preferring to be escorted instead by a small boy. Such informality reinforced his popularity with the public. His presence was always appreciated on charity and hospital committees, where he was called on to settle many an argument.

In August 1849 he went abroad for the last time to see the King of Hanover. The brothers had a pleasant time reminiscing over the past, but perhaps they recognized that they would never see each other again. The King could not face accompanying his brother to the station for fear of breaking down with emotion in public.

In June 1850, the Duke of Cambridge fell ill. The Duchess of Gloucester spent many hours visiting her brother, and the Queen came to call. After lingering for a few days during which time the doctors gave up all hopes of recovery, he died on the evening of 8 July, and was buried at Kew Church.

'Yesterday evening the good Duke of Cambridge died,' Prince Albert wrote to his stepmother, the Dowager Duchess of Saxe-Coburg; 'the family is plunged in grief . . . The poor old gentleman slept softly away at the last, after his strength had been quite exhausted by a three-weeks' fever.'[24]

During his eightieth year, the King of Hanover seemed to take on a new lease of life. He made a series of journeys around Germany early in the year, including visits to Mecklenburg to attend the christening of the Grand Duke's son, and to Luneburg to inspect his old regiment. His eightieth birthday on 5 June 1851 was marked by festivities which he enjoyed in the company of the King of Prussia, his own son and daughter-in-law, and grandchildren.

Silver one thaler of King Ernest Augustus of Hanover, 1849

He still took a keen interest in news from his homeland, and to Lord Strangford he remarked acidly on Prince Albert's Great Exhibition in 1851: 'The folly and absurdity of the Queen in allowing this trumpery show must strike every sensible and well-thinking mind, and I am astonished the ministers themselves do not insist on her at least going to Osborne during the Exhibition, as no human being can possibly answer for what may occur on the occasion. The idea of permitting 2000 National Guards to come over en corps, and parade in London their side-arms, must shock every honest and well-meaning Englishman. But it seems everything is combining to lower us in the eyes of Europe.'

The King had not been alone in predicting doom and catastrophe for the Crystal Palace Exhibition. Later he wrote, 'My opinion of the Exhibition has in no way changed, and the peace and good order, and regularity that has till now existed is owing entirely to the superior talents and vigilance and wise measures of that great man, the Duke,* for whose preservation everyone in Great Britain, and I may add in all Europe, must daily pray.'[23]

The last great occasion of his life was a visit to Göttingen that summer. He had been there in 1845, when he spoke of the pleasure it gave him to think that the troubles of 1837 were forgiven by both sides – overtures of peace had already been made to the exiled professors. He addressed academics and clergymen, opened a new hospital, inspected the zoological museum, joined in the singing at a torchlight procession, and returned to Hanover in a happy mood.

Afterwards a reaction set in, and he suddenly seemed very old and broken. He found it increasingly hard to keep awake; when not working, and sometimes during work, he would slip into a state between sleep and semi-consciousness. He spent much time in bed, as the effort of dressing and bathing was frequently too much for him. His last private visitors were entertained in his room towards the end of October 1851, by which time regular bulletins on his condition were being issued. His strength was declining, and on 18 November he sank into sleep for the very last time.

In the country of his birth, there was the customary empty formality of court mourning, and a grudging *Times* obituary remarking that 'the good which may be said of the royal dead is little or none.' In Hanover, the mourning was sincere, and a large bronze equestrian statue was raised by public subscription. On the plinth was chiselled DEM LANDES VATER SEIN TREUES VOLK ('To the father of his country from his faithful people').

His death left one surviving sister, the Duchess of Gloucester. She enjoyed a relatively cheerful and active old age, and in 1855 she contributed sixteen pictures to a Patriotic Fund exhibition staged on behalf of widows and orphans of officers engaged in the Crimean war. In August 1856 she had 'an attack of faintness and oppression' on returning from a drive. A month later she wrote to the Duchess of Cambridge, 'I am happy to tell you that I was up, and dressed,

---

* Of Wellington.

Queen Victoria, with Princess Mary, Duchess of Gloucester, the Prince of Wales, and Princess Alice, at Gloucester House, 30 June 1856, from a daguerreotype by Antoine Claudet. This was probably the only occasion on which a child of King George III was photographed

and in my room yesterday from half past two till near six o'clock – I am improving in a quiet way and beginning to employ myself.'[26]

On 25 April 1857, the Duchess celebrated her eighty-first birthday. 'Alas! we dared not keep it except *sacredly*, as it were,' wrote Princess Mary of Cambridge. The Duchess and her daughter were constantly at Gloucester House. Two days later, Mary related that her great-aunt, on being told that the Queen was about to come, 'looked round the room very much as dear Papa used to do in his last illness.'[27]

In the small hours of 30 April, the Duchess of Cambridge was by her side, and the daughters were summoned to join her. At a quarter past five, 'with another stretch and a momentary convulsive contraction of the face, all was over, and with the dawn of day the gentle spirit returned to God who gave it.'[28]

Over a century later, there is little reason to alter Fitzgerald's judgements substantially.* Though little of their correspondence has survived, there is enough left to show that they all had abilities and positive qualities. Despite misfortunes and their own mistakes, they were never the fools or knaves that their fiercest critics made them out to be. As parents, King George III and Queen Charlotte were conscientious but rarely understanding enough, and the daughters were undoubtedly stifled by their mother's possessiveness and lack of parental foresight. The sons all escaped to a greater extent, and it is tempting to speculate how each would have worn the crown in an age when the royal prerogative was visibly diminishing at the hands of Parliament. It seems unlikely that any of the brothers, despite differences in politics, character and personality, would have been less successful as constitutional monarchs than Kings George IV or William IV.

* See Foreword, pp. x–xi.

THE HOUSE OF HANOVER

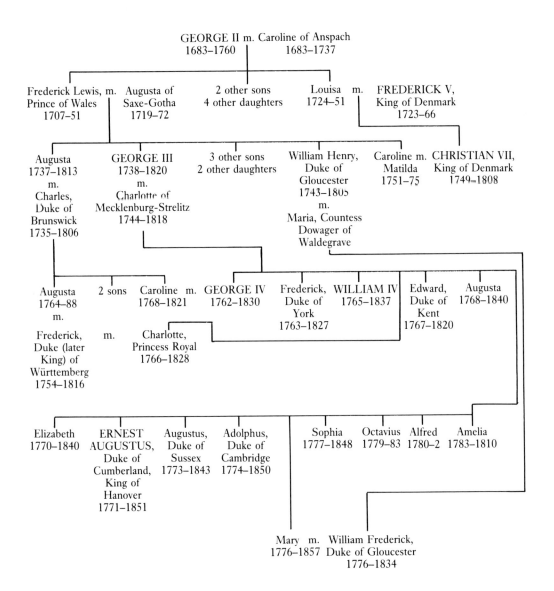

GEORGE II m. Caroline of Anspach
1683–1760 | 1683–1737

Frederick Lewis, m. Augusta of
Prince of Wales | Saxe-Gotha
1707–51 | 1719–72

2 other sons
4 other daughters

Louisa m. FREDERICK V,
1724–51 King of Denmark
1723–66

Augusta
1737–1813
m.
Charles,
Duke of
Brunswick
1735–1806

GEORGE III
1738–1820
m.
Charlotte of
Mecklenburg-Strelitz
1744–1818

3 other sons
2 other daughters

William Henry,
Duke of
Gloucester
1743–1805
m.
Maria, Countess
Dowager of
Waldegrave

Caroline m. CHRISTIAN VII,
Matilda King of Denmark
1751–75 1749–1808

Augusta
1764–88
m.

Frederick,
Duke (later
King) of
Württemberg
1754–1816

2 sons

Caroline m.
1768–1821

m. Charlotte,
Princess Royal
1766–1828

GEORGE IV
1762–1830

Frederick, WILLIAM IV
Duke of 1765–1837
York
1763–1827

Edward, Augusta
Duke of 1768–1840
Kent
1767–1820

Elizabeth
1770–1840

ERNEST
AUGUSTUS,
Duke of
Cumberland,
King of
Hanover
1771–1851

Augustus,
Duke of
Sussex
1773–1843

Adolphus,
Duke of
Cambridge
1774–1850

Sophia Octavius Alfred Amelia
1777–1848 1779–83 1780–2 1783–1810

Mary m. William Frederick,
1776–1857 Duke of Gloucester
1776–1834

THE HOUSES OF HANOVER AND SAXE-COBURG

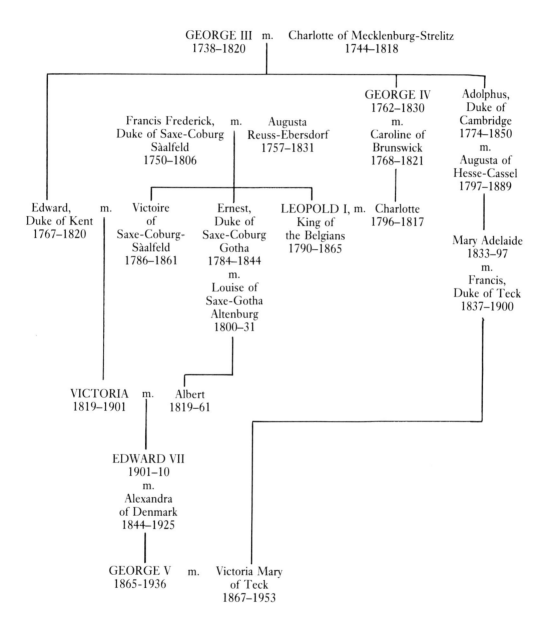

King George III's Children and Grandchildren

Note: for reasons of space, only marriages valid under the Royal Marriages Act, legitimate children, other marriages and illegitimate children publicly acknowledged at the time, are given below.

1. George Augustus Frederick, born 12 August 1762; created Prince of Wales, 1762; married Princess Caroline of Brunswick (1768–1821), 1795; ascended thrones of Great Britain and Hanover, as King George IV, 29 January 1820; crowned 19 July 1821; died 26 June 1830. Issue:
(1) Charlotte (1796–1817)

2. Frederick, born 16 August 1763; created Duke of York and Albany, and Earl of Ulster, 1784; married Princess Frederica of Prussia (1767–1820), 1791; died 5 January 1827 without issue.

3. William Henry, born 21 August 1765; created Duke of Clarence and St Andrews, and Earl of Ulster, 1789; lived with Mrs Dorothy Jordan (c. 1760–1816) for several years; married Princess Adelaide of Saxe-Meiningen (1792–1849), 1818; ascended thrones of Great Britain and Hanover as King William IV, 26 June 1830; crowned 8 September 1831; died 20 June 1837.
Issue by Mrs Jordan (all given the surname FitzClarence; younger sons and daughters given rank and title of the younger children of a Marquis in 1831, except those daughters who were already of a higher rank through their husbands):
(1) George Augustus Frederick, Earl of Munster (1794–1842)
(2) Henry (1795–1817)
(3) Frederick (1799–1854)
(4) Adolphus (1802–56)
(5) Augustus (1805–54)
(6) Sophia (1792–1837)
(7) Mary (1798–1864)
(8) Elizabeth (1801–56)
(9) Augusta (1803–65)
(10) Amelia (1807–58)
Issue by Princess Adelaide:
(1) Charlotte Augusta Louisa (born and died 27 March 1819)
(2) Elizabeth Georgina Adelaide (20 December 1820–4 March 1821)

4. Charlotte Augusta Matilda, Princess Royal, born 29 September 1766; married Frederick, Prince (later King) of Württemberg (1754–1816), 1797; died 5 October 1828 without issue.

5. Edward Augustus, born 2 November 1767; created Duke of Kent and Strathearn, and Earl of Dublin, 1799; married Princess Victoire of Saxe-Coburg (1786–1861), widow of Emich Charles, Prince of Leiningen, 1818; died 23 January 1820. Issue:
(1) Queen Victoria, born Princess Alexandrina Victoria (1819–1901)

6. Augusta Sophia, born 8 November 1768; died 22 September 1840.

7. Elizabeth, born 22 May 1770; married Frederick, Landgrave of Hesse-Homburg (1769–1829), 1818; died 10 January 1840 without issue.

8. Ernest Augustus, born 5 June 1771; created Duke of Cumberland and Teviotdale, and Earl of Armagh, 1799; married Princess Frederica of Mecklenburg-Strelitz (1778–1841), widow of Prince Frederick of Prussia, and of Frederick, Prince of Solms-Braunfels, 1815; ascended throne of Hanover as King Ernest, 20 June 1837; died 18 November 1851. Issue:
(1) George, King of Hanover (1819–78)

9. Augustus Frederick, born 27 January 1773; created Duke of Sussex and Earl of Inverness, 1801; married (1) Lady Augusta Murray (*c.* 1762–1830), 1793; (2) Lady Cecilia Buggin (1793–1873), 1831; died 21 April 1843. Issue by (1):
(1) Augustus Frederick d'Este (1794–1848)
(2) Augusta Emma d'Este, later Lady Truro (1801–66)

10. Adolphus Frederick, born 24 February 1774; created Duke of Cambridge, Earl of Tipperary, and Baron Culloden, 1801; married Princess Augusta of Hesse-Cassel (1797–1889), 1818; died 8 July 1850. Issue:
(1) George, Duke of Cambridge (1819–1904)
(2) Augusta, Duchess of Mecklenburg-Strelitz (1822–1916)
(3) Mary Adelaide, Duchess of Teck (1833–97)

11. Mary, born 25 April 1776; married William, Duke of Gloucester (1776–1834), 1816; died 30 April 1857 without issue.

12. Sophia, born 3 November 1777; died 27 May 1848.

13. Octavius, born 23 February 1779; died 3 May 1783.

14. Alfred, born 22 September 1780; died 26 August 1782.

15. Amelia, born 7 August 1783; died 2 November 1810.

Reference Notes

Abbreviations:
G III, *The later correspondence of George III, 1783–1810*, Aspinall (ed.), 5 vols, 1962–7.
G IV, *The letters of George IV, 1812–1830*, Aspinall (ed.), 3 vols, 1938.
PW, *Correspondence of George, Prince of Wales, 1770–1812*, Aspinall (ed.), 8 vols, 1963–70.
QV, *The letters of Queen Victoria, 1837–1861*, Benson and Esher (eds), 3 vols, 1907.

All references to Fitzgerald are to *Dukes and Princesses , , ,* unless stated otherwise.

Foreword (ix–xi)
  1 Iremonger 88
  2 Fitzgerald II 339–41

Prologue (pp. 1–8)
  1 Walpole III 432

Chapter 1 (pp. 9–18)
  1 Richardson 10
  2 Ziegler 16
  3 Papendiek I 78
  4 Ayling 214
  5 Stuart 207

Chapter 2 (pp. 19–34)
  1 PW I 26
  2 Ziegler 35
  3 Aspinall PW I 54
  4 Ziegler 42
  5 Stuart 324
  6 PW I 131
  7 G III I 77
  8 ibid I 124–5
  9 ibid I 152
  10 Hibbert *George IV 1762–1811* 63–4n
  11 G III I 129
  12 Fitzgerald II 188–9
  13 PW I 329
  13 Gillen *Royal Duke* 28
  15 PW I 329
  16 ibid I 336

Chapter 3 (pp. 35–49)
  1 D'Arblay III 76
  2 PW I 454
  3 G III I 514
  4 Gillen *Royal Duke* 41

  5 Fitzgerald II 109
  6 Gillen *Royal Duke* 37
  7 ibid 40
  8 ibid 44
  9 ibid 50
  10 Fitzgerald II 47
  11 PW III 14

Chapter 4 (pp. 50–64)
  1 Ayling 386
  2 Stuart 162
  3 ibid 150
  4 ibid 17
  5 ibid 19–20
  6 ibid 146
  7 Stuart 162–3
  8 ibid 87
  9 PW III 194
  10 ibid 200
  11 Stuart 25–6
  12 ibid 29–30
  13 ibid 32
  14 ibid 36
  15 ibid 36

Chapter 5 (pp. 65–79)
  1 Fitzgerald I 226–7
  2 Stuart 273–4
  3 Gillen *Royal Duke* 108
  4 Fitzgerald II 328–9
  5 Fulford *Royal Dukes* 177 (pbk ed.)
  6 Stuart 328
  7 ibid 329
  8 ibid 340
  9 Gillen *Royal Duke* 143
  10 PW IV 438
  11 Fulford *George IV* 89

Chapter 6 (pp. 80–92)
1 Gillen *Royal Duke* 180
2 Stuart 345–6
3 ibid 160
4 ibid 166–7
5 ibid 168–70
6 G III V 206
7 ibid 235
8 Stuart 352
9 ibid 356
10 ibid 357
11 Childe-Pemberton 209
12 Stuart 174
13 ibid 363
14 ibid 368
15 ibid 376
16 Brooke 383–4

Chapter 7 (pp. 93–113)
1 Ziegler 103–4
2 Stuart 286–7
3 ibid 98
4 ibid 100–1
5 ibid 101–2
6 ibid 216
7 G IV I 351
8 ibid II 301
9 Hibbert *George IV 1811–30* 108
10 Stuart 56
11 ibid 227
12 ibid 226
13 Gillen *Royal Duke* 187
14 ibid 150
15 Hibbert *George IV 1811–30* 110
16 Stuart 229
17 ibid 238
18 ibid 239
19 ibid 240–1

Chapter 8 (pp. 114–26)
1 Creevey 277
2 Stuart 179
3 Woodham-Smith 16
4 Ziegler 122
5 G IV II 251
6 Stuart 124
7 Hedley 298
8 G IV II 260
9 Gillen *Royal Duke* 160
10 G IV II 260
11 Gillen *Prince and his lady* 248
12 G IV II 298
13 Brooke 386

Chapter 9 (pp. 127–42)
1 G IV II 311

2 Stuart 247
3 Hopkirk 58
4 Plumb & Wheldon 228
5 QV I i 11–12
6 Fitzgerald II 156
7 ibid 161
8 ibid 172
9 ibid 179
10 Stuart 301
11 ibid 302
12 ibid 300
13 Ziegler 132
14 Rowse 190–1

Chapter 10 (pp. 143–56)
1 Stuart 63
2 ibid 64
3 ibid 64
4 QV I i 11
5 Stuart 68
6 G IV III 440
7 Bird 197
8 ibid 199
9 Stuart 191
10 Bird 207
11 Stuart 193

Chapter 11 (pp. 157–67)
1 Eden 198
2 Gillen *Royal Duke* 202
3 Fulford *Royal Dukes* 152 (pbk ed.)
4 Stuart 197
5 Greville I 412
6 Fitzgerald *William IV* II 376

Chapter 12 (pp. 168–86)
1 Lee 53
2 Bird 256
3 Gillen *Royal Duke* 212
4 Frampton 407
5 Stuart 132
6 ibid 198
7 Gillen *Royal Duke* 217
8 ibid 217
9 Woodham-Smith 193
10 Stuart 314
11 Gillen *Royal Duke* 227
12 Bolitho 21
13 Van Thal 252
14 Bird 281
15 Greville II 253
16 Bolitho 59
17 QV I i 481
18 Bird 291
19 Bolitho 60
20 Bird 292

21 Stuart 318
22 QV I ii 174
23 Stuart 318–9
24 Martin II 291

25 Fitzgerald II 298
26 Stuart 256
27 ibid 257
28 ibid 257

Bibliography

Allen, W. Gore, *King William IV.* Cresset, 1960

Ashdown, Dulcie M., *Royal Weddings.* Hale, 1981

Ayling, Stanley, *George the Third.* Collins, 1972

Bennett, Daphne, *King without a crown: Albert, Prince Consort of England, 1819–1861.* Heinemann, 1977

Berry, Paul, *By royal appointment: a biography of Mary Anne Clarke, mistress of the Duke of York.* Femina, 1970

Bird, Anthony, *The damnable Duke of Cumberland: a character study and vindication of Ernest Augustus, Duke of Cumberland and King of Hanover.* Barrie & Rockliff, 1966

Bolitho, Hector (ed.), *The Prince Consort and his Brother: two hundred new letters.* Cobden-Sanderson, 1933

Brooke, John, *King George III.* Constable, 1972

Childe-Pemberton, William S., *The romance of Princess Amelia, daughter of George III (1783–1810).* Eveleigh Nash, 1910

Clarke, John, *The life and times of George III.* Weidenfeld & Nicolson, 1972

Cooke, C. Kinloch, *A Memoir of Her Royal Highness Princess Mary Adelaide, Duchess of Teck,* 2 vols. John Murray, 1900

Creevey, Thomas, *The Creevey papers: a selection,* Herbert Maxwell (ed.). John Murray, 1905

D'Arblay, F. (Fanny Burney), *Diary and letters of Madame d'Arblay,* C.F. Barrett (ed.), 4 vols. Swan Sonnenschein, 1892

Eden, Emily, *Miss Eden's Letters,* Violet Dickinson (ed.). Macmillan, 1919

Elizabeth, Princess, *Letters of Princess Elizabeth of England, written for the most part to Miss Louise Swinburne,* Philip C. Yorke (ed.). Thomas Fisher Unwin, 1898

Fitzgerald, Percy, *Dukes and Princesses of the Family of George III,* 2 vols. Tinsley Bros, 1882

—— *The life and times of William IV,* 2 vols. Tinsley Bros, 1884

Frampton, Mary, *The journal of Mary Frampton from 1779 until 1846,* Harriet Georgina Mundy (ed.). Sampson Low, 1885

Fulford, Roger, *George the Fourth.* Duckworth, 1935

—— *Royal Dukes: the father and uncles of Queen Victoria.* Collins, 1973

George III, King, *The later correspondence of George III, 1783–1810,* A. Aspinall (ed.), 5 vols. Cambridge University Press, 1962–7

George III, Collector & Patron: an exhibition of paintings, drawings, furniture, etc. Queen's Gallery, Buckingham Palace (catalogue), 1974

George IV, King, *Correspondence of George, Prince of Wales, 1770–1812,* A. Aspinall (ed.), 8 vols. Cambridge University Press, 1963–70

George IV, King, *The letters of George IV, 1812–1830*, A. Aspinall (ed.), 3 vols. Cambridge University Press, 1938

Gillen, Mollie, *The Prince and his Lady: the love story of the Duke of Kent and Madame de St Laurent.* Sidgwick & Jackson, 1970

—— *Royal Duke: Augustus Frederick, Duke of Sussex (1773–1843).* Sidgwick & Jackson, 1976

Greville, Charles C.F., *The Greville diary, including passages hitherto withheld from publication*, Philip Whitwell Wilson (ed.), 2 vols. Heinemann, 1927

Hedley, Olwen, *Queen Charlotte.* John Murray, 1975

Hibbert, Christopher, *The court at Windsor: a domestic history.* Allen Lane, 1977

—— *George IV, Prince of Wales, 1762–1811.* Longman, 1972

—— *George IV, Regent and King, 1811–1830.* Allen Lane, 1973

Holme, Thea, *Caroline: a biography of Caroline of Brunswick.* Hamish Hamilton, 1979

Hopkirk, Mary, *Queen Adelaide.* John Murray, 1946

Iremonger, Lucille, *Love and the Princess.* Faber, 1958

Lee, Sidney, *Queen Victoria: a biography.* Smith, Elder, 1902

Longford, Elizabeth, *Victoria R.I.* Weidenfeld & Nicolson, 1964

Marples, Morris, *Six royal sisters: daughters of George III.* Michael Joseph, 1969

—— *Wicked uncles in love.* Michael Joseph, 1972

Pain, Nesta, *George III at home.* Eyre Methuen, 1975

Palmer, Alan, *The life and times of George IV.* Weidenfeld & Nicolson, 1972

Papendiek, Charlotte Louise Henrietta, *Court and Private Life in the Time of Queen Charlotte*, V.D. Broughton (ed.), 2 vols. Bentley, 1886

Plumb, J.H., *The first four Georges.* Batsford, 1956

Plumb, J.H. and Wheldon, Huw, *Royal heritage: the story of Britain's royal builders and collectors.* BBC, 1977

Richardson, Joanna, *George IV.* Sidgwick & Jackson, 1966

Roberts, Jane, *Royal artists: from Mary Queen of Scots to the present day.* Grafton, 1987

Rowse, A.L., *Windsor Castle in the history of the nation.* Weidenfeld & Nicolson, 1974

St Aubyn, Giles, *The Royal George: the life of Prince George, Duke of Cambridge, 1819–1904.* Constable, 1963

Somerset, Anne, *The life and times of William IV.* Weidenfeld & Nicolson, 1980

Stuart, Dorothy M., *Daughters of George III.* Macmillan, 1939

Van Thal, Herbert, *Ernest Augustus, Duke of Cumberland & King of Hanover.* Arthur Barker, 1936

Victoria, Queen, *The girlhood of Queen Victoria: a selection from Her Majesty's diaries between the years 1832 and 1840*, Viscount Esher (ed.), 2 vols. John Murray, 1912

—— *The letters of Queen Victoria: a selection from Her Majesty's correspondence between the years 1837 and 1861*, A.C. Benson and Viscount Esher (eds), 3 vols. John Murray, 1907

Vulliamy, C.E., *Royal George: a study of King George III.* Jonathan Cape, 1937

Walpole, Horace, *The letters of Horace Walpole*, P. Cunningham (ed.), 3 vols. Bentley, 1891

Woodham-Smith, Mrs Cecil, *Queen Victoria, her life and times, Vol. 1, 1819–1861.* Hamish Hamilton, 1972

Ziegler, Philip, *King William IV.* Collins, 1971

Index